What People Are Saying About
Chicken Soup for the Volunteer's Soul . . .

"Congratulations to the authors for capturing the spirit of neighbor helping neighbor in the pages of Chicken Soup for the Volunteer's Soul. It's the spirit of the human family that helps confirm the importance of our organization's mission to support and organize the vital work of the millions of volunteers in thousands of communities who are helping to solve some of our nation's most serious social problems. After experiencing the enlightening and inspiring stories, I hope readers share my enthusiasm and get connected to volunteer opportunities in their communities."

Robert K. Goodwin
president and CEO, Points of Light Foundation &
Volunteer Center National Network

"A great collection of heartwarming stories that both celebrates the heroism of volunteers and reveals the joy these actions can generate. Chicken Soup for the Volunteer's Soul will make you put down the remote control, go out and make a difference in someone's life."

Peggy Conlon
president and CEO, The Ad Council, Inc.

"Nearly 125 million Americans volunteer today, and a common reaction from these wonderful people—teens through seniors—is, 'I get back so much more than I give.' If you want to know what they mean, read this book! If you're not one of those 125 million, after reading it, you will be!"

Sara E. Meléndez
president and CEO, Independent Sector

"Chicken Soup for the Volunteer's Soul demonstrates an old truism—that by serving other people, you help yourself even more. Each of these stories is a testament to the power of volunteerism."

Edwin Fv
General Secretary, Rotary® Internatio

"*Chicken Soup for the Volunteer's Soul* is a vehicle that speaks to the dedicated volunteers who never have time to put the value of their work into words. It is a great compilation of blood, sweat and tears."

Jill Arahill Perez
former AmeriCorps project manager

"Absolutely incredible stories! Noble, generous, unsung heroes! Inspires not only volunteerism, but a thousand creative ways to do it."

Dr. Stephen R. Covey
author, *The 7 Habits of Highly Effective People*

"The stories in *Chicken Soup for the Volunteer's Soul* go far beyond volunteering. They are life lessons for us all. This may be the book that changes the world—at the very least, your little corner of it."

Diane Penola
helped in aftermath of the World Trade Center attacks
chairperson, Alliance for Substance Abuse Prevention

"The spirit of volunteerism is alive and well. This lovely and inspiring book offers wonderful examples of one of the most profound and basic of all human experiences—that is, the capacity for giving from the heart."

Jane Bluestein
author, *Creating Emotionally Safe Schools* and *Mentors, Masters and Mrs. MacGregor: Stories of Teachers Making a Difference*

"*Chicken Soup for the Volunteer's Soul* is a heartwarming ensemble of stories that will move your soul and rekindle your spirit for helping others. Every story will make an impact and tug on your emotional heartstrings. I was touched."

Lily DiSabatino
volunteer coordinator
Wilmington Hospital—Christiana Care Health System

CHICKEN SOUP FOR THE VOLUNTEER'S SOUL

Chicken Soup for the Volunteer's Soul
Stories to Celebrate the Spirit of Courage, Caring and Community
Jack Canfield, Mark Victor Hansen, Arline McGraw Oberst, John T. Boal,
Tom Lagana, Laura Lagana

Published by Backlist, LLC,
a unit of Chicken Soup for the Soul Publishing, LLC. www.chickensoup.com

Front cover artwork by Meganne Forbes
Front cover design by Lisa Camp
Originally published in 2002 by Health Communications, Inc.

Back cover and spine redesign by Pneuma Books, LLC

Distributed to the booktrade by Simon & Schuster. SAN: 200-2442

Publisher's Cataloging-in-Publication Data
(Prepared by The Donohue Group)

Chicken soup for the volunteer's soul : stories to celebrate the spirit of
  courage, caring and community / [compiled by] Jack Canfield ... [et al.].

  p. : ill. ; cm.

  Originally published: Deerfield Beach, FL : Health Communications, c2002.
  ISBN: 978-1-62361-001-2

  1. Voluntarism--Anecdotes. 2. Volunteers--Anecdotes. 3. Helping behav-
ior--Anecdotes. 4. Conduct of life--Anecdotes. 5. Anecdotes. I. Canfield,
Jack, 1944-

HN49.V64 C425 2012
361.3/7   2012944060

PRINTED IN THE UNITED STATES OF AMERICA
on acid free paper

21 20 19 18 17 16 15 14 13 12   01 02 03 04 05 06 07 08 09 10

CHICKEN SOUP FOR THE VOLUNTEER'S SOUL

Stories to Celebrate the Spirit of Courage, Caring and Community

Jack Canfield
Mark Victor Hansen
Arline McGraw Oberst
John T. Boal
Tom Lagana
Laura Lagana

Backlist, LLC, a unit of
Chicken Soup for the Soul Publishing, LLC
Cos Cob, CT
www.chickensoup.com

"I wrote to my folks last night and told them we were really able to dig into our first project!"

Contents

Volunteer's Creed *Tom Krause*..xii

Introduction...xiii

1. THE REWARDS OF VOLUNTEERING

When Two or More Gather *Maureen Murray*...2

Something Worthwhile *Tony Webb*..6

The Sounds of Hope *Cathryn Pearse Snyders*...9

The Yellow Birds *Karen Garrison*..13

Keep Your Head Up *Susana Herrera*...17

How Many Grapes Does It Take? *Natasha Friend*.....................................22

The Hug of a Child *Victoria Harnish Benson*..26

We've Got Mail *Gary K. Farlow*...29

With a Little Help from Her Friends *Eve M. Haverfield*.........................34

A Second Chance *Jenna Cassell*...38

Pegasus's Wings *Vera Nicholas-Gervais*..42

The Quilting Bee *Joan Wester Anderson*..46

Don't You Just Feel Like Singing? *Terry Paulson, Ph.D.*........................50

2. GIVING BACK

Roberto's Last At-Bat *John T. Boal*..55

Hurricane Donna *Arline McGraw Oberst*...60

Beyond the Huddle *Charlene Baldridge*..64

A Cure for Restlessness *Linda Jin Zou* 68

Giving Something Back *Wynell Glanton Britton*..............................72

Daddy Bruce Randolph *Pat Mendoza* 76

Coats for Kosovo *Debby Giusti*..78

I'll Never Forget *P. Christine Smith*..81

3. MAKING A DIFFERENCE

Dave *Jamie Winship*..89

A Touch of Love *Kayte Fairfax*..92

A Volunteer's Prayer *Lois Clark Suddath* 96

A Touch from Above *Melanie Washington*.......................................97

Treasured Visits *Rosemarie Riley*...101

A Brief and Shining Moment *George S. J. Anderson* 106

The Lady with the Smiley Voice *Diane Kelber* 110

Big Sisterhood *Beth Barrett*...113

What's a Big Brother? *Norma Reedy* 117

Drawing Out the Truth *Nate Klarfeld* 121

A Reason for Living *Ellen Javernick*...125

4. NEW APPRECIATION

The Pillow *Casey Crandall* 131

A Twist of Fate *Patsy Keech*..133

A Tiny Denim Dress *Jinny Pattison* 137

Reunion *LeAnn Thieman* 139

The Magic Key *David "Goose" Guzzetta* 142

The Reluctant Den Leader *Françoise Inman* 146

Volunteer's Lament *Mary Drew Adams* 150

Swinging for Respect *Sheila A. Bolin* 152

Just Obedience *Charles W. Colson* 155

5. LOVE AND KINDNESS

You Got Another One, Joey! *Bob Perks* 161

A Hug and a Kiss *Mack Emmert as told to Tom Lagana* 165

The Sign of the Rabbit *Pamela B. Silberman* 168

Grandmother's Gift *Ruth Hancock* 172

Her Spirit Lives On *Santina Lonergan* 176

A Child's Gift *Pamela Strome-Merewether* 179

One Step Ahead *Denise Peebles* 181

Thank Gawd fo' Y'all *Chris Bibbo* 185

The Children of Russia *Carolyn E. Jones* 189

Find That Child! *Tammie L. Failmezger* 193

A Friend for All Seasons *David Garnes* 196

My Brother, My Hero *Nansie Chapman* 201

Without a Word *Nancy Blain* 204

6. DEFINING MOMENTS

Forgive Me, Davey *Pooja Krishna* 209

One Whale of a Volunteer *Doc Blakely* 214

Residuals from Roger *Diane Rodecker* 218

An Armful of Love *Elaine L. Galit* 223

Conversation with a Wise Guy *Elizabeth T. Verbaas* 226

Volunteer 101 *Rusty Fischer* 231

Sap to Seedling *Tara Church* 237

Saving Grace *Rusty Fischer* 240

The Silent Breakthrough *Rod Delisle* 244

It Only Takes a Few *Dave Krause* 247

7. A MATTER OF PERSPECTIVE

Smashing Potato Chips *Father Domenic Jose Roscioli* 252

Christmas Presence *Laura Lagana* 255

The Eyes Have It *Cynthia Polansky Gallagher* 258

African Eyes *Stephanie Sheen* 262

No Batteries: No Survivors *Candace F. Abbott* 266

Coming Full Circle *George M. Roth* 270

Gentle Words *Karen Zangerle* 274

8. OVERCOMING OBSTACLES

He Taught Us to Love *Arline McGraw Oberst* 278

The Healing Power of Friendship *Barb Mestler* 281

Let the Games Begin! *Margaret Buckingham* 285

The Bread of Life *Ellen Javernick* 288

A Child's Voice *Sarah Hawkins* 291

The Real Treasure *Holly Frederickson* 295

One Determined Angel *Dorothy Rose* 298

If I Can Move I Can Win *Carl Hammerschlag, M.D.* 301

Ward C, Room 842 *Sarah Ainslie* 305

The Cry of a Woman's Heart *Johnnie Ann Gaskill* 310

Little Changes *Elaine Ingalls Hogg* 313

Hi, I'm Jane *Sandra J. Bunch* 316

9. ON WISDOM

Thanks, Mom *Liz Murad* 322

Twenty-One *Donna McDonnall* 327

Bless Every Evelyn! *Sally Fouhse* 330

Synergetic Souls *Malinda Carlile* 333
Top Ten List of Things a Volunteer Should Know
    Donald Patrick Dunn 336

Who Is Jack Canfield? 340
Who Is Mark Victor Hansen? 341
Who Is Arline McGraw Oberst? 342
Who Is John T. Boal? 343
Who Is Tom Lagana? 344
Who Is Laura Lagana? 345
Contributors 346
Permissions 358

Volunteer's Creed

Though my troubles and my worries
are sometimes all that I can see—
still I always must remember
life's not only about me.

Other souls are also hurting
and I know that it's God's plan
to reach out to help another—
to extend to them my hand.

With this purpose as my focus—
to be a comfort to a friend—
all my troubles and my worries
seem to fade out in the end.

It is one of God's true lessons—
how my walk is meant to be—
true happiness I find when
life's not only about me.

Tom Krause

Introduction

It is our deepest pleasure to offer you *Chicken Soup for the Volunteer's Soul.*

Over the years, volunteers have been treated, for the most part, with a nice pat on the back with the notion that the majority of people just didn't have the time nor the desire to get involved.

But as our society moves through economic cycles and recovers from acts of terrorism, the concept of volunteering to offer comfort, aid and, most importantly, *one's time* to "make a difference" has become validated as an accepted and natural part of daily life.

If you have not yet discovered the rewards of volunteering, our highest hope is that, as you read and absorb each story, you will feel inspired to reevaluate how you choose to spend your time.

Good stories, like the best mentors, guide but don't dictate: They are unique experiences, insights tied to emotional triggers that grab our attention and replay in our memories. They often free us from the chains of past decisions and motivate us to push harder to better the world. A really good story allows us to recognize the choices that are open to us and to see new alternatives we might not have considered before. It can give us permission and instill courage to try a new path of action, and, ideally, it can provide us with the motivation to join thousands of other volunteers on the same positive path.

For this book, we carefully selected stories that hopefully will make you feel as if you were actually present. From that virtual reality, we trust you will be inspired, empowered and, in some cases, even humbled to make a difference in the world on a sustained basis. We hope you will be moved from spectator to participant.

Many of the people you will meet in these pages are models of unconditional kindness, compassion and love. They chose hope over despair, optimism over cynicism, and caring over withdrawal or indifference by volunteering to help people in need.

Whether we are veteran or new volunteers, the result is clear: A single individual can make a significant difference in the lives of others, and thereby have a positive impact in creating a more equitable, civil and peaceful world.

1

THE REWARDS OF VOLUNTEERING

For it is in giving that we receive.

Saint Francis of Assisi

When Two or More Gather

You can't be brave if you've only had wonderful things happen to you.

Mary Tyler Moore

Three days after the terrorist attacks on New York and Washington, I was working in my home office, preparing for a speech I was slated to deliver. I struggled with how best to acknowledge the grief and shock of the recent tragedy, and still provide the content I was expected to present about positive perspective.

While I focused on this challenge, my mind occasionally turned to an e-mail I had received several times that morning and the previous evening, all from different people: "In an effort to demonstrate national unity, please stop for a minute at 7:00 P.M. on Friday, September 15th, and step outside your home or place of business and light a candle for peace."

I was moved by the idea. Candles signify gathering and ritual—sometimes to celebrate a birthday or to welcome a guest, sometimes to offer a prayerful petition, sometimes to mark passage into the next life. I forwarded the e-mail to my daughters at their respective colleges and retrieved two candles for my husband and myself from the buffet and laid them on the kitchen counter. Then I went back and got two more, intending to ask the young couple who live next door to join us. They were expecting their first child soon, and it occurred to me that they might welcome the chance to focus on something positive and uplifting.

When I stopped for lunch and discovered yet another e-mail about the candle lighting, I knew immediately that it should be more than just a private affair. It should be an opportunity for all our neighbors to gather together to share the grief and the disbelief, and to pray collectively for world peace. And it should provide a vehicle for all those who wanted to "do something" to help, so a basket for Red Cross donations seemed a good solution. I called my husband to bounce the idea off him.

"Let's go for it," came his unhesitating response. We both believed that there is great power and healing in group prayer.

Hastily printing flyers on my computer, I spent the next half-hour walking up and down our one-block-long street, distributing the invitation to gather in front of our home a little before 7:00 P.M. for candle lighting and nondenominational prayers for peace. We asked participants to bring candles, prayers, singing voices and, if they wished, a monetary donation. In an effort to avoid a somber or frightening tone for the many young children on the street, we noted on the flyer that everyone was to bring their best voices for a rousing "Three Cheers for America." And we made red, white and blue clothing optional.

At 6:50 P.M., the sidewalk in front of our house was empty, and I speculated that the typically busy Friday nights of suburban families had conflicted with our service. A few moments later, I stepped out the door and glanced up and down the street. More than forty people were converging from both directions, most of them sporting some form of red, white and blue, many carrying small flags with their candles.

One of the first people I spotted was a retired gentleman making his way very slowly up the street with his cane, his gait slowed by recent surgery. His petite wife, her face a picture of kindness and concern, accompanied him. We hastily moved the program toward their home. Another of the early arrivals was our neighbor from across the street whose celebration of new citizenship we had attended a scant few months ago.

But what moved me most was the presence of my neighbor, three doors down, on the same side. She had not attended any neighborhood gatherings since the death of her son three years previously. She had graciously declined invitations, explaining that she "wasn't ready."

"I wasn't sure if I could do this, but I really wanted to," she explained to me quietly. "You know, Michael was a Marine, and the talk of military action makes me think of him." She wore the sunglasses that so frequently hide the tears of a grieving heart.

"I'm so glad you came," I whispered. "Stay close to me." We stood shoulder to shoulder, holding hands during much of the service. I felt deeply privileged to witness both her courage and her wish to honor the memory of her son.

Our service was brief but meaningful. We welcomed our neighbors, said a prayer and petitions we had composed that afternoon, and asked for and received many spontaneous petitions. One woman brought a special prayer for our nation. We sang "God Bless America" and several other patriotic songs. When we finished with the songs we had planned, some of the older children led us in another. The "Three Cheers for America" generated great volume and enthusiasm, especially from the preschool participants. And the collection basket for the Red Cross brought a generous response.

I looked at the faces of my neighbors, awed by the power of the human connection that makes us feel a little more brave. I also knew in an instant that my message to audiences from this day forward would include service to others as a milestone on the path to perspective.

Maureen Murray

[EDITORS' NOTE: *For information on the American Red Cross, contact your local Red Cross chapter or visit their Web site:* www.redcross.org.]

Something Worthwhile

As a busy freshman college student who preferred entertainment and camaraderie, I decided to become a member of the university's Student Activity Committee. This committee was responsible for organizing and carrying out campus events, including community volunteer projects.

One of my first ventures with committee members consisted of boxing food items at the local food bank for delivery to low-income senior citizens. *It'll be fun to get away from studies and just hang out with my peers,* I thought. Yet, far beyond my wildest imagination, God had something much more meaningful in store for me.

Our first day out, students gathered at the food center. We packed boxes with some staples of life and loaded them into our vehicles. Then, in teams of three, we set out to predetermined destinations. My partners and I were assigned to the senior housing project on the south end of Salt Lake City.

Upon our arrival, we checked in at the monitor's desk and began moving from door to door with our grocery offerings. It quickly became evident to me that, although the residents were grateful for the food items, they were especially pleased to have young visitors. However, I sensed a longing in a few of them, perhaps for days of their youth.

One resident introduced himself as Loki and invited us into his humble dwelling. At the age of ninety-two, he carefully moved about with an aluminum walker. Loki explained that he lived alone since his wife, Ester, died in 1972. Around the small room were photographs of a young Ester and Loki, their children, grandchildren and great-grandchildren. Loki declared that he enjoyed his independence and preferred to live alone, not with family. Then, with downcast eyes, he said, "If life wasn't so hectic, I'd have plenty of family visitors." I wondered if his loved ones had forgotten about him.

We discussed sports, school and hobbies. As I made us some hot cocoa, Loki promised to teach us how to tie a fishing fly, in case we decided to visit again. Upon our departure, Loki smiled and gave us each a little hand-carved hickory flute. "This is to show my appreciation for your commendable service work," he announced proudly. By day's end, my selfish motives for participating in this project had slipped away. The sunlight of an unfamiliar spirit had begun to radiate in my heart.

As a windy fall began to turn into a frosty winter, I found myself returning frequently to the housing project for visits with the residents, especially Loki. Although he had little formal education, his wisdom was profound. Thanks to Loki, aside from mastering the arts of tying fishing flies and whittling flutes, I came to appreciate poetry, nature and God. Loki told me why I was unique and important—something that no one had ever impressed upon me. As my self-esteem increased, I began to gain interest in others. Soon, I felt a usefulness I had never known.

In late December of that year, bearing a Christmas gift, I went to see Loki. Upon my arrival at the senior housing project, John, the front-desk monitor, reluctantly informed me that my friend Loki had died during the night. My heart sank like a stone plummeting into a bottomless pit. I dropped Loki's present on the floor and staggered to a chair in the lobby. "God decides when it's our time to come home," Loki had recently told me, "and until then, we do the best we can on Earth." I vividly remembered his words.

Unaware that John had moved to my side, he placed a letter in my lap. My name was scrawled on the envelope in Loki's unsteady handwriting. "When I found him in bed this morning," John whispered, "he was holding this in his hands."

Trembling, I opened the envelope and removed the single page. As I read, tears welled up in my eyes. I began to cry and was unashamed, ". . . for this is natural and beneficial," my old friend had said. His letter of farewell was inscribed as follows:

> Dear Tony,
>
> It's my time to be with Ester. Although my body is very tired, my soul is soaring. I've lived a lot of years. But it was in my last days that the goodness in your heart, Tony, made for many of the most special moments. You were a good friend to an old man who ended up alone in this world. Thank you for being a valuable part of my life. Remember to always let God guide your journeys, and his angels will forever remain by your side.
>
> I love you,
> Loki

My service work allowed me to have a spiritual encounter with a ninety-two-year-old man who changed my attitude and outlook on life. God has blessed me with the gift of being a part of something worthwhile.

Tony Webb

The Sounds of Hope

Hope is the thing with feathers that perches in the soul, and sings the tune without the words, and never stops, at all.

Emily Dickinson

Regilene, a petite, shapely woman with long, thick, mocha-colored hair, moved with the slow, swaying style of women born to samba—the Brazilian dance of sensual hip gyrations. Her cinnamon skin and large, dark eyes seemed weary from twenty-seven years of negotiating a hard life.

When she first entered my exam room at the mission, her right hand was gently cupped over the center of her face. As she carefully removed that safeguard, her delicate fingers fell to her side revealing a sight that would provoke a wince, even in someone accustomed to working with maxillofacial disorders. Regilene had no mouth or nose, only a gaping hole where nature had played an evil trick, causing her palate and teeth to protrude from the chasm in a hideous countenance.

The plastic surgeons, nurses and dentists had already examined her. As a speech pathologist, I was familiar with cleft-palate speech and fluent enough in Portuguese to complete an evaluation and make an analysis as to how surgery might affect her speech.

I noted from her medical record that she was a young woman who lived in the interior of Brazil, a five-hour bus ride away. The fact that she was an adult was disturbing. The mission was based in a pediatric hospital, which meant that we only took children under the age of sixteen.

"Oi, Regilene, *como vai?"* I asked, as she sat down in my patient chair. "Hi, how are you?" The edges of her eyes turned up in what appeared to be a smile.

She produced a picture of a cherubic little boy. *"Meu filho"* ("My son"), she explained. Her nasal speech was intelligible only to those accustomed to cleft-palate conversation. She continued in Portuguese, using hand signals and gestures. "He was watching television and saw that Operation Smile was in this city. He begged me to come and get my face fixed. I am here for him and for me."

That night, after the team meeting, I searched for Dr. Bill Magee, the head of our mission and founder of Operation Smile. I wanted to be sure we would not turn this lady away. Surely we could do something for her.

To my relief, Dr. Magee had already sized up the situation and was working fervently with two Brazilian plastic surgeons and the hospital administration. Time was running out. We would be leaving in five days.

All week Regilene waited as a hundred children came and went, and returned for follow-up visits. Regilene, accompanied by a cousin, stayed in a crowded dorm-like room attached to the hospital.

In the middle of the week, I helped the team's Brazilian dentist fashion an obturator for Regilene—a dental prosthesis that would help close off the hole in her palate, improving her ability to eat and perhaps even her speech.

My colleagues and I taught her oral-motor exercises and showed her how to use her tongue and newly created palate to sound out letters. She practiced and wore her obturator faithfully. But the device failed to improve her appearance, and we were well aware it wasn't what she had come for.

While her cousin was away for a week, I looked in on Regilene every day. I usually found her among the children, drawing pictures of smiling girls with perfect faces. I brought inexpensive trinkets, like necklaces, lotion and bubbles, to keep her spirits up. Marc, the team photographer, gave her the most cherished gift of all: a radio headset to help her pass the time. All she could do for five interminable days was wait and hope.

Finally on the last day, the surgeons announced that they would operate. She was to be the last patient of the day. I reassured an anxious Regilene that I would accompany her into the operating room and hold her hand as she was put to sleep.

As promised, I spoke to her softly in Portuguese as the anesthesia took effect. I stayed for a while to watch the plastic surgeon, Dr. Henrique, as he created her new face. All I could see was a jumble of skin, cartilage, blood and teeth. It looked like a puzzle with missing pieces.

For the next few hours, I helped with the other patients in the recovery room, trying not to hope for too much. Suddenly, a voice summoned me from my reverie, "She's almost finished in surgery, Cathy."

I hurriedly put on my surgical mask, entered the room and carefully approached the sterile field. Dr. Henrique had just finished the last stitch. As I looked down, I saw an incredible sight. Where a horrendous abyss had once cursed Regilene's face, there was the semblance of a normal nose and mouth that would soon be capable of forming a real smile. Tears soaked my mask. Every one of the nurses and doctors shed tears of joy. For a full minute we just stood there in awe.

I sat with Regilene in the recovery room, as she slowly came to. With fear-filled eyes she took my hand. Later, a nurse and I wheeled Regilene out into the hallway to be taken to the post-operative area. Waiting at the end of the corridor were her cousin and the rest of the Operation Smile team. It seemed Regilene's timing was impeccable. Team members were already packing instruments for their return to the United States.

When Regilene appeared, everyone applauded and the sounds of hope echoed through the halls. As the nurse wheeled the cart toward the door, Regilene's cousin suddenly blocked their path, crying and yelling *"Pare!"* ("Stop!"). Next, she ran over to me, hugged me and said in Portuguese, "This is a miracle from God! Thanks to all of you for helping my Regilene." The cousin and the cart disappeared around the bend. I stood there, my body drained but my soul full.

Cathryn Pearse Snyders

[EDITORS' NOTE: *For information on Operation Smile, contact 6435 Tidewater Drive, Norfolk, VA 23509; 757-321-7645; fax: 757-321-7660; Web site:* www.operationsmile.org.]

The Yellow Birds

I was in the prima donna, self-centered phase of age seventeen, and my motives were simple—to enhance my final Health Assistant grade. To accomplish my goal, I volunteered at the nearby convalescent center.

For weeks, I grumbled to my boyfriend, "I can't believe I'm stuck with tending to old people for free." He agreed.

I soon realized that the bright yellow uniforms we were required to wear made matters even worse. On our first day at the center, the nurses took one look at our bright apparel and nicknamed us the "yellow birds."

On the days I was scheduled to work, I complained to the other "yellow birds" about how emptying bedpans, changing soiled linens and spoon-feeding pureed foods to mumbling mouths were not things any teenager should have to do.

One long and tedious month passed before I first met Lily Sturgeon, an eighty-seven-year-old resident who would change my life. I was given a tray of food and sent to her room. As I entered, Lily's bright blue eyes appraised me.

After talking with her for a few minutes, I realized why I hadn't noticed Lily before that day. I had walked past her room numerous times, but, unlike many of the other residents, Lily was soft-spoken and congenial. From my first day at the center, I learned that the nurses had their favorites, usually those who had outstanding characteristics. From joke-tellers to singers, the loud and rambunctious received more attention.

There was something about Lily that I liked immediately. Strangely, I began to enjoy our talks.

One rainy afternoon she smiled and said, "Come here, Karen. Sit down. I have something to show you." She lifted a small photo album and began to turn the pages. "This was my Albert. See him there? Such a handsome man."

Her voice softened as she pointed to a pretty little girl sitting on top of a fence. "And that was our darling Emmy when she was eight years old." Suddenly, a teardrop landed on the page.

I quickly turned to Lily. "What is it?" I whispered, placing my hand on hers. She turned the pages silently, and I noticed that Emmy was not in any of the other photographs.

Then Lily broke the silence. "She died from cancer that year," Lily said sadly. "She'd been in and out of hospitals most of her life, but that year her little body just couldn't take any more."

"I'm so sorry," I said, not knowing how to comfort her.

She smiled slightly as she turned to the last page. Inside the worn album was one more faded picture of a middle-aged Lily standing on tiptoes and kissing a clown's cheek. "That's my Albert," she laughed, recalling happier memories. "After Emmy died, we decided to help the children at the hospital. We were disturbed by the dismal surroundings while Emmy was hospitalized."

Lily stopped briefly to look at the photograph one more time. "That's when Albert decided to become 'Smiley the Clown.' Emmy was always smiling, even in the worst of times. I scraped together what fabric I could find and sewed this costume for Albert." She smiled and clapped her hands in joy. "The children loved it! Every weekend we'd volunteer at the hospitals to bring smiles and gifts to the children."

"But you said that you were poor," I reminded her. "How'd you manage that?"

"Well," she grinned, "smiles are *free*, and the gifts weren't anything fancy." She closed the album and leaned back against her pillows. "Sometimes the local bakers donated goodies. When we were really hurting for money, we'd bring a fresh litter of pups from our farm. The children loved petting them. After Albert died, I noticed how faded and worn the costume was, so I rented one and dressed as Smiley myself . . . that is, until my first heart attack, about ten years ago. Smiley was then forced into retirement."

When I left Lily's room that day, I couldn't think of anything but how generous she and Albert had been to children who weren't even their own.

Graduation day neared and, on my last day, I hurried to Lily's room. She was asleep, curled into a fetal position from stomach discomfort. I stroked her brow and worried about who would take care of her the way I did. She didn't have any surviving family members, and most of the staff were too busy to give her the extra love and attention I had grown to so willingly share.

At times, I wanted to proclaim Lily's virtues to the staff. She would stop me and remind me that the good things she'd done were done without thoughts of self. "Besides," she would say, "doesn't the good Lord tell us to store our treasures in heaven and not on this Earth?"

Lily must have sensed my anguish that day as I stood by her bed. Opening her eyes, she asked in a concerned voice laced with pain, "What is it, dear?"

"I'll be back in two weeks," I responded, explaining

about high-school graduation. "And then I'll visit you every day. I promise."

She sighed and squeezed my fingers. "I can't wait for you to tell me all about it."

Two weeks later, I rushed back to the center with a bouquet of lilies in my hand. As I stepped into her clean, neat, *unoccupied* room, I searched for an answer to Lily's whereabouts. My heart already knew the answer.

I threw the flowers on the bed and wept.

A nurse came in and gently touched my shoulder. "Were you one of the yellow birds?" she asked. "Is your name Karen?"

I nodded, and she handed me a gift-wrapped box. "Lily wanted you to have this. We've had it since she died because we didn't know how to get in touch with you."

It was her photo album. Clutching it tightly to my chest, I quickly left.

Three weeks later, my horrified boyfriend stood before me. "You can't be serious!" he said, pacing back and forth. "You look ridiculous!"

As I tried to look at myself in the mirror, he blocked my reflection. "You can't be serious!" he repeated. "How in the world did you pay for that thing anyway?"

"With my graduation money," I answered.

"What?" he exclaimed, shaking his head. "You spent the money that we saved for New York on *that?*"

"Yep," I said. "Life is more about giving than receiving."

"This is just great," he muttered, helping me tie the back of my costume. "And what am I supposed to say when someone asks me what my girlfriend's name is? Bozo?"

Looking at my watch, I realized I needed to hurry if I wanted to make it on time to the Children's Hospital. "Nope," I answered, kissing him on the cheek. "Tell them it's Smiley . . . Smiley the Clown."

Karen Garrison

Keep Your Head Up

No one can make you feel inferior but yourself.
Eleanor Roosevelt

I am a volunteer teacher in Africa. I am not here to change anything, I say to myself on the way home from school. Yet today the boys made it clear that girls aren't allowed to participate in class. The girls don't even try. They are outnumbered: 102 boys and five girls. The girls sit squished on two cement bricks in the back of the class, pretending to be invisible.

As I pass the well, I wave to the women working and smile at my student, Lydie. She sees me, stops pumping water then approaches. In class, she's the only girl out of the five who leans forward, listening to my lesson, looking as if she wants to raise her hand, take a risk and participate.

"Miss?" Lydie asks. "Will you teach me to ride your bike?" She is so shy, almost shaking, and her eyes are squinting as though she's afraid I'll slap her for merely asking the question.

"When do you want to start?" I ask.

Lydie's eyes flutter as if there's a butterfly trapped

inside, longing to be set free. "No one must know, Miss. You must teach me in the darkness of the morning. Please, Miss, promise not to tell."

"I promise, Lydie, but why?"

"Women don't ride bikes. They say we won't be able to make baby. And no one would want to marry me if he thought I could ride a bike across the village and get into trouble."

I don't understand what it means to be an African woman. I don't understand how to be a volunteer teacher. How do I teach her what she wants to know without causing waves? How do I set her mind free without getting us both in trouble?

The next morning, Lydie arrives at four-thirty. She insists on guiding the bike through the darkness toward our remote destination. Lydie's shoulders are high and tense as we head out from the village.

"I want to be strong, like you, Miss," Lydie says.

She is so nervous that I now understand why this is an activity where we better not be caught.

"Which direction is Nigeria?" Lydie asks. I point west toward the bridge. Lydie's eyes fill with tears. She clears her throat, then says, "I have watched you cross that bridge so many times."

Lydie fixes her eyes on the horizon. Here, women learn to put their secret hopes in the distance and wait for the wind to change and blow their dreams closer.

"How far is it to Nigeria?" she asks, dreaming of the freedom to have an adventure of her own someday. "Miss, you come only once in my life. I want to learn from you," she says.

"This is a good place," I say and Lydie confronts the bicycle. She lifts her head and for the first time, swings her right leg over the bicycle.

"Okay," I say, "you pedal, and I'll push."

"Don't let go, Miss."

I don't say a word. I just begin to push. She glides along for twenty yards or so without doing a thing.

"Pedal, Lydie, pedal!"

She begins to pedal. I try to maintain the balance myself, while increasing the speed so she can gain momentum. But Lydie is steering wildly and twists the bike from my grasp. I'm forced to let go and fall to the ground as she crashes.

Lydie lies sprawling on the sand as I quickly get up and run to her.

"Miss! You let go!"

"The bike was swerving, and I couldn't hold on," I say.

"I will never be able to steer!"

"Steering will come."

"I can't do this."

"Lydie, you will learn!"

Lydie climbs back onto the bike. As I push again, running behind and steadying her with both hands, Lydie pedals furiously.

"That's it, Lydie. That's the way!"

"Don't let go, Miss!"

When she has a rhythm, I let go. But this time she falls hard, screams on impact, then quickly throws a hand over her mouth in panic. We both look around to see if anyone is nearby.

Lydie looks up at me bitterly.

"I'm sorry, Lydie, but it's the only way."

"I can't do this! When I look down and see how fast I'm going, I get scared."

I haven't yet told Lydie about needing to find a balance. Here I am trying to find the balance for her, and it doesn't matter how she pedals or how she steers if she doesn't have a balance of her own.

And then I realize, African women grow up learning that skill. I think back to the well when I tried to find a balance carrying a bucket of water.

"Lydie, imagine carrying a bucket of water on your head. You don't look down when you're carrying water. You look at what's in front of you."

Lydie winces as she mounts the bike. Both knees are bleeding, and her elbows are badly scraped.

"Imagine a bucket of water right here," I tell her. As I touch the top of her head, she looks into my eyes and, finally, smiles.

Lydie begins pedaling confidently. Her steering is better, and her head is up. The seat is steady in my hands now, and I'm no longer struggling to maintain a grip. In a moment, we're gliding through the fields.

"Keep that bucket of water on your head!"

Lydie raises her chin. The imaginary bucket is there, sitting atop her head like a crown. Lydie gets it and flies with it.

And when I finally let go, she doesn't even notice. She just pedals on. What seems like an eternity is perhaps only one triumphant minute. I hold my breath, watching Lydie flow through the desert like a graceful sailboat driven by a steady wind. Lydie has found her moment of victory. She is free!

I realize this is Lydie's achievement, not mine. I recognize that Lydie has found the door to freedom on her own. I let go of the "American volunteer hero" concept that I carried with me in Africa. I am no longer Peace Corps, no longer a volunteer, nor am I Lydie's teacher. I am simply a woman. And Lydie is no longer of the developing world. She's not African, not Cameroonian and not a student.

We're only two women, and each of us is struggling to learn something new.

It feels right, and I let out a joyful cry.

Lydie hears and realizes that my voice has come from a distance. As she turns her head and looks back at me, she loses control of the bike and crashes.

But this time it doesn't matter. Lydie has had a victory, and I can't wait to tell her how proud I am and how brave she is.

I run to her and lift the bike away. Then, on my knees, I lift her from the sand and into my arms. "You did it, Lydie!" I exclaim, as I rock her in my arms. "You did it!"

As the realization comes crashing down on her, Lydie begins to cry. Then she smiles. She can do it. She can do anything.

Susana Herrera

[EDITORS' NOTE: *For more information on the Peace Corps, contact 1111 20th Street, N.W., Washington, DC 20526; 800-424-8580; Web site:* www.peacecorps.org.]

How Many Grapes Does It Take?

Melissa lived in a trailer park, miles from my campus, in one of a dozen turquoise units wedged between a bowling alley and the turnpike. Beer cans and abandoned clothing speckled the lawn outside #9—a scene not unfamiliar to your average college student, *if* this were the aftermath of a frat party. But those rusted training wheels? That Barbie lying face down in the mud?

"Mol," I said. "What are we doing here?"

Molly nosed the car up to the only patch of ground not littered with anything and replied, in that deliberate way that only a best friend can, "We're making a difference. Remember?"

Three weeks before, propelled by the fervor of the liberal-arts curriculum, I had charged back to my dorm room with all the righteousness of Robin Hood. "I'm signing us up for 'Big Brothers Big Sisters,'" I told Molly. "What's an $85,000 education worth if we don't use it to make a difference?"

Molly smiled at me, the same smile she always wears because she knows me so well she can read my mind: *Who do we think we are—with our J. Crew barn jackets and our name-brand educations? Who do we think we are, showing up on this family's doorstep and kidnapping their daughter?*

Fearing the awkward moment of face-to-face economic disparity, we knocked on the door. Much to our relief, the parents didn't answer. Melissa did, in all her kindergarten splendor. Tiny and stick-limbed, she peered up at us and wrinkled her nose like a rabbit. Sniff. Sniff. Could these big girls be trusted?

Behind her stood two older children, each with Melissa's shaggy blonde hair and blue eyes. They hung back as she gave us a tour of the trailer.

"Here is the TV. Here is the beanbag chair. Here is the picture I drawed in art."

Melissa's parents, quiet in chairs, watched her flit about. They smiled with the amused detachment of any parent watching a child take the spotlight.

"Here is me when I was a little baby. Here is my twin baby, Mark, that died."

Molly and I leaned in closer to see the photos clearly: one baby dressed in pink, one in blue.

"Missy," the mother said softly, beckoning with her finger. Melissa walked over to her mother and leaned in to hear the secret. Missy regarded us solemnly. "Mama said he's in heaven with the other angels."

There was a shuffling silence from the agnostics in the room. Molly and I tried to fill the air. We offered unbidden assurances: seatbelts fastened, the four food groups, home by eight.

Then the older sister piped up, "How come Missy gets extra sisters and we don't?"

"Yeah," chimed the brother. "How come *she* gets a dinner at college?"

From his chair at the opposite end of the room, the father spoke for the first time. His voice was deep and strong. "Tonight is Missy's night."

Melissa grabbed one of my hands, one of Molly's and

started bouncing. "Katie . . . Dusty, I'll eat for you," she announced.

Walking to the car, Melissa still held onto our hands. She managed to turn around and wave, with her foot, to Katie and Dusty who had their noses pressed against the windows.

"They wanted to come," said Melissa as we tucked her into the back seat of the car.

"Next time, kiddo. Tonight's your own special night," we told her. Melissa spent the drive to campus bouncing in the back seat: *Tonight's my special night, my special night, my special night.*

In our cafeteria, Melissa was about the same size as the dining-hall tray she was carrying. Since she insisted on carrying it herself, she was oblivious to the throng of students towering over her, thundering past her. She only saw the food.

"Can I eat . . . *anything?*" she asked.

"Sure," we told her. "Pizza, pasta, cereal, soup, salad . . ."

Melissa turned in circles for a few minutes, open-mouthed, until we guided her over to the salad bar in the middle of the Commons where she rested her tray along the slide and thought for a minute.

She pointed to items in a metal tin. "What are them things?"

"Grapes. Green grapes."

Over Melissa's head, I mouthed to Molly: *She's never had grapes?*

"They good?" Melissa asked.

"Delicious," we told her, relieved she didn't go straight for the ice-cream machine.

I lifted Melissa up so she could reach the grapes with a pair of salad tongs. She piled enough on her plate to feed a large colony of fruit flies. "Whoooa, cowgirl," I said.

That was all she wanted. Grapes. From the staggering

display of food in our dining hall, all Missy wanted were grapes. She thought they were "the *most prettiest,*" "the *most yummiest*" thing she had ever encountered in her life. She wanted to eat them every day of the week for every meal.

We finally had to tell Melissa, ever so gently, that too many grapes would equal one very big stomachache, and that now would be a very good time to *stop.* The look on her face was priceless.

"But I ain't never gonna eat grapes *again.* I gotta eat enough for *everyone.*"

"Missy," I affirmed, "there will always be enough grapes."

All three of us walked back to the salad bar and started filling plastic cups with grapes—one for each member of Melissa's family, one for her *for tomorrow,* one for Molly and one for me. We promised there would be grapes the next time we brought her to dinner, and the next, and the next.

Our drive home was a quiet one. Melissa sat very still in the back seat, careful not to spill her bounty, smiling down at the cups with reverence.

We drove out onto the turnpike, past the bowling alley, through the trailer park and up onto the only patch of ground not littered with anything, before Melissa spoke.

"Guys," she said, "are there grapes in heaven?"

Molly reached over and squeezed my hand, silently saying this question was all mine.

"At every meal, baby," I told her. "At every meal."

Natasha Friend

[EDITORS' NOTE: *For more information, contact Big Brothers Big Sisters of America, 230 N. 13th St., Philadelphia, PA 19107; 215-567-7000; fax: 215-567-0394; e-mail:* national@bbbsa.org; *Web site:* www.bbbsa.org.]

The Hug of a Child

As we drove across town, I prepared my two children for what they were about to see. A lady from our new church was dying of cancer, and I had volunteered to help her with the housework. "Annie has a tumor in her head, which has disfigured her face," I cautioned them.

Annie invited me to bring my children with me one day, as I had told her so much about them. "Most children are frightened by my appearance," she said. "But I will understand if they don't want to meet me."

I struggled for the words to describe Annie's appearance to my son and daughter. Then I remembered a movie I'd seen two years earlier with my son, when he was ten. I wanted him to understand that disabled people are like anyone else—their feelings can be hurt, too.

"David, remember the movie *Mask* about the boy with the facial deformity?"

"Yes, Mom. I think I know what to expect." His tone told me it was time to stop mothering him so much.

"What does a tumor look like?" Diane asked me.

Answering my nine-year-old daughter would be tricky. In order to prevent Diane's revulsion when she met

Annie, I needed to prepare her just enough but not too much. I didn't want to frighten the child.

"Her tumor looks like the skin on the inside of your mouth. It sticks out from under her tongue and makes it hard for her to talk. You'll see it as soon as you meet her, but there's nothing to be afraid of. Remember, don't stare. I know you'll want to look at it . . . that's all right . . . just don't stare." Diane nodded. I knew she was trying to picture a tumor in her mind.

"Are you kids ready for this?" I asked as we pulled up to the curb.

"Yes, Mom," David said, sighing as only a preteen can.

Diane nodded and tried to reassure me. "Don't worry, Mommy. I'm not scared."

We entered the living room, where Annie was sitting in her recliner, her lap covered with note cards for her friends. I stood across the room with my children, aware that anything could happen next.

At the sight of my children, Annie's face brightened. "Oh, I'm so glad you came to visit," she said, dabbing a tissue at the drops of saliva that escaped from her twisted mouth.

Then it happened. I watched David stride across the room to Annie's chair, wrap his arms around her shoulders and press his cheek to her misshapen face. Smiling, he looked into her eyes and said, "I'm happy to meet you."

Just when I didn't think I could be more proud, Diane copied her big brother and gave Annie the precious, accepting hug of a child.

My throat tightened with emotion as I saw Annie's eyes well up with grateful tears. I had nothing to worry about.

Victoria Harnish Benson

The Deep End   by Matt Matteo

We've Got Mail

A small blur flew a few scant millimeters past my nose. "I don't eat these!" Mrs. Clara Anthony wailed. This spry eighty-six-year-young resident of the Golden Years Nursing Center had quite a reputation. Glancing down at my feet, I discovered a single-serving box of cornflakes that she had just launched from her bed.

It was my first day on the job as the new activity director, fresh from college and full of ideas. I was determined to give my residents more than the traditional three Bs of nursing-home activities: Bibles, Baskets and Bingo.

Every attempt I made to pry Mrs. Anthony out of her bed and socialize with others met with failure. She would lift her glasses to her eyes and say, "I don't do *those* things." Shopping trips, travelogues, drama club—nothing could budge Clara.

"She's a crotchety old cuss," said Annie, a nurse's aide. "She could join in on the activities, but she prefers to sit in her dark room and wait for mail."

"Mail?" I asked.

"Ever since her only son and his family moved to Texas,

all Mrs. Anthony does is wait on mail. She misses them somethin' fierce."

Each week saw more and more residents up, dressed and ready to participate in the "goings-on," but Mrs. Anthony continued to withdraw.

"I give up," I admitted to Pam, the Adult Basic Education teacher. "I don't know what to do."

"You must be talking about Clara Anthony," said Rachel, my assistant.

"Gary, Mrs. Anthony's only interested in mail. If a day passes without a letter, watch out!" added Pam.

"What do you mean?" I asked.

Rachel replied, "If either Pam or I pass her room empty-handed, she throws the nearest thing."

"I've seen books, cups, even flowers come sailing out of her room," added Pam.

"She sounds unhappy," I speculated.

"Unhappy?" Rachel said incredulously. "After she's thrown out half her room, she breaks down in writhing sobs."

"She misses her grandchildren," Pam mused.

Several days later, I walked into the activity room amid boisterous giggles. Rachel, Pam and a dozen residents were trying on an assortment of baseball caps. "Where did these come from?" I inquired. "There must be hundreds."

"A hundred and twenty, to be exact," replied Robert, a retired airline pilot, who visited regularly to do travelogues for our residents.

"After the residents told me about the garden club and their need to wear hats in the sun, I decided to clean out my closets," said Robert. The unused caps were emblazoned with a variety of emblems.

"Hey, check me out, Gary. I'm a mailman." Stephen grinned as he displayed his new blue cap with the words "U.S. Mail" affixed across the front. This ten-year-old son of a staff nurse would occasionally volunteer and help with arts and crafts.

As I stared at his cap, Rachel asked, "What's wrong?"

"Rachel, have you delivered today's mail to the residents yet?"

"No. Why?"

"I've got an idea. Stephen, would you like to be our new mailman?" Stephen nodded in agreement.

Pam asked, "Gary, what are you doing?"

"Mrs. Anthony loves getting mail, and she misses her grandkids. Why not let Stephen deliver her mail?"

"But she doesn't always get mail," Rachel pointed out. "Besides, I don't think Stephen really wants a pillow thrown at him."

"Why don't we see?" I concluded.

As luck would have it, Mrs. Anthony did have a letter that day. Stephen donned his mailcap, and Rachel, Pam and I trooped down the hallway to Clara's room together.

"We can't all go in," I warned, stopping in front of her door. "Knock first, Stephen, then go in."

Stephen tapped twice on Clara's door.

A delicate voice responded, "Come in."

"I've got mail for you, Mrs. Anthony," Stephen said proudly.

"Oh my, what have we here? Aren't you a dear."

"She wouldn't be saying that if he didn't have a letter," Pam whispered.

"Hush!" I hissed, leaning closer to the half-open door. Looking more like a covert CIA operative, I whispered, "I'm trying to listen."

Clara continued, "What grade are you in?"

"Fourth grade," replied Stephen.

"I taught school for forty years."

"Wow! I'd sure hate to be in school that long," Stephen quipped.

The laughter spilled into the hallway as the three of us stood spellbound by the sudden change in Mrs. Anthony.

"What's your name?" Clara inquired.

"Stephen."

"Would you read my letter to me, Stephen? My eyes aren't so good."

"Sure."

Rachel broke the silence in the hallway. "Gary, there's nothing wrong with her eyes."

"Shh . . . it doesn't matter," I whispered. "It's working."

"What's working?" Pam asked.

Pointing toward Clara's room I said, "Look."

Peering around the corner, we saw Stephen reading to Clara. Her smile spoke a thousand words.

"Thank you, dear," Clara said after Stephen finished.

"You're welcome. I'll come back tomorrow if you get another letter."

"You don't have to wait for me to get mail, Stephen. Come any time. In fact, I have a grandson just about your age."

"You do?"

"Yes, but he lives in Texas. I don't see him much anymore."

"That's sad. I miss my Nana, too."

"Where is your grandmother, Stephen?"

"She's gone to heaven." Stephen hesitated for a moment before asking, "Would you be my Nana?"

Clara chuckled. "Oh my. How would your mother feel about that?"

"She wouldn't mind. She works here."

"Well, honey, you come visit me any time."

No mail came for Clara over the next few days, but the staff began to notice a dramatic change taking place.

"She quit throwing things," Rachel reported.

Pam added, "And she stopped crying all the time."

While the staff and I discussed Mrs. Anthony in my

office behind closed doors, we heard a gentle knock. "Come in," I said.

Stephen smiled and said timidly, "Hi."

As he opened the door we heard a familiar feminine voice. "I hope we're not disturbing you." There sat Clara in her wheelchair with Stephen at the helm, both of them wearing "U.S. Mail" caps.

"We're off to deliver the mail," Stephen proclaimed proudly. "Aren't we, Mrs. Anthony?"

She winked at us and smiled. "Yes . . . that is . . . if it's all right?"

We were speechless. In one week, Clara had gone from a sullen, sorrowful recluse to a smiling social butterfly.

After a few seconds, I managed to say, "Rachel, please give them the mail."

The mailbag perched in Mrs. Anthony's lap, Stephen announced, "Come on. We've got mail to deliver."

"Let's ride!" Mrs. Anthony shouted.

We heard the pair chanting as they disappeared down the hall. "Through rain, sleet . . . snow."

Pam uttered, "How about that?"

"Amazing," I added.

Stephen and Clara became a common sight. When they weren't delivering mail, Clara helped Stephen with his homework. When they weren't too busy, he showed Clara how to play Nintendo.

Stephen became our first volunteer to "Adopt a Grandparent." While he couldn't replace Clara's grandson, just as Clara couldn't replace Stephen's grandmother, they discovered the value of a little time and love between two people.

Gary K. Farlow

[EDITORS' NOTE: *For information on Adopt-A-Grandparent Foundation, visit the Web site:* www.adopt-a-grandparent.org.]

With a Little Help from Her Friends

I drove slowly along the moonlit beach that night in July, looking, as always, for the telltale tracks of giant nesting sea turtles.

My mission was to apply a special tracking tag on these imperiled marine creatures that are dangerously close to extinction.

As I watched and listened to the surf's gentle lapping on the shore, my eye suddenly caught the movement of a form emerging from the water. I watched as the silhouette slowly began to ascend the beach. It was a loggerhead sea turtle, repeating the ancient ritual of returning to the beach to lay her eggs near the very place where she was hatched, perhaps fifty or more years ago.

From a distance, I watched as she reached the top of the dune. There, she nestled into the sand using her flippers to clear the area until she created a body pit. For the next thirty minutes, she excavated a nest chamber with her rear flippers, piling sand to either side of her. I heard her labored breathing as she created her nest.

Once the digging stopped, her rear flippers curled up slightly and then relaxed. She had begun to lay her eggs.

They dropped into the chamber too fast to count. She might lay 120 or more Ping-Pong–ball-sized eggs, which she never sees. When the chamber was full, she scooped the sand over her eggs, packing it down with her powerful flippers, then wildly casting more sand over the site and over herself to hide her precious eggs. With her nest safely tucked away, she slowly turned and crawled back to the ocean once again.

Quickly, I attached tag number S7113 to her flipper just before the waves washed the sand away from her shell. In an instant, she was gone. Several seconds passed, and suddenly her head reappeared. She exhaled, then disappeared into the moonlit waters. Even after twenty-two years as a volunteer working for the recovery of endangered sea turtles, my heart still felt that indescribable exhilaration as I stood peering into the darkness, hoping for just one more glimpse of her. Nature and timing took care of that.

Two weeks later, several other volunteers joined me, eager to see one of these elusive, mysterious creatures that visit our beaches. We searched for hours under the starry summer night sky. Nothing.

Suddenly, there she was at the edge of a wave, pausing as if to scrutinize for hazards lurking on land, or perhaps, to make sure this was "her" beach. We kept still, hoping she would not notice us, that she would come ashore and nest as her ancestors had done for millions of years. Slowly and arduously, she crawled up the beach toward the dune vegetation.

Although graceful in the water, sea turtles on land are slow and awkward, expending enormous energy nesting, then returning to the sea. This turtle, however, seemed to be moving more slowly, haltingly, then exhaling more loudly, struggling all the more. Three times she started a body pit only to abandon her efforts. Cautiously, and out of her line of vision, I approached her as she was going through the rhythmic motions of creating a body pit for yet a fourth time. My heart was pounding as I moved toward her, praying I would not frighten her away. Just then, I made the most amazing discovery. It was S7113; she had found her way back. Our paths crossed once again, like finding a dear old friend.

But something was wrong—terribly wrong!

As I looked closer at her ponderous shell, it was heartbreakingly clear: Her rear flippers had been completely severed—ripped off—most likely by a shark! Where her flippers had been, there were only bloodied, raw stumps. It was impossible for her to dig her nest! Still, she labored, the instinct to complete her procreative urge so strong, as if she knew this would be her last legacy. What pain she must have felt!

Turtles shed tears while nesting, partly to remove sand from their eyes; but I shed tears of sorrow for S7113, now so vulnerable not only on land but at sea as well. For centuries, we humans have been anything but kind to these magnificent mariners. Perhaps only one out of ten thousand turtles reaches adulthood. S7113 was that rare one who made it. She beat all odds. And now she was facing even greater suffering just to survive.

Gone was the strength and agility to protect herself at sea.

Gone was the autonomy to create a nest for her offspring.

Gone was the carefree ability to navigate the seas at will.

Her wounds would heal remarkably quickly but forevermore, her life at sea was drastically altered.

We were all overcome with compassion and sadness for this hapless animal. Without completing her nesting, S7113 would receive yet another blow to her species' tenuous future. I had to do something!

Gingerly, I positioned myself flat on the sand so I could mirror her sideways movements and began scooping out sand for her, my hands becoming the flippers she had lost. For at least thirty minutes, we continued in unison, moving side-to-side, digging deeper and deeper. Finally, she stopped and with an audible sigh, began filling the chamber with her glistening, white pliable eggs.

What joy it was to see her future generation fall gently into the sandy cradle. S7113 . . . you did it! We did it! For a fleeting moment, I felt like a sea-turtle midwife! When she finished laying eggs, she and I replaced the sand once again and then, like a blessing, her strong front flippers cast the final spray of sand over her nest. Exhausted, she dragged herself back to the sea, clawing at the sand with only her front flippers, her life-giving task completed perhaps for the very last time.

We all gazed in sheer awe as S7113 disappeared into the watery darkness filled with a sense of sadness as well as joy for having lent a hand in the eternal process of renewal. We knew she might never again be able to nest without a human's help. All the volunteers left the beach in silent rapture that night, each of us imbedded with a deeper understanding and determination for the mission we had undertaken—to fight for the survival of this threatened gentle mariner, the sea turtle.

I never saw S7113 again. Two months later, her nest hatched and there they were: one hundred or so tiny tracks in the sand made by her hatchlings as they left their nest and bravely headed home to the sea, the cycle now completed. My heart smiled again.

Eve M. Haverfield

[EDITORS' NOTE: *For more information on Turtle Time, Inc., contact P.O. Box 2621, Fort Myers Beach, FL 33932; 941-481-5566; e-mail:* whaverfi@peganet.com; *Web site:* www.turtletime.org.]

A Second Chance

As she drove to the Humane Society, Catherine wondered, *What in the world am I doing?* It was the middle of a busy morning, of a busy day, of a busy month, of her busy life. With grueling, eighteen-hour workdays, she barely found time to eat lunch. Here she was, a corporate president, driving away from her office at 10:00 A.M. to walk dogs as a kennel volunteer.

No one was surprised when the company she started exploded with success. What did surprise Catherine was that the more "successful" she became on the outside, the more her soul seemed to be shrinking.

She drove faster toward the kennel for fear that good sense would override her inner drive to be with the dogs. When she entered, amid the loud barking of the dogs vying for her attention, Catherine heard a quiet, constant whimpering. For several long minutes she searched, until she was looking into two sad eyes.

Alone in kennel number 32 was a beautiful springer spaniel with long, snow-white hair painted with patches of brown and tan. She had an underbelly that looked like overfilled cow's udders. "Oh, honey, where are your babies?" Catherine asked lovingly. The dog responded with a loud cry.

Catherine went to the puppy room where she found nine small replicas of their mother, happily bouncing on top of each other, competing for a chance to visit. They were as soft and beautiful as their mother.

Joe, the kennel supervisor, came into the room and said, "Someone just dropped off the mother and all her puppies last night. I expect the puppies will go fast."

Catherine kept her eyes on the litter. "What about the mother? She really misses her pups terribly. Can I bring her in for a visit?"

"No," Joe said quickly. "Separating the pups from their mother was traumatic enough. If we let them see each other, we'll have to do it all over again. Finding the mother a new home is the most difficult task we have now."

Catherine vowed, "I'll find their mom a new home before the last of these puppies is taken."

Joe laughed. "That's a tall order. I'd encourage you to try, but don't be disappointed if it doesn't happen."

"Oh, it *will* happen!" Even Catherine was surprised at the certainty of her voice as she made this declaration.

She returned to the mother's kennel, opened the cage slowly and invited the dog for a walk. The dog came to Catherine cautiously, with her head low to the ground. Once outside, the dog burst into a fury of movement, running from side to side, as far as the leash would allow. Catherine, surprised by all this activity, realized that the poor dog was looking for her babies.

Catherine sat down on the curb and placed her arms around the dog's soft body as she spoke lovingly into her ear. "I don't know why one as sweet and beautiful as you has to suffer the loss of your home, your freedom, your name and especially your precious babies. But I promise to help you find a new home. Let's begin by giving you a name. How about Mattie?"

In response to her new name, Mattie turned her head toward Catherine so that their deep blue eyes were perfectly aligned. She gently licked Catherine's face, sensing she had found a friend. Then the corporate president and homeless mother dog sat together quietly.

Catherine managed to steal time out of her busy corporate life every day that week to be with Mattie. Before she left on Friday, she checked the puppy room to find that just two puppies remained. Her plan was to come back to the shelter on the weekend to match Mattie with the best family she could find.

Arriving at the shelter on Saturday, even before it opened, she took Mattie for a walk and brushed her coat. Then she carefully fastened the new red collar she had bought around Mattie's neck.

Catherine decided to visit the puppy room next, since most people looking for a pet usually start there. After helping several people find dogs that were best suited to their families, Catherine noticed a middle-aged couple enter the puppy room. The petite woman seemed kind, although her husband was large and bearlike. But the way he held his wife's hand and gazed lovingly into her eyes suggested he was a teddy bear. They were both eyeing the last remaining springer spaniel puppy. After introducing himself as Mr. Goodwin, he asked, "Can you tell me how big this puppy will be when fully grown?"

Catherine, smiling with delight, responded, "*Tell* you! I can *show* you exactly how big she will be. And, at the same time, I will introduce you to the best dog we have—this puppy's mother." They nodded enthusiastically.

"I'll bring Mattie out to the exercise pen so you can have a visit," Catherine offered.

Catherine whispered into Mattie's upright ear as she

walked her to the pen. "This is it! This is your chance for a nice, new family. Be sweet to them, and you'll go home today, girl." But when they entered the pen, Mattie was only interested in being with Catherine. The bond between them was so strong that Mattie didn't even notice the Goodwins.

"I need to make a call. Why don't you take the leash and see how it feels to walk Mattie? I'll be right back." Leaving quickly, Catherine crossed her fingers and held her breath. As she spied at them through the window, she was relieved to see Mattie responding to the couple. The Goodwins took turns walking her, and with each passing moment, it was obvious that they were bonding. When Catherine returned, the couple announced, "We want to take her home."

As the Goodwins completed the paperwork, Catherine sat with Mattie. Mattie leaned against her as if to offer a last good-bye. Catherine held her close and began to cry. Rather than tears of sadness, they were tears of sheer joy that Mattie was getting a second chance.

She also cried tears of joy for herself because it was through her volunteer experience that she was able to reconnect to a part of herself that had been dying for a long time. Catherine's heart was now open wide. She remembered what it was like to be a whole and loving human being. And she knew she would bring this wholeness to her work. She had saved one life and changed her own forever.

Jenna Cassell

[EDITORS' NOTE: *For information on The Humane Society of the United States, contact 2100 L Street, N.W., Washington, DC 20037; 202-452-1100; Web site:* www.hsus.org.]

Pegasus's Wings

Each handicap is like a hurdle in a steeplechase, and when you ride up to it, if you throw your heart over, the horse will go along, too.

Lawrence Bixby

I've always loved horses, and for some time I'd been looking for a volunteer opportunity in my new community. The idea that I might be able to pursue both interests at once hadn't actually crossed my mind. So I couldn't get to the phone fast enough when I saw an ad in the paper about a search for volunteers at a therapeutic riding center for handicapped children.

"Yes, we're still looking for people," the woman told me. "We're having a training session for new volunteers this Saturday. You're welcome to come."

"Thanks," I answered, barely containing my enthusiasm. "I'll be there."

I joined a small group of new volunteers that day. We were perfect strangers with an instant connection, all drawn there by the same potent mix of heart and soul—a passion for helping, a passion for horses, and a simple knowing that we had come to the right place. By the end of the training session, we all knew we'd be back for the first of many weekly riding classes together.

That first Saturday, ten children between the ages of eight and twelve showed up. Ten struggling young bodies and ten eager, loving smiles greeted us. "This is Robbie," said the instructor, placing a gentle hand on each small shoulder as she conducted a round of introductions. "And this is Christine." We went around the circle of excited faces. All the children faced some level of physical or mental challenge—sometimes both. Jenny had multiple sclerosis, Kevin lived with cerebral palsy, Christine with Down's syndrome, and Robbie a spinal-cord injury. I marveled at these children, healthy souls and wholesome appetites for living shining through their bodily constraints.

The following Saturday, I arrived at the stables in time to groom my assigned horse before class, put on his tack and ensure that he was sound, calm and ready for his small rider. This week, I would be handling Stripe, a speckled-gray Appaloosa with comfortably rounded sides and an indulgent, ever-patient nature. Today, Stripe was the designated therapy horse for nine-year-old Katie, a victim of muscular dystrophy.

Curly auburn hair framing her delicate, pale face, Katie arrived at the stables in a wheelchair. The spokes glistened in the sun as her mother helped her up, steadied her and introduced us. My eyes met Katie's—an exchange full of shared excitement and anticipation. "Katie has been waiting impatiently for hours," her mother explained with a smile.

We set about preparing for the ride. I fitted and attached Katie's safety helmet and adjusted Stripe's specially adapted saddlery. I helped her mount and shared her triumphant grin as she settled into the saddle, perched above and beyond her limitations. I led Stripe around the arena during the class, quietly coaching both horse and rider as the instructor led the group from the center of the ring. We walked, trotted and moved together for an hour. Katie's tortured body gradually relaxed into Stripe's fluid movements, becoming one with the animal.

In silent awe, I let the wordless, poignant communication between Katie and Stripe unfold. Acutely sensitive to her well-being, Stripe intuitively softened his gait at the slightest perception of Katie's imbalance or discomfort in the saddle. The tone of her voice induced the same effect, even though she was unable to use verbal commands that the horse was trained to recognize. Surprise, delight, hesitation, fear—Stripe understood and responded patiently, lovingly—like a great teacher.

At the end of the class, I helped Katie dismount. Color in her cheeks now, she smiled radiantly and arched her thin arms around Stripe's lowered neck. He kept his head down. Burying her face in his mane, Katie murmured softly, "I love you, Stripe." I stood motionless a few feet away, touched by a moment of uncommon beauty.

The magic drew me back each week. No two Saturdays were the same. Rotations of therapy horses and riders gave volunteers the opportunity to get to know each animal and child. Every Saturday offered a glimpse of an intensely intimate connection between equine and human spirit. Every Saturday revealed the power of this fabled four-legged creature to triumph over a child's physical and mental adversity. Every Saturday, a child held the reins of freedom and borrowed Pegasus's wings.

For me, volunteering was a personal journey into unexpected enrichment and inspiration. I helped small children revel in another realm of physical and spiritual being, a space only their horses could create for them. I saw these children empowered and renewed by their equine companions. I rediscovered my deep love for horses and drew lessons from their gentle ways. And last but not least, I learned that giving yields greater generosity than it asks.

Inspired by my experience, I picked up the phone one day and called my brother at the family farm where I had spent my teenage years. "How's Cowboy doing?" I asked of my own horse.

"He's just fine," my brother replied, "but I think he feels a bit forgotten."

And that's why, a week later, Cowboy came out of semi-retirement and was transported to his new home hundreds of miles away—with me. Now Cowboy—my retired showhorse with huge brown eyes, a stripe down his back and a penchant for pleasing people—volunteers, too.

Vera Nicholas-Gervais

[EDITORS' NOTE: *For information on the North American Riding for the Handicapped Association, contact P.O. Box 33150, Denver, CO 80233; 800-369-RIDE; e-mail: narha@narha.org; Web site:* www.narha.org.]

The Quilting Bee

We are each of us angels with only one wing.
And we can only fly by embracing each other.
Luciano deCrescenzo

"This is a good idea," my friend Sandy mused, reading the bulletin board in the church vestibule. "I wonder what our neighborhood could contribute."

I sidestepped our three-year-olds and leaned over her shoulder to look at the announcement. A parishioner's child had hemophilia, the blood transfusions were becoming expensive, and in addition to requests for donors, the parish had decided to run a raffle on the child's behalf. Neighborhoods were encouraged to get together and donate suitable items.

"You'd never get anyone on our block to participate," I reminded Sandy. She and I, brought together by our toddlers and a mutual need for companionship, were probably the only neighbors who shared any time together. Socializing among the women on our street seemed limited to casual waves while dashing to the office, quick over-the-fence comments and brief greetings at the supermarket. And Mrs. Witkowski, the middle-aged woman in the yellow bungalow, was downright irritable. More than once she had glared at Sandy and me—or actually gone in the house and slammed the door—when we pushed our strollers past her well-tended lawn.

Sandy was still staring at the notice. "Well, we ought to try something, at least. How about a sewing bee where everyone sits around and makes a quilt? A lot of the older women know how to do that sort of thing."

"I think you're out of your mind," I told her affectionately, "and you know I can't thread a needle. But I'd be glad to cut squares or serve lemonade. Hopefully, Mrs. Witkowski won't come—she makes me nervous."

"She never goes anywhere," Sandy reassured me. "Don't worry."

We were wrong on all counts. Not only did several neighbors like the idea and volunteer their help, but at the first meeting Mrs. Witkowski appeared, too, bearing a bag of old fabric scraps and wearing her usual stern expression. She said little but went right to work, tacitly taking charge of the project.

There was something restful about the soft, rhythmic work that encouraged communication. At first, we talked in general terms. Except for Mrs. Witkowski, who stitched without comment, the rest of us chatted about food prices, the state of the union and the new house being built at the end of the street. Slowly we got to know more about each other.

Then one evening Mrs. Witkowski picked up a scrap of red-and-white cloth, and tears filled her eyes. Conversation came to a halt as everyone looked at her. "I remember this material," she murmured finally. "It's from a dress I made for my daughter when she was ten."

There was an uncomfortable silence, and I blundered

into it. "I didn't know you had a daughter, Mrs. Witkowski," I told her.

"I don't. Not anymore." The words were blunt. "She died of leukemia four years ago."

The silence grew even more unbearable, and then another woman spontaneously reached over and took Mrs. Witkowski's hand. "Carol was a darling girl," the woman said, "and I miss her. It's a shame these younger neighbors never met her. You must have some wonderful memories."

The entire room seemed to hold its breath. And then, slowly, Mrs. Witkowski's face relaxed. "Why . . . yes, I do," she said hesitantly. "I remember the time . . . " Her words stumbled at first. Then, as the rest of us listened intently, she went on, reliving some of the special moments, savoring the joy that a beloved child had brought to her.

Gently, other neighbors added their own memories of Carol—her beautiful brown hair, her boyfriends, her graduation from high school. . . . How long, I wondered, had Mrs. Witkowski kept her feelings bottled up because no one had offered her the time, the affirmation, the loving permission to express them? Perhaps she had seemed so angry with Sandy and me because our children were a reminder of her loss.

From that point on, the quality of our relationships in the quilting group changed. As barriers came down, we began to share deeper concerns. Midlife mothers voiced their fears about teens away at college: Would their family's values stay with them, or would they be vulnerable to other ideas? An elderly widow confided her desire to remain independent during her final years. Sandy and I voiced our frustrations in coping with endless diapers and toddler demands. We talked about God, about our plans and dreams. And everyone, even Mrs. Witkowski, laughed—healing laughter all the more precious because it was shared.

We didn't always agree, of course, and we didn't solve any of the world's problems. But during those sewing sessions, we gained something very special. We learned to care for each other, to suspend judgment, drop the facade of polite disinterest and explore each other's spirits. We learned that being a friend meant sustaining each other in times of trouble, rejoicing together in moments of happiness, allowing our own weaknesses to show so that others might comfort us. As our quilt took shape, so too did our friendships with one another.

The day came, of course, when our project was finished, and we all went together to deliver it. The woman at the church hall was astonished when we told her how it had been made. "All of you?" she asked. "All sewing together?"

We nodded. "And we're going to make another," Sandy announced. "We need the therapy!"

Mrs. Witkowski and I exchanged smiles, then watched with the others as the quilt was folded and carefully packaged. Yellow corduroy, blue-and-white gingham, pink-dotted dimity—the fabrics of our lives now forever connected. It had started as a work for charity. But the quilt had made us rich.

Joan Wester Anderson
Originally published in Catholic Digest

Don't You Just Feel Like Singing?

Humor is, in fact, a prelude to faith, and laughter is the beginning of prayer.

Reinhold Niebuhr

According to Westlake Lutheran Church's tradition, our small but spirited band of off-tune singers left the church for a night of singing and good cheer for the sick members of our church. But it was quickly apparent that, because few were sick this year, we'd be back to the cider and cookies all too soon. It was time for some merry magic to weave an insightful strategy.

After finishing our repertoire of songs at the last home, our group of teens and good-natured sponsors huddled together at my request. "I've a got a crazy idea," I said. "Let's go caroling at the supermarket."

The blank stares of the teens were matched only by the alarming and skeptical look of my wife. Not one for making a scene in public, particularly in *her* market, she was ready with a quick veto. But before she could speak, I shared the rest of my plan.

"No," I said, "it won't be our usual caroling experience."

My voice turned almost secretive as if plotting a fiendish act. "Each of us goes into the market alone. We each take a cart and march through the store. Then we meet in the fruits-and-nuts section." The kids were excited, but my wife's expression said otherwise.

My voice picking up speed as the plan emerged, I continued, "We meet in the produce section. Then I'll turn to you and shout, 'Don't you just feel like singing?' Then so as not to leave me alone and looking like a fool, you say, 'Yes!' At that precise moment, we break into song with 'We Wish You a Merry Christmas'!" That seemed to be the only song we were able to hit on key with any regularity.

Before my wife could turn the tide, we were off to Von's market with a renewed sense of mission. We wandered the aisles with our empty carts, trying to look normal. My wife, on the other hand, chose to wander a bit further away, hoping not to be identified with this band of crazy Lutherans.

Although my plan was well thought-out, I was not prepared for the multitude of shoppers already in the fruits-and-nuts section.

There is no way this is going to be a clean performance, I thought. *There are too many unsuspecting shoppers in the way to gather our throng of singers.* I looked across the aisle at my wife, whose look reflected more horror than support. The teens were confused and unsure of what to do. Wearing my "Just Do It!" sneakers, I knew there was only one alternative—stick to the plan.

My enthusiastic question reached the ears of a woman in front of me, right about the time her hand reached a ripe tomato. With as much sincerity and Christmas cheer as I could muster, I looked her in the eye and asked, "Don't you just feel like singing?" The woman recoiled as if attacked, and the unsuspecting tomato fell victim to her death grip.

She looked confused, as if trying to figure out whether I was a mad-hatter or serial killer. As a somewhat shocked and strained smile appeared on her lips, she uttered cautiously, "Well . . . yes!"

With her guarded approval, I turned to the throng in the produce section. With arms open wide, I asked, "Don't the rest of you just feel like singing?"

As the voices of our small but spirited band of off-tune singers blended with the glassy-eyed crowd, they shouted, "Yes!" in unison.

At my direction, we all turned and faced the checkout lines, singing, "We wish you a Merry Christmas, We wish you a Merry Christmas, We wish you a Merry Christmas, and a Happy New Year!"

In a flash, like elves scurrying for cover, our merry band left our carts and immediately ran for the doors, leaving the explanations to the puzzled participants.

Today, many of those young people now work in church groups across the country. We still get an occasional call from a "teen"—now in an older person's body—who will leave a message on our answering machine: "We did a Von's!"

These are the best memories of all.

Terry Paulson, Ph.D.

2

GIVING BACK

Service is the rent that you pay for room on this Earth.

Shirley Chisholm

"It's quite obvious, Tom, that the town can't afford to give you a raise, so we're promoting you to volunteer."

Roberto's Last At-Bat

The only thing necessary for the triumph of evil is for good men to do nothing.

Edmund Burke

As one who wore his first baseball uniform at age three, who slept with his glove under his pillow, who loved the taste of dirt while diving to knock down a ball, who during the 1960s tiptoed around Forbes Field in Pittsburgh like it was a shrine, who marveled at the extraordinary skills of Pirates' rightfielder Roberto Clemente and, unfortunately, as one whose bat could never figure out the physics of a curveball in the Pony League, I did the next best thing to keep my flame for the game alive.

I became a beer vendor at Three Rivers Stadium when it opened in July 1970.

During the summer of the 1972 season, Roberto's last, I was returning to the commissary for another load of beer when Clemente, known as "The Great One," was getting up from a table where he was signing autographs.

As he was dressed in a crisp, white Pirates' home uniform,

I approached him in my dorky, neon-green ZumZum uniform. Our eyes locked, and I briefly asked him in Spanish how he was feeling today.

In an instant, Roberto—with supernatural forces of explosive energy and extreme dignity emanating from his compact body—focused all of his concern on me and respectfully asked how I was doing.

Even though we were worlds apart in careers and years, there was not one drop of condescension, just Roberto's singular concentration for a fellow human being that pierced through me like a laser beam. It was a moment in time that has transcended throughout my life. Yet I was by no means alone.

"Roberto identified with the struggler—the poor man, the taxi driver and the factory worker," explained Luis Mayoral-Rodriguez, a liaison for Latin American ballplayers, in *Pittsburgh Weekly*. "The people who have to suffer, he used to say, the people who have to work."

Despite Roberto's incredibly acrobatic ability for running down fly balls in the gap, his low-slung "basket catches", his unequaled cannonlike arm, his flailing, all-out base-running style, and his beloved, thirty-six-ounce knobless bat with his ferocious, helmet-spinning corkscrew swing, his greatest and lasting memory will always be what he selflessly accomplished and showed by example off the diamond.

Throughout his life, Roberto continually helped people wherever he was—on Pittsburgh's Hill District where he doled out money to homeless people—or throughout Puerto Rico where he passed out fifty-cent pieces to kids.

Roberto was a man who was extremely vigorous to his word. He once said, "If you have a chance to do something for somebody and do not make the most of it, you are wasting your time on Earth." He could never say "no" if he were asked to help or if he felt something better could be done to help those less fortunate.

While being honored by the large Puerto Rican community in New York, Clemente was reluctant to accept a Cadillac as a gift. He insisted the money could be better spent helping charitable organizations and later got promises from the sponsors to help his two favorite causes: mentally-challenged children and kids with physical handicaps.

At the end of that 1972 season, the thirty-eight-year-old Clemente stroked his three-thousandth hit, a double off the left-centerfield wall. I remember it well. I was carrying a load of Iron City beer with my left arm and raising my right fist in the air whooping it up with the rest of the slim crowd. That was Roberto's last official hit, which in retrospect became all too symmetrical and memorable as it capped his illustrious career.

Two months later, while back in Puerto Rico, Clemente eerily woke up one morning and told his wife, Vera, that he'd seen his own funeral in a dream.

Then, during almost the entire month of November, he was in Nicaragua, managing a Puerto Rican baseball team in an amateur World Series. While he was there, he befriended a fourteen-year-old legless orphan and made arrangements for him to be fitted with artificial limbs.

Clemente's compassion combined with being a man of action came to full force after a powerful earthquake rocked Managua, Nicaragua, on December 23, 1972. It killed over 7,000 people and left 250,000 homeless.

This motivated Clemente into becoming head of the Puerto Rican relief committee. He worked fourteen-hour days, gathering food and supplies, filming TV spots, making calls and even going door-to-door to collect donations. His Christmas presents lay unopened as he worked straight through the holidays. In all, he collected $150,000 and twenty-three tons of food, medicine and supplies.

Clemente also made arrangements to lease a cargo plane for three round-trips to Nicaragua at a cost of $11,000.

But then a desperate call came in from Managua for sugar and even more medical supplies. Again, Clemente made the arrangements. This time for a rickety-old, DC-7 cargo plane.

Despite the pleas of Vera and his best friends, Manny Sanguillen and Jose Pagan, Clemente was committed to complete his mission of mercy by going on the second plane as he had heard reports that the rebels in Nicaragua were confiscating shipments.

When asked why he had to leave on New Year's Eve, a highly revered holiday in Puerto Rico, Clemente simply responded, "For me, every day is the same."

With eight tons of supplies haphazardly loaded on the DC-7, the plane took off. An engine caught fire, and it crashed into the Atlantic Ocean at 9:22 P.M. sending Clemente and four others to their premature deaths.

That New Year's Eve, back in Pittsburgh, I had left my radio on all night to a soft music station. For some strange reason, I awoke at 4:00 A.M. just as the first news of his death was being broadcast. Stunned, I can only remember those next couple of weeks as a blur of widespread and deeply felt community grief throughout Pittsburgh and Puerto Rico.

It was just ninety-one days after his three-thousandth hit and only a month after he foresaw his death in a dream. But just as he played the game, Roberto's passing was not only dramatic, it made a statement as well.

It's a statement that has flourished over the years as a bridge, dozens of schools, health centers, ball fields, parks, streets and even a thoroughbred have been named in his honor all over the world.

In 1973, Major League Baseball changed the name of the

Commissioner's Award to the Roberto Clemente Award to annually honor a player who best exemplifies the game of baseball through his involvement in the community.

And as just one example of how he touched so many people, an eight-story-high school in Chicago opened its doors in June 1974, as Roberto Clemente High School. Explaining the name change, the school declared, "This extraordinary man is remembered by most people as one who gave all he had to give, including his life, to help his fellow man."

Yet while most baseball fans were in awe of the exterior Clemente—his gifted physical skills—his enduring legacy will always be the interior Clemente, who as a compassionate humanitarian was, and still is, symbolic of the highest level of human potential for passionate caring and giving within all of us.

Helping people he didn't know, at their greatest time of need, Roberto Clemente, in his last at-bat, died as a volunteer.

John T. Boal

Hurricane Donna

Truly, it is in the darkness that one finds the light, so when we are in sorrow, then this light is nearest of all to us.

Meister Eckhart

When I named my daughter Donna after the hurricane that swept up the East Coast in 1960, little did I know that one day she would have to pass through a hurricane of her own that was every bit as devastating as Hurricane Donna.

The storm in Donna's life began in the summer of 1988. Donna had married four years earlier, and now she was to give birth to a baby. My husband and I, as well as Donna and her husband, began to anticipate a happy time in all our lives.

But things didn't turn out how we had hoped. Although Donna was healthy and strong, and the pregnancy had gone well, Austin was born with a very rare, incurable syndrome. It was very unlikely that he would be with us for long. Perhaps a year, the doctors said.

All of a sudden, the warm glow of having a new son, and

for me a grandson, turned into something very different. It was a stern, heartrending challenge for everyone.

Of course, Austin stole all our hearts. He was a courageous little boy, and he helped to teach us the lessons we needed to learn. Donna was a tower of strength for the family and all our friends. As she cared for her son, she made his every breath count. It was extremely taxing for her, but she seemed to gather strength from it. If a hurricane was going on around our Hurricane Donna, she seemed to have found a way of remaining calm in the midst of it.

When Austin was one year old, he was enrolled at Child Development Resources, Inc., a preschool for special-needs children in Norge, Virginia. This gave Donna a break for a few hours a day, and she would frequently go to the school to watch the way the therapists worked with Austin. He received wonderful care and was totally accepted by all the staff. Austin was not an easy child to care for—he was almost always in pain—but at CDR they loved him and for all the right reasons.

Austin battled hard to make the best of what he had been given, and he managed to outlive his predicted life span.

But it could not last forever. Donna's little boy died when he was three years old. We knew that what had kept him alive for so long was the wonderful nurturing and care he received.

It is hard to explain how it feels to lose a grandson in such circumstances. Or how it feels to lose a son. Donna managed to cope, I could only guess how, but I knew there was an emptiness in her life. There had to be.

One day, a few months after Austin died, Donna called me. It was one of our regular mother-daughter chats. "Mom," she blurted out, eagerness in her voice. "I'm going to volunteer at the school!"

"Oh," I replied, puzzled. "What school's that, Donna?"

"Austin's school!" Her excitement was fairly buzzing down the phone line. "It was where he was happiest. I want to help other special-needs children feel loved, too."

I was speechless. How could Donna have the strength to even contemplate doing that? Reviving all those sad memories. Seeing all those other children with similar conditions. To be where Austin used to be but wasn't any longer.

"Donna . . . " I began. I wasn't sure she should expose herself to all that pain again. I had difficulty just looking at Austin's pictures or the video we had of him from his first birthday.

But Donna knew with certainty what she wanted to do. "He loved being there, with all the other children, remember? He felt so accepted there. I can help because I know what it feels like to be a parent with a special-needs child."

There was a lump in my throat. I was so proud of her. I knew then that she was making the right decision.

And so it turned out. Donna lent her special, hard-won skills to those special-needs children. She knew how to give strength to the parents, too. She had walked in their shoes, and they knew this and loved her for it. Donna felt strongly that the parents should know that the people who were caring for their children loved them. "Not for what's wrong with them, but for what's right with them," she told me.

And although Donna never told me this directly, I think she felt once again connected to Austin during the time she worked at the school, as if his spirit was still present. Austin may no longer be in this world, but he was still making an impact, through Donna, on hearts that needed strength and comfort and inspiration.

Donna's volunteering turned out to be a life-changing event. After discovering the fulfillment in serving others, she decided to train as an occupational therapist. There was nothing in her background previous to this that would have indicated such a course in life. But her precious son Austin had given her the means to discover where her gifts lay. And as an occupational therapist at Norfolk General Hospital, Donna's been giving the gift ever since.

Arline McGraw Oberst
Dedicated to the memory of Austin Lee Hanning

Beyond the Huddle

Unless you try to do something beyond what you already mastered, you will never grow.

Ronald E. Osborn

Realizing that she needed an occupation, Ruth Henricks moved to San Diego and began working for tips in her sister-in-law's neighborhood restaurant, The Huddle.

Ruth took to waitressing like a duck to water. It put her in touch with people, and Ruth loved people.

"I found I was a valuable person," she admits. "I had already raised my children and had a home. But I needed to feel the kind of self-worth you get from being able to say, 'Here's something I can do well!'"

Getting into the restaurant business was just the beginning for Ruth. Eventually, she and her sister-in-law became partners in an additional coffee shop at the downtown San Diego YMCA, which offered affordable rooms to single men. In 1981, Ruth noticed that an excessive number of customers were becoming sick and dying. "It was very hush-hush," Ruth says. "No one ever said they were dying of AIDS, but looking back, I know that was the case."

When her sister-in-law retired, Ruth purchased The Huddle. Among her loyal customers was a darling young man named Scott, who came in for meals every day. Six-feet tall, long blond hair and friendly blue eyes, Scott was very good-looking. He told Ruth he had AIDS. He seemed to grow weaker every day, despite Ruth's hearty meals. As he steadily deteriorated, Ruth became his sounding board. He talked with her each day, explaining a little bit of what was happening to him.

Scott was appreciative for the treatment he received at The Huddle. He would drag himself into the restaurant and say, "When I come in, I'm greeted by everyone. They know my name, and they pat me on the back and ask how it's going today—no matter how I look. I'm so grateful for you and the home-cooked meals."

Scott admitted he no longer had the energy to shop or to prepare food. "I depend on you for my meals, Ruth. If I'm not at The Huddle, you'll know I'm not eating."

One day Scott failed to come to The Huddle. When he didn't come on the second day, Ruth became worried. His haunting words echoed in her ear. She realized she didn't even know his last name or where he lived. Agonizing over Scott's disappearance and feeling totally helpless for days, she finally confided in her regular customers and friends.

Among the customers was a doctor from the nearby medical center. He suggested that she post a note on the cash register, offering to deliver meals to people with AIDS. The response was overwhelming to an unmet need. Ruth, the physician and her supporters met in The Huddle's little dining room and signed papers of incorporation giving birth to the San Diego Special Delivery.

In addition to running The Huddle, Ruth also manages her "troops"—a cadre of 200 volunteers, 100 of them drivers—who prepare, wrap and deliver home-cooked

Huddle meals to about 175 people living with AIDS. "Special Delivery" is a 100 percent volunteer organization.

Through her association with Scott, Ruth has touched the lives of thousands. "I'm amazed at the heart I find in each of my volunteers," she says proudly. "All of us realize we have some kind of talent. Although we can't do everything, there is at least one thing we can do. Scott's probably looking down from heaven right now. He came to me a stranger and changed my life. He got me to look way beyond our little family restaurant."

Ruth Henricks found something she could do well—for others.

Charlene Baldridge

The Deep End

by Matt Matteo

A Cure for Restlessness

Love cures people—both the ones who give it and the ones who receive it.

Dr. Karl Menninger

Last year, when I went back to China, I paid a visit to Xiaotao, my college friend. He wasn't home, but his wife, Malan, greeted me warmly and led me into their home. As I answered her questions about my life in the United States, I glanced at the expansive living room with elegant furnishings. I knew that what I had heard over the years was true. As China continued to prosper in the last decade, so did my friends.

Half an hour later, when Xiaotao still had not returned, I asked, "Do you think he had to work late?"

"Ah, no," Malan answered pleasantly, pouring tea into my cup. "He's at the orphanage this afternoon."

"Orphanage?"

"Yes," she nodded with a smile. "He began volunteering there three years ago."

During my visit, I heard many things about my friends:

Zhang attained wealth; Li obtained a divorce; Wang was laid off . . . but volunteering in an orphanage sounded alien. I wanted to ask her why, but I didn't. The look on my face must have betrayed my amazement because Malan began telling me the story.

In 1987, she and Xiaotao married. She worked as a copy editor at a magazine, while he taught at our alma mater. Malan gave birth to their son a year later, and their life was good.

But when the government began to allow private enterprise in 1992, Xiaotao became restless. He wanted to make money—lots of it. Borrowing funds from his parents, he quit his job and opened his first restaurant. He was very good at what he did. No one knew how he had learned his business savvy—both his parents were teachers.

After the triumph of the first restaurant, he opened another, then a clothing store, an ice-cream parlor and a string of other successful enterprises. In five years, he became a very wealthy man.

Malan momentarily paused. Her smiling face quickly turned somber as she continued. "But trouble began soon after that. Xiaotao's businesses were thriving, and he had more free time on his hands and more money in his pockets than he knew what to do with. He began to frequent bars and discos and spend less and less time with me and our son."

Pausing to control her emotion, she continued. "Then one night he didn't come home. The next morning, he walked in reeking of perfume and liquor. That's when I asked for a divorce. He was so angry that he stormed out of the house, got back into his car and drove away. As he was driving to a nearby village, he hit an old woman.

"That was another turning point in our lives," she said. "The old woman suffered a fractured arm, and Xiaotao visited her every day at the hospital. He was fond of her.

They exchanged their life stories, and before long, we called her Aunt Liu.

"On the day she was released from the hospital, Aunt Liu suggested a cure for his restlessness. She told him to spend some time at the orphanage where she worked. He laughed loudly, patted her on the shoulder and assured her he would donate plenty of money. Aunt Liu shook her head and told him that spending time at the orphanage would be more helpful to *him* than to the orphanage."

Then, looking at me with a proud smile, she said, "After his first visit, he embraced it with his heart and soul. He helped to make cribs and additional rooms for new arrivals. He held the babies when they cried and played with the older children, spending most of his free time there."

An hour later, Xiaotao came home. "Sorry I'm late," he said, shaking my hands with a vise-like grip. "I was about to leave when an abandoned baby girl was brought in."

"What did you do with her?" I asked, my heart in my throat.

"I held her and rocked her until she stopped crying."

Swallowing hard, I tried not to cry. We visited a while longer before I had to take my leave.

The week before my departure, I got a call from Malan asking me to attend Xiaotao's mother's funeral. When I arrived in the old neighborhood, the procession for the funeral was already a mile long and the cry was heard a mile wide. Colorful paper money flew about in the breeze like butterflies. *Some things in China will never change,* I thought.

As I entered the courtyard and bowed in front of his mother's coffin, Xiaotao came over to shake my hand. "Thanks for coming," he said. He looked somber and pensive.

"My condolences," I said softly.

He nodded. "My mother lived a long life."

"I want you to know something," I said. "Of all the

things new in China, what impresses me the most is how the orphanage helped you to regain your life and how you are helping these children."

His lips quivered. "The night before my mother died, she told me about a secret she had kept," he said, staring into the distance. "One night, thirty-seven years ago, she found me lying in a basket on the doorstep . . . of an orphans' home."

Linda Jin Zou

Giving Something Back

We make a living by what we get, but we make a life by what we give.

Winston Churchill

After thirty-three years of managing the office for our auto-parts store in our small hometown of Athens, Alabama, we decided to sell our business and retire. We also raised beef cattle on the farm where we live, so I knew my husband would find plenty to do to keep busy, but what about me? I needed something to fill my days and most of all to feel needed. Our two children were married and had homes and careers of their own. Oh, I knew I'd be busy gardening, freezing vegetables and all the other things farm wives do, but I was used to being with people, and I loved the many friendships we shared with our customers and friends. How could I retire and still have a feeling of connection with our community? After all, these were the people who supported our efforts when we first opened our business, two young people scared to death we wouldn't make it on a shoestring budget. We had been so blessed, and I wanted to give something back.

Knowing my dilemma, a friend told me about a hospice meeting and asked if I would be interested in taking the training class and becoming a hospice volunteer. I was so excited! Here was my opportunity to serve my community, give back to it, maintain friendships and begin new ones. The only thing I worried about was that all my patients would be terminally ill and in their doctor's opinion would not live more than six months. Was I up to the task?

I could certainly sympathize with their families. I had lost both my parents when they were in their prime of life. I had been a young mother myself, and I desperately needed my mother's love and advice when she was stricken with cancer. I longed for my children to have the opportunity to get to know her gentle ways and to remember her kisses on their skinned knees, but that was not to be. I spent many days and nights alone or sometimes out on the old porch swing with a cup of coffee, feeling as if no one knew or cared for me. How I wished for an understanding arm around my shoulder while my mother slipped quietly into eternity. Yes, I knew grief firsthand. If my experience had taught me anything, it was to share compassion to the dying and their families. So I became a hospice volunteer, and my journey began.

Equipped with information from my new training class, my desire to serve and a willingness to learn, I was assigned my first patient. With shaking knees, I knocked on the door of an elderly gentleman who was thrilled to see me. I recognized him at once as one of our former customers. Mr. Adams, a humble man, could neither read nor write, nor could his wife. She had never learned to drive a car; therefore, I drove him into the nearest town for his cancer treatments. I took him for drives through the countryside to his boyhood home and stopped occasionally for a cool drink of water from the sweet spring there.

His wife found it too difficult to help him prepare for the inevitable, so it was I who helped him in the making of his last will and testament, pre-planned his funeral and helped him with his final wish—to accept the Lord as his Savior before he died. Mr. Adams taught us all the power of faith by living two years from the time I first knocked on his door instead of the usual six months.

My next knock found my knees shaking, just not as hard. Imagine my surprise when I was answered by a caregiver and led to the bedside of my favorite high-school teacher, whom I had not seen in many years. Her body was terribly frail but her memory still vivid. We had many days of joyful remembrances, and I was able to notify several of her former students of her condition, so she had many visits and calls.

My greatest challenge was my childhood friend, who had remained a dear friend and confidant, and was diagnosed with inoperable brain cancer. By her bedside, we shared our feelings about life and how it seems to slip away unnoticed, so many things left undone and unsaid.

Then came the elderly couple who were struggling to care for each other. At first, they were a little reluctant to let anyone into their lives, but they soon appreciated the loaves of homemade bread and fresh vegetables from my garden. Their favorite gifts were the big bouquets from my rose garden. My rose garden was my greatest asset. I found that all my patients and their families loved my roses. A fresh bouquet of vibrant red "Dolly Partons" or the creamy pink "Barbara Bushes" always seemed to brighten up a dismal sick room. My garden of eight to ten bushes, inspired by my patients' enthusiasm, began to grow. Twenty, then forty, then sixty-five bushes, a whole corner of my yard in wonderful fragrant colorful roses just waiting to be cut while the early morning dew still lingered on their petals. They seemed to know their purpose and outdid themselves with some blooms as big as saucers. Soon, my garden became known as my Hospice Rose Garden. Word soon spread about the Dollys and Barbaras. They began to appear at weddings, teas and other social gatherings in our community. Just another way I found to give back.

My greatest reward is being requested by a patient or family to be their volunteer. When I get a call from our director with the words, "Someone has asked for you," I am filled with great humility. Each assignment holds a new challenge. I have learned from every family. We are all God's children, and he has a plan for each life. A smile is the same in every language, and "I love you" is really very easy to say if you mean it.

Wynell Glanton Britton

[EDITORS' NOTE: *For information on Hospice Net, contact Suite 51, 401 Bowling Ave., Nashville, TN 37205; Web site:* www. hospicenet.org.]

Daddy Bruce Randolph

During the times of maladies, true bodhisattvas become the best holy men medicine; . . . during the times of famine they become food and drink. Having first alleviated thirst and hunger, they teach the dharma to living beings.

The Buddha Vimalakirinirdesha Sutra 8

"Daddy" Bruce Randolph was a chain smoker who used a white filter on his Winstons. It was his only vice. Mostly, the dapper man—around five-feet-eight and slightly built, who would never be seen in public without his hat, vest and coat—fed people.

At age sixty-one, he opened Daddy Bruce's Barbecue Restaurant in the "Five Points" area, a poor section of Denver.

There is debate about whether his ribs were the best in town but no debate on the man himself. He was a gentle man, and he started a tradition that died with him, some thirty years after he opened his restaurant. He fed people—not just his customers, but the poor and the homeless.

Every Thanksgiving, Daddy and his son began cooking for the multitudes of homeless. He wanted them to have a great dinner on the one day this country celebrates its bounty.

About a week before, Daddy began making all the "fixin's." In the early years of his project, he paid for everything out-of-pocket. But as time went by, the costs skyrocketed as the crowds grew. That's when Daddy's admirers stepped in to help.

They donated tons of turkeys, potatoes, yams and ribs. And they donated their time to stand behind and beside the old man. Professional athletes, politicians, cops, nuns and clergy, as well as others volunteered to cook and serve. It was a rare moment to witness a Denver Bronco serving food to a man who lived in a cardboard box underneath a viaduct.

It seems there was an endless supply of food to feed the multitudes. No one ever walked away hungry from Daddy Bruce. It was Daddy who started the whole thing and supervised it until a few years ago when he edged toward ninety. He had become too old to work anymore.

He was one of the few people who lived to see a city street named in his honor. In 1991, Mayor Federico Peña renamed East Twenty-third Avenue "Bruce Randolph Boulevard." A couple of years later, Daddy Bruce died. He lived modestly but well.

When asked why he volunteered to feed the thousands of poor and hungry people for over twenty-five years, his reply was simple. "You can't beat love. Nothing beats love. If you give just one thing, you get three things back. That's why I do it." And he did it well.

Pat Mendoza

Coats for Kosovo

Compassion is the chief law of human existence.
Fyodor Dostoyevsky

My son was deployed to Kosovo in 1999, and he phoned home shortly after arriving at Camp Monteith in the eastern section of the country. The call was relayed through Germany and then sent to an army post in the United States before being patched through to my house. He spoke enthusiastically about his base camp and his new job, but there was concern in his voice when he told me about the Kosovar children.

"They'd break your heart, Mom, if you could see them. When we drive through town, they stand in the streets in their frayed coats and worn shoes and wave at us as we pass by. Smiles cover their faces, but it's so cold. And they don't have warm clothing to wear."

When he called the following week, the children were still on his mind. "They need coats, Mom. Maybe some of the people from church could send their kids' used clothing."

Ironically, our parish had sponsored a refugee family from Kosovo. Many people had worked to resettle the eleven Albanians by donating food, clothing and money to help them get back on their feet. I hated to ask the parishioners to do more, and so I failed to respond to Joseph's request. He was quick to remind me of the need for action when we spoke the next time.

"The snowdrifts are more than five feet high," he said. "The children play outside, yet it's freezing. And they have so little."

Wood-burning stoves had been sent in by the relief services, and his unit had distributed them to the people in the area. They were working with the town's mayor to build a market and to get an old mine back in operation. But it was the children who continued to tug at Joseph's heart.

"They're cold and don't have enough to wear. Won't someone send coats?"

No longer able to ignore his insistent pleas, I arranged a notice in our church bulletin. A few hours after returning home from Mass that Sunday, the phone rang.

"I have coats," a woman said. "Tell me where to mail them." Another call soon followed. "I'll clean out my kids' closets and drop the things off at church."

One woman approached me later that week. "I found a coat on sale," she said as she slipped it into my hands. Fire-engine red with black diagonal stripes, the jacket was water-repellent and down-filled. "It's only one coat but . . . ," she shrugged, "maybe it will help."

A friend who always puts words into action and responds quickly to the needs of others canvassed her neighborhood. "I have eight shopping bags filled with coats," she told me over the phone.

I smiled at her success. "Bring them over. We'll box them up and mail them together." The clothing was in good condition and would provide warmth even in the coldest weather. As we carefully tucked the coats into boxes, we prayed for the children who would wear them and for their protection in the midst of conflict.

Ten days later, the phone rang, and I heard Joseph's voice. "The boxes have started to arrive. The coats are perfect, Mom. The kids will love them."

My son wasn't the only one seeking help for the children. Many of the other soldiers' families were sending donations. Joseph's company commander's wife, a mother with three little ones, sent gloves and hats along with coats. Clothing was pouring in from the battalion chaplain's stateside congregation.

Then, to my surprise, digital photos arrived as an attachment to Joe's e-mail. I downloaded them onto a disc and eagerly opened the file. Slowly the photos unfolded across my monitor. I saw a muddy road and bullet-scarred walls and the faces of beautiful children receiving gifts from the United States. I didn't need to hear their voices, for their eyes—filled with amazement at the bounty they had been given—said it all. And there was Joseph in the midst of them, dressed in a Kevlar helmet, bulletproof vest and mud-smeared boots, with an M-16 rifle slung over his shoulder and a wide smile plastered on his full face.

"Tell the people at church how much their gifts mean to the children, Mom. They're the greatest!"

Debby Giusti

I'll Never Forget

*It is when we forget ourselves that we do things
that are remembered.*

Eugene P. Bertin

It was a brisk fall day in 1970—brisk by Southern
California standards. Mary and Ellen, sisters in their late-
forties, stepped off the bus and onto the sidewalk to enjoy
the sunlit stroll toward the USO (United Service Organization) building. Rounding the corner, they were immediately startled by the scene unfolding before them.

In the center of a violent crowd, a splash of "olive drab"
color was barely distinguishable. "A soldier!" Mary gasped.
The women tried to shove their way through the raucous
crowd of Vietnam War protesters.

"Oh my gosh!" cried Ellen. "They're beating him." The
women, desperate to break up the group and help the
young man, were repeatedly jostled and elbowed. Unable
to get close enough to help, they could do little more than
watch the young soldier as the crowd repeatedly kicked
him and spat on him.

With a lunge, Ellen tried to break through the enraged

crowd, only to receive an elbow in the face. Mary rushed to her sister's aid, and while nursing Ellen's bleeding nose, the two women watched as a protester suddenly produced a knife, plunging it into the back of the outnumbered soldier who lay curled up on the sidewalk, trying to shield his body from his attackers.

With that a police whistle blew, and the crowd of protesters attempted to scatter. The police in riot gear grabbed as many of the protesters as they could, including the young man with the bloody knife still in his hand.

As additional police officers ran to the soldier's aid, Mary and Ellen quickly sunk to the sidewalk. "I can't believe it," muttered Ellen, horrified by their violent encounter. Tears were streaming down both their faces.

"How could they do that? He's just doing his job," Mary said between sobs.

A paramedic knelt next to Ellen and tried to examine her bleeding nose. "I'm fine," she said stiffly, pulling away and rising to her feet. "Let's go, Mary!"

Still in shock, Ellen and Mary stumbled toward the USO building, arm in arm, glancing back over their shoulders every few seconds to see the paramedics who continued to work on the wounded soldier. Once inside, John, the director of the facility, helped Ellen to a chair while Mary ran off in search of a washcloth for her sister.

With tears in his eyes, John asked, "Did you see what they did to that young soldier?" John's attempt to display strength couldn't conceal the pain written clearly on his face.

"Yes, we both saw it," Ellen replied. "We tried to help him, but with that vicious mob we couldn't get close enough."

"When I realized what was happening, I called the police," John began. "I hope it wasn't too late."

"Something must be done," Ellen said vehemently.

Later that afternoon Ellen, Mary and John sat in the lounge, sipped coffee and tried to settle their nerves. Ellen looked toward Mary and said softly, "Remember the old days, Mare?"

"Sure do," Mary replied with a small smile. "Those were glorious days when Mother and Daddy helped to start the first USO back in 1942. World War II was awful, but at least we stuck together as a nation. Everyone supported our boys back then."

Ellen nodded in agreement. "What has this country come to . . . wanting to kill the very people who defend us? These protesters don't understand the respect that we owe our men and women in uniform. Because of them we enjoy our freedom."

Ellen and Mary, together with John, devised a plan so that they would never again have to witness the horror that occurred right outside their doors. They distributed messages and flyers to all the military bases in the area, urging them to warn military personnel not to walk the city streets in uniform.

In 1970, any man with a short military-type haircut was sure to be a target. Once Ellen and Mary got the word out, young men with long hair began slipping through the front doors of the USO, dressed in tie-dye T-shirts, torn jeans and sunglasses. But once inside, the wigs and sunglasses came off, revealing the soldier or sailor within.

A few weeks later a "hippie" entered the USO's main lobby while Ellen and Mary were stationed at the front desk. After writing his name on the sign-in sheet, the handsome young man pulled off the sunglasses and wig, revealing a peach-fuzz head and bright blue eyes. With a hearty laugh and a colossal grin he asked, "Hey, how much do they pay you women to work here?"

Ellen smiled back and replied, "Not even a penny."

With a look of concern the soldier said, "You mean, in

this day and age, women volunteer to help U.S. military personnel? You could get into trouble. I hope you're careful."

"Don't worry about us, dear," Ellen replied reassuringly.

"And what about those pretty young women that come to dance with us on Saturday nights? What do they pay them?" the soldier inquired.

Tickled by the young man's questions, Ellen responded with a chuckle, "Nothing."

"No way!" The young man exclaimed. "Why would they spend their time here?"

"Some of us do care, dear," Ellen said unwaveringly.

The young man stooped down, unzipped his backpack, and as he stood up once again he smiled and presented Ellen and Mary with two small floral bouquets. As he handed over the flowers he said, "Three weeks ago I saw you being pummeled out here on the sidewalk, when the soldier was stabbed." The two women hung on his every word as he continued. "I saw what you tried to do. You were the only ones who tried to help." Just then he pulled down the top of his T-shirt to reveal a large bandage stuck neatly to his left shoulder and upper chest. "Thank you for trying to help me," he said with great sincerity. "I will never forget you."

The two women immediately ran out from behind the counter; as they cautiously threw their arms around him, they burst into tears. "It was you!" they exclaimed in unison. "It was you! Thank goodness you're alive!"

Twenty years later the United States found itself embroiled in conflict in the Persian Gulf region. Ellen and Mary, in their late sixties by then, were still tirelessly volunteering at the USO. As the women finished tying another bundle of yellow ribbons to distribute to local residents and businesses to show their support for the U.S. military troops, they heard that the war had ended.

A few weeks later the city sponsored an elaborate

parade for the returning heroes. Ellen and Mary were riding atop the USO float. As they waved to the cheering crowd, they noticed a cluster of people gathered near a Vietnam Veterans' banner. As their float passed, a middle-aged man, his lovely wife and their two teenage children ran over to the float. Standing with his hands behind his back, the grinning man winked. "I promised I would never forget you. Thank you for all you've done," and instantly produced a bouquet of flowers for both Ellen and Mary.

P. Christine Smith

[EDITORS' NOTE: *For information on United Service Organization World Headquarters, contact 1008 Eberle Place, S.E., Suite 301, Washington Navy Yard, DC 20374-5096; 202-610-5700; e-mail:* info@uso.org; *Web site:* www.uso.org.]

The Deep End
by Matt Matteo

$\overline{3}$

MAKING A DIFFERENCE

Somewhere out there is a unique place for you to help others—a unique life role for you to fill that only you can fill.

Thomas Kinkade

"It's just until we get the car back!"

Dave

For what does it profit a man if he gains the whole world but forfeits his soul.

Jesus of Nazareth

"Remember that nothing carries more potential for change than individual acts of human kindness, even though corporate enterprise is important to the economies of developing countries." The keynote speaker had just concluded his lecture entitled "Business Opportunities in Southeast Asia."

Impressed as I was by the speaker's business savvy and his obvious understanding of international markets, I believed his last statement to be somewhat disingenuous.

What did an American, dressed in an expensive suit, lecturing in a five-star hotel, know about individual acts of human kindness in the developing world? Judging from the cynical expressions on the faces of my fellow conferees, I was not alone in my skepticism.

The following day, while touring the Indonesian city where the conference was being held, the taxi in which I was riding passed through a dilapidated block that consisted almost entirely of trash. I rolled down the cab window in an effort to grasp the squalor I had only seen on TV in the United States, but the stench of the surroundings forced me to retreat. Before passing on to less disturbing scenery, I saw a shabbily dressed woman and two small children rummaging among fly-infested debris, eating discarded scraps.

The image of the pitiable woman and her children filled me with a sense of hopelessness and an even darker skepticism toward the words of the speaker from the previous night. *No act of personal volunteerism, however noble or kind, could change the plight of a family like that,* I thought.

Eighteen months later, I had the occasion to return to that city and, having spent a year and a half in the creature comforts of the West, had forgotten about the images of the woman and her children. It wasn't until the taxi was passing through the very same section of the city that I remembered the family. Though I was certain I was in the same location as before, the area looked cleaner.

I explained to the driver what I had seen eighteen months earlier and asked him if he knew a woman with two children who lived among the refuse.

"Ibu Lani," he said.

Fearing the worst, I asked what had become of her.

"I'll show you."

Maneuvering the taxi between piles of discarded cardboard boxes and newspapers, the driver stopped in front of a small wooden shack hidden behind a mountain of empty bottles and rusty cans.

"She's probably in there," the driver said pointing at the shack.

"Is that where she lives?" I asked, hesitant to get out and see for myself.

"No," the driver answered, laughing. "That's her office. She has a house near where her children go to school."

"Office?" I asked. "I thought she was so poor she had to search among the trash for food."

The driver smiled at me through his rearview mirror.

"She was, but a foreigner taught her how to collect the trash and sell it to companies to recycle. He even brought people to meet her so she could find out what they wanted. I know because he was in my taxi the first time he saw this place and Ibu Lani."

"Who is this guy?" I wanted to know.

"That's him behind us with Ibu Lani."

I turned to look where the driver was pointing and gasped when I saw the transformation that had occurred in Ibu Lani. There was no doubt she was the same woman, but she was well-dressed and carried herself with a graceful confidence not present when I had seen her eighteen months earlier.

And who was the foreigner who had taken the time to teach this woman that she could rise above the poverty and despair which surrounded her? Dressed in filthy coveralls and carrying a dripping trash bag filled with greasy newspapers, it was none other than the conference speaker himself.

I was too embarrassed to tell this man that I was aware of his humble act of service to this woman. I think Dave is one of those rare individuals who would rather remain obscure.

Thinking back on it now, after I spent the next seven years serving the people of Indonesia, I wonder who Dave's act of volunteerism impacted the most?

Jamie Winship

A Touch of Love

*If we pray, we will believe; if we believe, we will
love; if we love, we will serve.*

Mother Teresa

I'd already been a research volunteer in India for a year
when I decided to volunteer at the Mother Teresa Home
for the Sick, Dying and Destitute in Calcutta. I knew my
research was useful, but I couldn't help feeling that India
was calling me to do something else. I felt my place was in
Calcutta among the poorest of the poor. One day, I finally
gathered the courage to follow my heart and caught the
train to Calcutta.

There is something about Calcutta that I will always
love. Despite the dirt, cracked pavements, dusty trees and
belching traffic fumes, there is such an overwhelming
sense of the human spirit that I walk its streets with joy.
But, the day I arrived on the dusty street outside the
Home, I was overcome with doubt.

My eyes filled with tears as I faced the place my heart
had led me, but I couldn't join the volunteers who were
going in. I was terrified of what was inside and of failing to

help. I stood outside alone until I couldn't delay any longer. I walked up to the narrow wooden door and stepped in.

The first thing I saw was a dead man, wrapped in a sheet, waiting to be moved. I had never seen anything like it before; only deceased relatives in coffins. I paused at his skinny, crooked shape. A nun asked me what I wanted. When I looked at her simple smock and rough, callused hands, I realized that she dealt with death every day. She didn't need me wasting her time. So I promised myself I'd be strong and not let her down. "I am here for the day," I said. "What can I do?"

She instantly bundled me into a room with a mostly empty medicine cupboard and flung open a larger cupboard with sheets and diapers. With no instructions, she pointed me toward the women's wing and bustled off. As I looked for an apron, a two-year-old started to scream behind me as a volunteer cleaned the burns covering half the child's body. Two other volunteers were cleaning a hole in a woman's foot. I could see a bone protruding from the bloody, red flesh. I couldn't believe her courage nor the skill of the volunteers. *A dead body, a burnt child, a foot cut to the bone—what on earth can I offer here? I'm a researcher not a doctor.*

An American volunteer called to me, "Come here and help, will you?" She was trying to wash an elderly lady who was squirming in pain. I helped lift her and dried her off. But no sooner was she out than another was brought in. Over the next few minutes I realized the work had a pattern.

In front of me stretched two rows of women on simple cots. Volunteers were scurrying back and forth, washing, scrubbing, lifting, feeding and diaper changing. They seemed to work in pairs. Everybody was constantly coming and going. I felt lost. The American didn't need me anymore, and I didn't know where else to begin. The volunteers looked friendly but were too busy to explain much to a late newcomer. As I wondered if I should leave, a German woman threw me a cloth.

For the next two hours, I washed, wiped and tried to keep the women's dignity as I changed diaper after diaper. Some women cried out in pain in Hindi; others glared silently. They no doubt resented this young Western girl fumbling about with their bodies, and I didn't blame them.

At mid-morning the volunteers had tea and biscuits on the roof. How wonderful to meet some of the faces that had raced around me at three times the pace I could manage. But, I felt shy and disappointed that I couldn't make a real difference to the women downstairs. Once again, my mind told me that my actions were useful, yet my heart and spirit felt empty. As I looked down at the flower and fruit *wallahs* (sellers), who sat all day on the street, I decided to find meaning in whatever I did that day.

I ran downstairs, full of energy for more scrubbing. To my surprise, a volunteer told me this was *quiet time* when I could spend a couple of hours with one woman. I could brush her hair, talk to her or hold her hand. I started walking along the beds and asked the universe to direct me to someone. A few of the women were sleeping, and most who were wide awake turned away from me. But one woman looked straight at me and called to me in her language.

I sat on her bed, reaching for her hand, but she grabbed my wrist first, holding me in a ferocious grip. Her stringy, tangled hair was slick with grease, and her bumpy skin sagged into her cheeks. She looked fiercely into my eyes for a minute, then two minutes—maybe longer. I didn't know what to do. I wanted to help her. Feeling embarrassed, I turned to ask a volunteer. Suddenly, the woman grabbed my wrist even harder, as if to say, *No, you can't go. Your time's not done here.*

Taking a deep breath, I looked into her eyes and realized that my challenge was to love without fear. I began to do the only thing I could think of—stroke her arm. As she lay her head back on the pillow, I took her other arm and rubbed that, too. Her eyes were closed. Finding some moisturizer, I massaged her shoulders. She suddenly pulled up her tunic and pointed to her belly, which was as twisted as her face had been a moment earlier; I massaged that as well. As her body eased itself into my touch, her face began to soften. Over the next hour I massaged her legs, her back and finally her head and face.

During that hour, years melted from her face. When she finally opened her eyes, they were so full of peace that I started to cry. It seemed incredible that only a few hours before I had felt useless. I had forgotten how I love to share the healing power of touch. But she saw through my fear and gave me the best gift of all—the opportunity to love another human being so completely that we were both transformed. I will always remember that moment as the most beautiful and powerful in my life and honor her as one of my greatest teachers.

Kayte Fairfax

A Volunteer's Prayer

O, God,

Today I will be with those who are suffering and frightened, and possibly alone. Some will have no one to talk to today, Lord, but me.

May my arms be strong to give someone a hug, my hands comforting and warm to hold another's hand, and through my eyes and smile may someone know I care.

But most of all, Lord, give my heart the compassion and understanding that will calm another's fears, dry a tear, and give strength to face what lies ahead.

I am only one person, Lord, but you and I know one person can and will make a difference in another's life.

And if I can do that for someone today, when my head lies upon my pillow tonight, and my eyes close, I will be at peace.

Amen and Amen.

Lois Clark Suddath

A Touch from Above

Always forgive your enemies ... nothing annoys them so much.

Oscar Wilde

The phone rang at three-thirty A.M.

Thinking it was my son playing a joke, I blurted, "What's up?"

"Mrs. Washington?" the unfamiliar voice asked.

"Yes."

"I'm from the Medical Examiner's office. Do you have a son named Grub?"

"Yes, sir, I do."

"I'm sorry to tell you this, but your son's been shot several times."

I immediately sat up. "Go on ..."

"I'm sorry, ma'am, but your son is dead."

At that moment, I felt like my life had ended. My son, whose real name was Damon, was only nineteen and had two children he loved very much. I got up and went to my other child and told him his brother was dead. We fell into each other's arms and cried harder than I had ever cried in my life.

By mid-morning, the house was full of people from my church and family. I sat in a frozen daze wondering what I had done to deserve this numbing pain that was all too familiar.

When I was ten, I witnessed the murders of my mother and my sixteen-year-old sister at the hands of my step-father. I was to die that day, too, but the gun didn't go off when he fired at me. Then a short time after my last son was born, his father, the love of my life, was murdered. And now the fourth murder in my immediate family. I hurt with heartaches and headaches that defied medical description. It was like being pummeled by cinder blocks that just wouldn't stop falling on me.

Somehow, as I can't really recall, I slowly started gathering myself over the next few months. While getting updates from "we have a suspect" to "captured and arrested," I realized we have a hurting world of young people. Deciding to take some kind of control of the accumulated tragedy in my life, I researched the backgrounds of my perpetrators and found they had all spent time in criminal institutions without any type of rehabilitation to dissolve the anger that drove them to kill another human being. I wrote the young man who killed my son, asking him for his forgiveness for hating him for what he had done to my life. In return, I forgave him for brutally murdering my son. He didn't respond with anything positive for some time. Then one day I received a letter that thanked me for forgiving him. He calls me "Mom" today, and we still write each other as often as we can.

To continue to help myself heal, I began a program called "Mentoring A Touch From Above" that works with youth ages thirteen to eighteen in the California Youth Authority. I took on numerous youths but one in particular became my focus.

His name was Pony. He was a Cambodian who was

serving time for armed robbery and assaults while in a Vietnamese gang.

Although Pony was a brutally bitter man, he and I became instant friends after I told him my story. He wrote a touching poem about Damon and, in turn, told me his life story.

The oldest of three brothers, Pony was the focal point for the future of his family. While Pony's father was like many older Asian men in the United States, meek and quiet, Pony's mother was in constant distress, a troubled woman in a strange land, who didn't speak unless she was hollering and cursing.

Through my program, Pony completed his high school education in prison and earned his diploma. When he was released, I visited him in a halfway house where the older men were beating him. Driven from there, he went right back to the streets.

But from the skills he learned in my modest program, Pony began to look for jobs and joined a youth church group. After weeks of trying, he finally landed a job working with one of my company's suppliers. He helped pay the bills in his home, mentored his younger brothers and was considered one of the best employees this company had hired.

If I had not volunteered to take Pony on so vigorously as a client, he would have been just one more number shuffling through the revolving door of the California Youth Authority. Today we have over two hundred "Ponys" involved in the program with two hundred to three hundred more on our waiting list grasping for a one-way ticket to exit this violent circle and reenter society.

So far, we've helped thirty youth who are now living permanently at home and who have returned to the mainstream by going back to school, getting jobs and working with their families. These thirty "adopted" sons are helping me, in turn, work through my compound losses by insuring their futures will not end in premature death.

Life is still going to throw them some punches, but with renewed hope and constant encouragement, Pony, like the others, will make it and will always have me to call on in times of need.

While my son's life was tragically lost at nineteen, as a surrogate mother to Pony, those in my program and the hundreds behind them just itching to join, I can proudly say Damon did not die in vain.

Melanie Washington

[EDITORS' NOTE: *For more information on Mentoring A Touch From Above, contact 3970 S. Atlantic Ave., Suites 208–209, Long Beach, CA 90807; 562-490-2402; fax: 562-981-0512; e-mail:* melbel11@msn.com; *Web site:* www.matfa.com.]

Treasured Visits

I met her on my first day as a volunteer ombudsman—
a patient's advocate at an assisted living facility. As the
elevator doors on the first floor opened, I saw her—a large
woman with graying hair, no more than fifty and seated
on a bed in the room ahead. She was staring at something
in her hands. I headed for the nurses' station.

"Could I have the name of the woman in room 212?"

"Room 212?" murmured the nurse, glancing at a sheet in
front of her. "That's Jeannie," said the young nurse with a
smile. "She arrived today."

Knowing how one feels in a strange place, I headed for
the room and knocked. "Is there anything I can do for
you?" I asked with a smile.

She glanced toward the door but didn't return my
smile. *Well,* I told myself, *you can't expect a smile on your first
visit. After all, you are a stranger.* "I am Mrs. Riley," I said. "I am
an ombudsman."

"Ombudsman?" A frown crossed Jeannie's face. "What
do you want with me?"

"I heard it is your first day." I waited for her to say something. When she didn't, I continued. "Maybe there is

something you would like me to get for you to make you more comfortable?"

Ignoring my question, she held out the photo. "My daughter and grandchildren. Aren't they beautiful?"

I took the picture and agreed. The smiling faces were enough to brighten any room, especially this resident's room. Her room was no more than ten by ten feet with a bed, a wardrobe and one easy chair. A small brown wooden table stood in front of the window. There were no pictures on the walls and no rugs on the floor—not even a colored cushion on the bed or chair. The only color in the room was the forget-me-not blue bedspread, compliments of the facility. *Very little to show for fifty years of life,* I remember thinking at the time.

"My daughter will be back to visit this weekend. Then I will get to see my grandchildren." The woman's face lit up, as she uttered the words, but her brown eyes never developed the warmth I had seen in the eyes of other proud grandmothers when they talked about their families. "She will bring my belongings."

I nodded. *No doubt the room would look better on my next visit,* I thought. For the next fifteen minutes Jeannie told me about her childhood and growing up in Fresno. She described her old neighborhood. "All of us on my street attended the same schools together, married and when the babies came along, we got to baby-sit each other's children."

Fascinated, I couldn't help but wonder why a woman of her stature and obvious independence was in an assisted living environment. From where I sat, she looked very capable. She rose and holding onto the bed and then the wall, made her way to the window. Spreading the curtains, she gazed out. "Everyone tells me the garden is beautiful this time of the year."

As if sensing my thoughts, she turned and stared in my

direction. "I suppose you're wondering why I'm here."
Before I could speak, she continued. "I didn't want to be a
burden to my family after my husband died."

"Burden?" I asked somewhat confused. As I met her
steady gaze, I couldn't imagine her being a burden on anyone. She was still young, independent and able to move
by herself. The few residents I had seen when I entered
the building were anything but independent; some were
confined to wheelchairs, while others managed to walk
with the aid of walking frames. This resident was different.
I had witnessed it myself as she clutched the bedpost and
the wall, making her way to the window.

As I reflected on what I had seen, a cannon went off in
my head. How could I have missed it? Her staring eyes
that didn't have warmth, her failure to smile when I
walked in, her need to clutch the bed and then the wall,
finally, her comments about the beautiful garden? Jeannie
was blind.

Each week for the remainder of the month, I made sure
I didn't miss a visit with Jeannie. I'd listen while she told
me about her family and how well her grandchildren were
doing in school. On one occasion, she told me about her
granddaughter's forthcoming piano recital. "My daughter
is coming this Saturday to take me to hear Annie play,"
Jeannie said excitedly.

Several days later, when I asked Jeannie about the
recital, a frown crossed her face. "I didn't get to the recital."

I saw the disappointment on her face and heard the sadness in her voice. "My daughter called to say she was running late. Work had kept her longer than she had planned.
Coming here would have made her even later, and she
didn't want to miss the recital." She paused then smiled.
"Not to worry," she said, "I'll get to hear about it when the
family comes to visit."

Over the next month, I found myself looking more and

more forward to my chats with Jeannie. Despite her hand-
icap, she always managed to have a cheery smile for me as
I entered the room. "Hi, Rosemarie," she'd say as I entered.
She recognized my footsteps before I had time to ask,
"How are you, Jeannie? Have you heard from your family
this week?"

Then the following week, I arrived early at the facility.
Leaving the elevator at the first floor, I approached
Jeannie's room. Pushing open the door, I halted. The room
was empty. Disappointed, I inquired at the nurses' station.
"Has Jeannie gone out with her daughter? It's such a nice
day to be outdoors," I said, remembering the warmth of
the summer sun on my arms as I made my way toward the
building.

The nurse shook her head. "The only person to visit
Jeannie is you. Her family has managed to visit only once
since she has been here."

"But Jeannie tells me about their visits. What about the
rugs and the pictures on the wall?" I had noticed Jeannie's
room taking on color since my first visit.

"Oh those things? We found some pictures and rugs in a
storeroom. Thought they would brighten up the room."
The nurse made a note in a book. "It's really so sad. The residents look forward to visitors, and Jeannie's no exception."

"Where's Jeannie now?"

"You'll find her in the community hall," said the nurse.
"It's sing-along today. Jeannie loves to sing."

Sure enough as I entered the hall, I saw Jeannie sitting
in the front row singing heartily. I made my way down the
aisle. "Hi," I whispered.

Jeannie smiled and beckoned me to join her. For the
next thirty minutes we sang together, her melodious con-
tralto voice hiding my high-pitched off-key one. At the
end of the show Jeannie took me aside. "I just wanted to

tell you I had a call from my daughter. Annie got straight A's. I knew she could do it."

Two weeks later, I stepped out of the elevator and headed for Jeannie's room. Outside the open door, I stopped. The room looked different. The bed had a different coverlet—a floral one, not the blue one I had grown accustomed to seeing when I entered. A white painted desk stood under the window and a matching rocker sat in the corner. Two framed pictures sat on the table next to a vase of fresh zinnias. Gone were the flowered rugs. Instead, a large red Persian rug square covered the floor.

Her daughter must have bought new furniture for her, I thought. But a strange feeling swept over me as I stared at the photos. My heart beat faster as I retreated down the hallway. At the nurses' station I paused. "Has Jeannie moved?"

The nurses exchanged glances. "We were going to call you. Early yesterday morning, she passed away."

"Jeannie's dead?"

The nurse nodded. "She had a bad heart."

"I didn't know," I mumbled dumbfounded and turned to go. "If it's any consolation, Mrs. Riley," said one of the nurses, "you were the highlight of her week. She looked forward to your visits."

A warm glow flowed over me. I turned back and saw the nurses smiling. "She did?"

"Sure," the nurses chorused. "She was always asking us the time and how much longer before you'd arrive. Then she'd go and sit on her bed to wait."

Though I knew I would miss our talks, I felt comforted by the knowledge that for a short time, I had been a friend to Jeannie, and maybe, just maybe, I had made a difference in her life.

Rosemarie Riley

A Brief and Shining Moment

My philosophy is that not only are you responsible for your life but doing the best at this moment puts you in the best place for the next moment.

Oprah Winfrey

Almost eight years ago, my wife was diagnosed with a rare form of breast cancer, and that's when I learned to pray. My prayers for her return to good health still persist, although the damning prophecies of medical science can't predict just how long Lois will live.

When she asked me to start a support group for the husbands of breast cancer survivors, I was hesitant at first. I didn't want to endure the pain all over again. But knowing the kind of pain that other husbands were going through, and the mere fact that this was what Lois wanted, I finally consented.

People often ask, "How do you do this? Doesn't it get depressing? Some of these women aren't going to make it. What are you going to do or say that is going to make any difference?"

I respond with yet another question. "Would you like to endure the process of watching your wife, sister, mother or daughter battle the ravages of breast cancer all alone, with nobody to talk to, or to rely on for support?"

By running a husband's support group for the women who have been affected by breast cancer, I have found more than I've lost, gained more than I've given and realized that hope shines in a world where hopelessness prevails.

Some years ago, Sandy, an attractive fifty-year-old woman, asked my wife if she could speak with me before the support group started. I knew both Sandy and her husband from previous encounters with the group. She looked like a model, certainly not someone that most people would think of as being a breast-cancer survivor.

Although Sandy's treatment consisted of a mastectomy without chemotherapy, she still withstood the agonizing process of disfiguring surgery, the tribulations of hormone therapy and the reality of her own death. She was dealing with it fairly well, but I knew that Mike, her husband, wasn't.

Sandy wanted to speak with me because she was upset with Mike. Apparently, he would come home from work and then go out for hours, without explanation. Whenever she tried to talk to him about it, he would give her the cold shoulder and walk away in silence. She worried that her husband couldn't accept her after the disfiguring surgery, and they were drifting apart. Through grievous tears, Sandy confided, "I think he's having an affair."

"I'll try to draw Mike out at the meeting tonight," I promised, adding, "but if he does tell me anything, I'm obligated to hold it in the strictest confidence between the two of us."

Sandy said that she understood and hoped I could help him.

That evening, I took the sparse gathering of five men to our small meeting room, while their wives were escorted by another volunteer to a separate meeting room. After the men were seated in a wide semicircle, I asked them how they were coping. Everyone was able to verbalize their feelings and talk about their situations; everyone except Mike, who remained silent.

I offered my own personal suggestions, to the group, of how I got through my wife's illness. "There were times when I just started to cry for no apparent reason, like while I was driving to work. One time I absent-mindedly drove to The Galleria, when I had no intention of even going there. I got so wrapped up in my own thoughts of despair that I lost all sense of time."

Listening with interest, the men eventually began telling stories of their own struggles. Some told chilling stories of how they just needed to get away from the house, and their wives, because they couldn't deal with it. Almost everyone admitted to attacks of overwhelming sadness where they would cry alone for hours. Others spoke of crushing hopelessness that hindered them from assuming full responsibility for the household chores that their wives could no longer perform.

Mike kept his head down throughout the discussion, his hands clasped in front of him on his lap. As the discussion progressed, I directed a question at Mike. "We haven't heard from you yet, Mike. Have you experienced any of these things we've been talking about?" As he looked up, we all saw the damp streaks that stained his cheeks. He quickly wiped them away, rejecting their existence. I sensed that he didn't want to let on that he'd been crying.

Mike said, "I don't know what else to do. I just drive around for hours." I thought, *Well, that explains why he leaves. I wonder what else he'll tell us?*

"What do you do when you drive around, Mike?" I

inquired. "Do you go out and cry, or have a beer, or do you have a special place to go and just think?"

It seemed like he wanted to answer, but something was holding him back. Finally Mike stood up and shouted, "I go out and scream. I go out in my car and scream for hours, and when I get back home I can't talk because I'm hoarse."

Stunned, and trying to comprehend what I had just heard, I said, "Mike, you'll have to tell Sandy all of this. She's worried about you. You have no idea. I mean it. When we leave here, you need to tell Sandy what you just told me."

When both groups finished, I watched as Mike approached Sandy. He spoke to her for a few moments, and then she cried silently on his chest. I could tell Mike was moved, but somehow he remained stoic, stereotypically male to the end. I was proud of him just the same.

Sandy finally knew that it wasn't her fault, but rather Mike's inability to break out of that terrible, unresolved sadness and anger over her illness. It was a brief and shining moment that night as Lois, nestled against my side, and I watched Mike and Sandy walk slowly down the quiet corridor toward the parking lot, arm in arm.

Over the next several months, we saw Mike and Sandy at almost all of our support group meetings. But suddenly they stopped coming. Through mutual friends, we heard that Sandy's cancer had metastasized to another part of her body, and she lost the battle. Mike stayed with her to the very end.

As clearly as if it were only yesterday, I can still see Sandy and Mike holding one another in that quiet hallway together. This memory sustains me, reassuring me that, in those last, precious days together, they were able to love, cherish and support one another.

George S. J. Anderson
Dedicated to Mike and Sandy Sexton

The Lady with the Smiley Voice

People are always good company when they are doing what they really enjoy.

Samuel Butler

My mom, Rosie, began her first real volunteering in the late 1950s. With five rambunctious children being . . . well . . . children, she had to find a regular, temporary escape out of the house.

I was the youngest of those brats who helped chase her into becoming a volunteer. But it was without regrets as it shaped both of our lives for the next four decades.

Since one of my mom's favorite nieces was blind, she chose to sign up as one of the first volunteers at the national nonprofit organization known as Recording for the Blind & Dyslexic (RFB&D) at their Upland, California studio.

Immersing herself completely into her "work," Rosie became Board chair (five times), a leading fundraiser and their star volunteer recruiter. Her passion was so contagious no one could turn her down.

When Rosie realized blind students needed to identify the textbooks on audiotape, she learned Braille and made tags to identify the tapes. She then founded the Pomona Valley Transcriber's Guild and taught Braille to sighted adults, vision-impaired children and local college students.

My mother had two passions: one for our family and the other for the visually impaired. She was fiercely committed to all students having equal opportunity and flew to Sacramento, our state capital, more than once to picket for the cause. In addition, she graduated from college a year before I did because, as she said in words I can still hear, "Recording for the Blind prefers volunteers with college degrees, honey."

On one occasion, Rosie had the opportunity to meet a blind "borrower" of RFB&D's audio textbooks. As soon as she introduced herself to the young man, he exclaimed, "Oh I know you. You're the lady with the smiley voice!"

The last year of my mom's life was extremely painful and frustrating. Cancer had taken over inside, and pain was something she couldn't understand or bend to. After forty years of steady volunteering—including weekly trips to the recording studio—the RFB&D staff came to my mother's house to set up a home recording station since trips to nearby Upland were too much for her to endure.

On her "good" days, she would spend an average of fifteen minutes recording textbooks in her living room for the kids she wanted to make sure stayed in school. She actually became embarrassed that was all she could give. Finally too weak to record and riddled with pain, she spent her last days proofreading Braille lessons for the blind college students who had come to depend on her.

But before my mother died, she made us swear not to hold a funeral. If we did, she promised to haunt us.

Waiting until I got home from a trip to Sacramento and then eking out one more day of life so my brother, Richard, could celebrate his birthday on June third in peace every year, Rose Betty Kelber—a volunteer for most of her life—

died on June 4, 1998. She was willful, vibrant, caring and always put others before herself.

Our family pulled together and got around the haunting threat by holding a "Celebration of Life." As my siblings, father and I numbly filed into the front row at Temple Beth Israel, as if orphaned children had taken over our middle-aged bodies, we were stunned to see more than two hundred people filling the seats behind us. In a moment's notice, the community had come to bid goodbye to my mom. We had no idea her years of volunteering had meant so much to those who depended on her.

I'll never forget the faces. They were bereft at the loss of one who had given so selflessly. The lady "with the smiley voice" who had inspired them and whipped them into shape would be heard no more.

As one of her dear friends said, "I've never known a more unselfish person than Rosie. Her remarkable energy and talent were given with the deepest kind of compassion for the welfare of others. Her life was a gift to all who knew her." That was my mom.

I've now been on the staff at the Los Angeles unit of RFB&D for over six years. Not a day goes by without hearing echoes of her voice: "Oh honey, it's such a wonderful organization. You *have* to take the job!"

Now I see myself in a staff position with the heart and soul of a volunteer. It is my mom's everlasting memory driving me to tell the world that each one of us has some special gift that can change a myriad of lives.

Diane Kelber

[EDITORS' NOTE: *For more information on Recording for the Blind & Dyslexic, contact 20 Roszel Rd., Princeton, NJ 08450; 800-221-4792; Web site:* www.rfbd.org.]

Big Sisterhood

Each friend represents a world in us, a world possibly not born until they arrive.

Anaïs Nin

The Big Brothers and Big Sisters program always sounded like a worthwhile cause. I thought, *One day, when I'm not such a busy trial lawyer, I would like to volunteer to be a Big Sister.*

One month later, in the local Bar Association newsletter, I noticed a desperate plea for men and women to volunteer. Many children had been waiting well over a year. Even though it seemed like a great imposition on my time, I decided that this request was directed at me.

The next question that popped into my mind was whether the program would want me. Because of a nerve disorder, I could only walk with the aid of crutches. I called and spoke to a caseworker who assured me that a perfect physique was not one of the criteria in order to be accepted into the program.

After completing the initial orientation process, Mandy, my caseworker, told me she would get back to me in a few weeks after a potential Little Sister match was made. A short time later, Mandy called and said, "I have the perfect Little Sister for you. Her name is Karen, and she is eight years old."

Perfect, I thought, *what a great age—young enough for Disney movies and old enough to have amusing conversations.*

Mandy continued, "The reason I think she is so perfect for you is because she is legally blind."

Usually I'm pretty good at keeping my thoughts from blurting out of my mouth, but in this case, I couldn't. "Are you nuts?" I said. "Me leading the blind? What kind of match is that? I can't even hold her hand because I have to hold onto my crutches. This is a crazy idea, Mandy!"

"I knew you would say that, Beth, but let me tell you why I'm convinced you're the right match. Karen's mother is blind, and her older sisters are legally blind, too. I want Karen exposed to someone with a disability that doesn't let it affect her life. You'd be such a good role model for her. You can show her that she can be anything she wants to be and do anything she wants to do, despite a physical challenge."

That was a pretty hard rationale to resist, so I agreed to meet with Karen. Over a soda, this adorable little eight-year-old, with thick magnifying glasses, and I discussed how we could adapt our special needs to each other. "Could you hang on to my shirt or coat instead of my hand and promise you would never run away from me?" She nodded in agreement. She asked if I could let her know when land was uneven or whether stairs went up or down. That seemed reasonable enough for me to accomplish, so, on a handshake of agreement, we became sisters.

When Karen was ten, she said to me one day, "Do you know why we get along so well, Beth?"

"What do you think?" I responded.

"We both have the same haircut, we both love art, we

both wear glasses, we're both handicapped, and we don't even mind that we are," she answered with a smile. Karen's remark was proof-positive that Mandy had made a wise choice in this unlikely pairing.

During our years together, Karen and I have had a lot of fun. We have tasted different foods of the world at ethnic restaurants and fairs, attended concerts ranging from classical to jazz to rock, gone on marine biology and rock-hunting expeditions and visited museums and zoos. We've done countless other activities ranging from the more mundane tasks of planting gardens and cooking to the excitement of day-trips to explore New York City.

Today, Karen is fifteen, and I still get incredible joy listening to her share her dreams and goals—just like any other fifteen-year-old. One day she is going to be a writer, another day a teacher or a seeing-eye dog trainer. Karen has a practical approach. She knows there will be challenges, but she also knows there is no limit as to how far she can go if she doesn't limit herself.

Beth Barrett

[EDITORS' NOTE: *For information on Big Brothers Big Sisters of America, contact 230 N. 13th St., Philadelphia, PA 19107; 215-567-7000; fax: 215-567-0394; e-mail:* national@bbbsa.org; *Web site:* www.bbbsa.org.]

"I'd like to trade in my big sister for another one."

Reprinted by permission of Tom Prisk.

What's a Big Brother?

Ward LeHardy was first paired with my son, Phil Reedy, in May 1990. There was no way that Ward could know his first match would be an opportunity to not only influence a boy and prepare him for life, but also to help him deal with sickness and eventual death.

In 1989, a family counselor recommended that I seek a Big Brother for my thirteen-year-old son, Phil. Reluctant at first, I eventually contacted Big Brothers and initiated the preliminary process. By December, we received word that a match would be forthcoming, as soon as the final background check had been completed.

In January 1990, my son was diagnosed with leukemia. Thus began our journey into a frightening world—a place of uncertainty and fear, where many bald children lived out their brief existence attached to intravenous poles.

When I called the organization and told them about Phil's illness, the match was put on hold because of the emotional impact it might have on the Big Brother. "I believe that decision should be made by the prospective Big Brother, not the organization," I countered.

Shortly after that conversation, the coordinator called me back. "Ward LeHardy of Arlington, Virginia, wants to be your son's Big Brother. He's excited about meeting Phil."

When Phil and I first met Ward, I scrutinized, examined and cross-examined him with downright invasive questioning. In the end, I knew in my heart this man was right for my son.

Phil had to have a bone-marrow transplant in June 1990. Because of his fragile immune system, few people were allowed to enter his isolation room. Ward had a contagious skin condition, but that didn't prevent him from driving thirty miles so he could stand outside the glass door and let Phil know that he was there for him.

I stood lookout for nurses while Ward donned a mask and opened the door a crack so he could converse with Phil. A cherished photograph shows a smiling Phil communicating through this crevice with his Big Brother.

In late July, Phil was allowed to go on short passes from Children's Hospital to the Ronald McDonald House, where I stayed. Ward came over and played Nintendo with Phil, who delighted in beating Ward's socks off.

After Ward discovered their common interest in art, he enrolled in Phil's private art classes, which gave them the opportunity to enhance their artistic skills and their relationship on a weekly basis.

In time, because of severe organ rejection and resultant lung damage, Phil had to be hospitalized frequently. Ward arranged their outings around Phil's medical needs. No matter what they did together, from sharing a favorite sandwich to art projects, they both enjoyed just "hanging out." They were comfortable with one another and talked about everything. But some of their most difficult discussions involved God and death.

On May 5, 1994, Phil turned eighteen, the age at which the role of Big Brother typically ceases, but Ward remained his close friend. When Phil was unable to receive the lung transplant that would have ensured his future, his friend stood by his side in the ICU. Ward prayed for his "Little Buddy" to pull through after an episode of near-fatal respiratory distress.

As Phil survived crisis after crisis, his Big Brother remained one of his main cheerleaders. Nurtured by consistency and commitment, they shared a special relationship.

Ward captured the excitement of Phil's high-school graduation, in June 1995, on video. After Phil's death, Ward, who also owned his own production company, produced a video tribute to his Little Brother.

As the single mother of a very ill child, Ward's commitment to Phil meant the world to me and to my son. I don't know whether Ward fully realized the awesome responsibility he had accepted, but I do know that he took his commitment seriously, regardless of the circumstances.

I witnessed the transformation of a thirteen-year-old boy into a man. Even though Phil's mission on Earth was drawing to a close, he was unafraid of death—partly because of the dedication, love and commitment of his Big Brother.

If Big Brothers held an essay contest asking their Little Brothers to write about "Why my Big Brother should be National Big Brother of the Year," Phil probably would have written something like this:

My Big Brother's a gnarly kind of guy. He picked me, knowing that I might go and die on him. I was an uncouth, angry, snotty-nosed brat. He lectured me about everything from treating my mom better to taking my medicines. When I was bald, "The Wardmeister" treated me like I was normal. He played Nintendo when he knew I'd whip his butt. And when I was sick, he'd clean up after me. When I was puffed up because of the strong medication, he acted like I was just as good-looking as ever. (Smile!) And when I went down to

eighty pounds and was on life support, he acted like he
didn't even notice.

Though I rarely let him know how much I loved him,
he taught me how to love and give to others and not be
so selfish. He did this by example. If you ask me, he's
earned the title "National Big Brother of the Year"!

Norma Reedy

[EDITORS' NOTE: For information on Big Brothers Big Sisters
of America, contact 230 N. 13th St., Philadelphia, PA 19107; 215-
567-7000; fax: 215-567-0394; e-mail: national@bbbsa.org; Web
site: www.bbbsa.org. For information on Ronald McDonald
House Charities, contact One Kroc Drive, Oak Brook, IL 60523;
Web site: www.rmhc.com.]

Drawing Out the Truth

A man wears a mask and his face grows to fit it.
George Orwell

It was my first month on the job as a Child Life Volunteer at Children's Mercy Hospital in Kansas City, Missouri.

As a retired, forty-five-year-old dentist who was financially secure, I was also a cancer survivor from non-Hodgkin's lymphoma, stage 3. When I, a computer-literate male, showed up, the volunteer department welcomed me with open arms.

In my third week, I met Darren, a thirteen-year-old kidney transplant patient who would be admitted many times over the next eighteen months. Darren was quite small for his age. He weighed about sixty pounds, was hearing impaired and was somewhat developmentally disabled.

Yet Darren had the biggest smile with eyes so huge they almost resembled a cartoon character.

When he'd see you coming, his expression would light up the room, and his arms would go out with all the energy his frail body could muster. He was literally a human magnet, and I connected with Darren in a nano-second. No introductions were needed. Although he could be difficult, I knew this was the kid I was going to stick with.

My supervisor noted that while he was a sweet kid, he usually didn't participate in group activities and would reject bedside projects with a resounding "NO!"

I purposely didn't do the computer activity because it negated one-on-one contact. In the beginning, Darren completely ignored me. He was in pain as he was just coming off a procedure. So I started working my way into his life through his oldest brother, Brian, who was fifteen.

On my first visit, I noticed Brian's hero of the week was the wrestler, Sting, who looked similar to the way that the members of the rock band KISS paint their faces. And every week, Brian would show up in a different T-shirt depicting a new "hero" of the World Wrestling Federation (WWF). So I knew if I started faking some knowledge about the characters in the WWF, I might be able to shoe-horn my way into their acceptance.

On the advice of the volunteer coordinator—who thought I was "too fresh from the trenches" for the oncology floor—I hit Tower 5 armed with a basket of art materials. It contained coloring sheets, crayons and paints to work with patients ranging in age from two months to early twenties.

So one day, I said, "Let's see who can paint the best Sting face mask."

I picked up a few colors from my nontoxic liquid tempera paints and drew an oval outline for a face.

I asked, "What are Sting's colors?" After some discussion, we decided to use red, black and white. I gave each of them sheets of paper and the Sting coloring contest began. I told them I would put their artwork up in the playroom so everyone could marvel at their drawings. A booming "Cool!" from Darren was my clue that ice was breaking.

The next few weeks were tortuous for Darren and his family. While his body was rejecting a second kidney transplant, his mother—who lived 150 miles away—learned she was pregnant, which meant fewer trips to Children's Mercy.

Some weeks after I arrived, my supervisor put a star next to Darren's name on the status report meaning "must see." An ongoing game of curling into the fetal position, weeping into his pillow and then shooting me a wide grin when I least expected it kept me glued to his side for weeks on end. In fact, I didn't see any other kids after a while. I would spend three to six hours a week just with Darren over an eight-month period. I even asked for additional days to spend with him, but they said I was getting too emotionally involved. And I was.

My wife was working full-time; my son was away at college; I never bonded with a pet; I was a cancer survivor; and I didn't have to be a dentist with that "professional" bedside manner anymore. I just fell in love with Darren's personality; he was a funny, funny kid. In return, he uncovered a childlike innocence that had been lurking inside me all these years.

One day, I came and the nurses told me Darren was "not doing very well." They were prepping him for a biopsy, and he had been down all morning.

With a deep breath and a broad smile, I barged in as usual with a booming "What's up, guys?" Darren turned and wrinkled his face at me. His mother patted his head, and the family was in a numbed trance.

The doctors came in with clipboards meaning "patient consent forms" and wanted to speak to the family in the conference room. There was some swelling in his spine, and they were going to take out some fatty tumor.

I told them I would stay with Darren until they returned. Darren was depressed and crying.

"I don't want a biopsy," he yelled.

I said, "Do you want to play a trick on the doctors?"

"Yeah, man!"

So I painted his face like Sting's in red, black and white. With his war paint on, I then told him I'd put a tattoo on his little belly.

He held his bed sheet up and I worked "under cover" in case anyone showed up unexpectedly. Darren giggled as we worked quickly together. The tattoo I drew was a giant ZIPPER on his belly from top to bottom with lettering on his side and chest. We both blew on the paint and then covered him up just as the aides and doctors came strolling into the room.

Everyone laughed when they saw his painted face. They all thought that was the joke. While they wheeled Darren away on a stretcher, he had a triumphant smirk as he was anticipating the moment when the doctors and nurses lifted the sheet downstairs and saw a painted zipper defying all of them even more.

As his body rejected the second kidney transplant, Darren unfortunately went downhill from there. They even tried cord blood from his mother's new baby and put him on drugs I had taken during my cancer treatment. But still, there was nothing more they could do and he later died. But Darren gave me something all volunteers crave: For a very, very discrete period, you can walk into someone's life and make a difference.

After he passed away, I immediately flew to Philadelphia to see my own son. Darren also inspired me to get my certificate to teach inner-city, high-school students to try and recapture those step-by-step, inch-by-inch moments of sheer delight that the underserved and underdogs in life can give back so innocently and honestly to those who try to draw them out.

Nate Klarfeld

A Reason for Living

To everything there is a season, and a time to every purpose under heaven.

Ecclesiastes 3:1

"What do you think of suicide?" asked the frail feminine voice on the other end of the line.

I didn't expect a suicide call at 8:59 in the morning, one minute before the Helpline Office opened. Usually suicide calls startled me from a sound sleep after midnight. My caller probably anticipated getting through to the office staff instead of a volunteer who was finishing a shift at home.

During our crisis training, I learned to listen, rather than respond with something flippant like, "I'm against it." I simply waited. The caller continued. As she talked, I checked the proper boxes on her profile sheet.

"I live in a nursing home in a nearby city," she said. " I'm seventy-six and . . . and I'm dying." Her fragile voice faded away as she struggled to catch her next breath. "I have cancer and emphysema. There's no hope that I'll recover. I don't want to burden my family any longer. I just want to die," she said as she burst into tears.

Although I'd answered the Helpline phones for several years, suicide calls still scared me. Life is precious. I was sure that there was no instance where I could condone suicide as a solution.

"Have you talked to anyone at the nursing home about this?" I inquired.

The caller responded, "When I mentioned suicide to one of the nurses here, she got scared and called my doctor, my family and my minister. Everybody rushed in but nobody . . . listened. So I phoned you." Once again, her weak voice trailed off for a few moments.

"I'm listening," I said softly.

"My husband's been gone for nine years now. When I tell them how much I miss him, they *say* they understand." She continued, "But they *can't* understand. When I speak of the pain, they promise to up my dose of medication. The medicine only makes me feel groggy." Stopping to cough, she resumed hesitantly, "I told them I'm ready to go home to God. They said suicide was a sin, so I promised I wouldn't think of killing myself again, but I do . . . all the time. I have no reason for living any longer."

Confused and searching for the right thing to say, I asked myself, *What can I say to this sweet lady that will help her?* Before, I never doubted for a second that suicide was wrong. However, I was disturbed to find myself sympathizing with her reasoning. Certainly the quality of her life would not improve.

I remembered a young man who had called one New Year's Eve—gun in hand. After we talked throughout that lonely night, he said he finally felt a ray of hope. *What hope can I offer this distressed caller?* I wondered.

I decided to stall for time. "Tell me about your family."

She talked lovingly of her children and grandchildren. They came to visit her often at the nursing home. She loved to see them but felt guilty for taking them away from their own families and activities.

Andrew, her rebellious middle child, had gotten especially close to her during her illness. When he first heard she was dying, he apologized for the times he'd been thoughtless during his young adult years.

As she talked, my mind raced. I thought back to when I was visiting my Grandma Florence in the hospital every day. One evening, just after returning home, I received a call. Grandma Florence had taken a turn for the worse, and they wanted me to come back immediately. As I sat by her bedside, silent tears spilled from my eyes. The nurse tried to console me by saying, "She's ready to die."

Angrily, I retorted, "But I'm not ready to *let* her die!" Grandma Florence died six weeks later. By then, I was ready to let her go. I was glad God had given me a little more time.

Maybe someone in my caller's life needs more time, I thought. I told her of my experience and said, "Perhaps God is giving someone in your family more time."

She was silent for a few moments before she mentioned Andrew again. "I'm glad I didn't die six months ago, although I'd considered suicide even then."

During our conversation, I learned that during the months after her diagnosis of cancer, Andrew, a skilled woodworker, made her a beautiful casket. Although she never doubted his love, he needed those months to show her just how much he cared about her. But now the casket was finished, and he had time to reconcile.

"Maybe God is allowing you to suffer a little longer for someone else in the family," I suggested.

"Yes, of course . . . it must be Sarah," she answered sadly.

I didn't remember her mentioning a Sarah. "Who is Sarah?" I inquired.

"Sarah is my granddaughter. She just gave birth to a stillborn baby. I'm so worried about her. Her loss seems overwhelming. Perhaps God knows that Sarah couldn't deal with another death right now."

As she talked, this sweet lady's voice grew a little stronger. From my training, I learned this is sometimes an indication that a person is beginning to see a ray of hope. My caller's hope came not from the prospect of her own life improving, but from her perception that God had a purpose for her life. He needed her help on Earth just a little longer.

Ellen Javernick

4
NEW APPRECIATION

Ultimately, the only way to experience the richness of life is to live in an attitude of gratitude: to appreciate what you have and what you can give. The best way to ensure your happiness is to assist others in experiencing their own.

Anthony Robbins

"But I want to volunteer too, Dad!"

The Pillow

For twelve years, my church has participated in the Appalachia Service Project. One week each summer, volunteers travel to Kentucky, Tennessee, Virginia or West Virginia to repair or build homes for families.

At the age of sixteen, I went on my first volunteer project in West Virginia. On the night we arrived, we discovered that "our family" was living in a trailer that was in poor condition, no bigger than two parking spaces. A crew had been working on it for two weeks, but every time they finished one problem, another surfaced.

The staff soon decided that the only reasonable solution was to build a new house—something highly unusual but necessary under these circumstances. Normally the goal is to repair existing homes. Our family was overjoyed with their new house that was twenty by thirty feet with three bedrooms, a bath and a kitchen/family room.

On Tuesday of that week, while we all ate lunch together, I asked our family's three boys, Josh, Eric and Ryan, "What do you want for your new room?" Anticipating posters, toys and other gadgets that children usually ask for, we were surprised when Josh, the oldest, responded, "I just want a bed."

We were stunned. The boys had never slept in a bed. They were accustomed only to foam pads. That night we had a meeting and decided that beds would be the perfect gift. On Thursday night, a few adults in our group drove to the nearest city and bought beds and new bedding. They arranged for everything to be delivered on Friday.

When Friday arrived, we could hardly contain ourselves. After lunch, when we saw the delivery truck coming, we told our family about the surprise. It was like watching ecstatic children on Christmas morning.

That afternoon, we set up the beds as we finished each room. Josh, who had his own room, wanted to put his bed together by himself. Eric and Ryan shared a room and got a new bunk bed. As we fitted the frames together, Eric, who had been working outside, ran into the house to watch us. Too dirty to enter his room, he observed with wide-eyed enthusiasm from the doorway.

As Meggan, a member of our group, slipped a pillowcase onto one of the pillows, Eric asked, "What is that?"

"A pillow," she replied.

"What do you do with it?" Eric persisted.

"When you go to sleep, you put your head on it," Meggan answered softly. Tears came to our eyes as she handed Eric the pillow.

"Oh . . . that's soft," he said, hugging it tightly.

Now, when my sister or I start to ask for something that seems urgent, my dad gently asks, "Do you have a pillow?"

We know exactly what he means.

Casey Crandall

[EDITORS' NOTE: *For information on the Appalachia Service Project, Inc., contact 4523 Bristol Highway, Johnson City, TN 37601; 423-854-8800; fax: 423-854-9771; e-mail:* asp@asphome.org; *Web site:* www.asphome.org.]

A Twist of Fate

Every child comes with the message that God is not yet discouraged of man.

Rabindranath Tagore

"Would you care for a glass of milk?" I asked innocently.

As he nodded yes, I saw dirt matted in his hair and smelled the stench of stale cigarette smoke embedded in his coat.

"How's it going today?" I continued as I handed over the carton of milk.

No response. "Is there anything else you need?" Nothing.

This just didn't happen once; it happened dozens of times. As a teenager, I was the cheerleader for Loaves and Fishes, a program my mother started at our church. We served meals to anyone who showed up, primarily street people in the Minneapolis/St. Paul area.

No matter how much I tried to raise their spirits, I was often puzzled by the way "those" people reacted to me. They didn't look me in the eye when I spoke to them, and they were rarely grateful. I wanted to shout, "Hey, we're doing a great thing here. You could at least thank us!"

After I stopped volunteering at Loaves and Fishes, I took control of my own destiny. Over the next ten years, I strove for the picture-perfect life: a college degree, teaching career, wonderful husband and then our first child, Derian.

The excitement of his arrival was instantly shattered when the doctors discovered Derian had a heart condition that required immediate surgery. *How could this possibly happen?* I asked myself in total shock and denial.

Later, Derian was diagnosed with CHARGE Syndrome, a nongenetic condition that strikes about one in every twelve thousand births. Coming out of the hospital, I soon discovered, unlike every other aspect of my life, I was not in control. The name of Derian's condition was a telling irony to who was really in charge now.

Affecting not only his heart but also his eyes, ears, nose and general growth and development, Derian's deficiencies put him in constant need of repair, which meant a steady stream of doctor visits and considerable time spent in the hospital.

Thirteen months after Derian was born, Connor, our second son, was born, thankfully with a healthy body.

Amidst all the doctor appointments, hospital surgeries and having a second child, I naturally had to take an unpaid leave from teaching. While insurance covered some of our medical bills, other people came forth to help with a variety of support. One time, my students raised sixteen hundred dollars in only twenty-four hours. It was enough to cover two months' mortgage payments enabling me to spend more time with Derian.

Even though Robb was a manager at a clothing store, the mounting financial, medical and parenting responsibilities began to take its toll. We had done the best we could for as long as we could. In the spring of 1995, we decided to seek help.

I had heard about a program that assists mothers

and children with food vouchers. I put my pride aside and made an appointment.

On the morning of my appointment, I debated over and over on what to wear so we didn't look too well off, but not too poor either. We tried at least three different sets of clothes. Once we were dressed, I knew I would be judged on my mothering ability: not too firm, look in control and confident, hoping all along the boys cooperated.

With four toddler legs, it was a long walk into the building. I signed in and looked around at the other people in the waiting area, wondering what their stories were. In that single moment, I felt that treacherous twist of fate and was ashamed of all the ignorant stereotypes I once had about being poor. Now it was my turn to be poor. I didn't like it. I didn't deserve it, and I couldn't handle it. I was tempted to grab the boys and run. But looking into their bright eyes, I knew why I had to stay.

For the first time in my life, I understood why the people I once served at Loaves and Fishes were not grateful. Who wants to be this down and out? It is incredibly humbling and what makes it worse is when people—like I was as a teenager—act like they are doing you a favor, and you owe them gratitude.

Asking for help when it's needed most is so difficult! I never really wanted a "relationship" with the people who were helping me with the services I desperately needed. It was so much easier to stay aloof and keep things on an impersonal level.

I clenched my teeth as my name was called. What if someone recognized me? I would be humiliated if anyone knew I was getting vouchers. After three hours of questions and exams, I finally got what I came for. That began a day-by-day quest for survival; we were determined to make it.

After a two-and-a-half-year struggle, Derian's soul left

his tattered little body on May 9, 1996. I know he came to us for many reasons, and I'll never forget those lessons: compassion and understanding for the poor, not just momentary sympathy and a handout.

After experiencing life from the other side, Robb and I created the Spare Key Foundation in memory of Derian. Its mission is to help Minnesota families with critically ill children undergoing long hospitalizations by making a one-time mortgage payment. During our first four years, we made over 100 grants averaging $850. We were also recognized by Oprah's Angel Network and received a "Use Your Life" award.

We are not always thanked when we grant a mortgage payment. But it doesn't bother me, as I quickly remember what life was like when we walked in their shoes.

It is now that I fully understand the joy of volunteering is not found in a "thank-you" or in that feel-good feeling, but rather from the awesome privilege of being able to help a fellow human being in his or her time of need.

Patsy Keech

[EDITORS' NOTE: *For more information on the Spare Key Foundation, contact 820 South View Blvd., Suite 202, South St. Paul, MN 55075; 651-457-2607; fax: 651-306-0229; e-mail:* contact@sparekey.org; *Web site:* www.sparekey.org.]

A Tiny Denim Dress

Our rickety truck climbed the steep hill to the fertile coffee land in the Honduran mountains. To the right was a beautiful countryside. Unless you looked closely, you couldn't see the crumbled homes. Off to the left were shacks belonging to seventeen devastated coffee farmers who lost everything when Hurricane Mitch swept through this land nine months earlier.

Unable to buy back their expensive coffee land, the government took ownership of the land after their homes were evacuated in October 1998. Two days after the hurricane, missionaries and relief agencies rushed food to these mountain families. But the temporary relief didn't provide new homes or new sources of income.

We unloaded the twenty bags of clothing sent from American missionary barrels. My teammates and I each grabbed a bag while our leader announced to the villagers, *"Vamos a dar ropa. Venga."* We are going to give clothes. Come.

The dark-eyed people swarmed around our bags. I looked around trying to size up a tiny denim dress. A small girl with lightened streaks of hair—probably from malnutrition—shyly put out her hands. I held the dress to her shoulders. It looked right. I helped her slip on the dress and button it up. A perfect fit. A girl, who once wore only panties and sandals, walked away wearing a dress and a beaming smile.

I watched her trek up the hill and wander into the door of her one-room shack. She kept looking down and holding out her dress. Her fingers caressed it, as if amazed to actually own something so beautiful. I hung my head in shame. At home, my closet bulged with clothes. How many times had I complained about my lack of clothes? Would I ever dare to wear the same shirt two days in a row to school, or would I still be embarrassed?

When I signed up for this Teen Missions International summer trip to Honduras, learning humility was not what I had bargained for. Heat, thundershowers, mosquitoes and different foods challenged us. Each night of our two-week training ended with a rally filled with cheers, singing and inspirational speaking. Our team learned brick-laying, concrete mixing, carpentry, steel-tying and even puppetry in preparation for our four weeks in Honduras.

Why should I slave away under the hot sun in a foreign country when I could be relaxing at the lake? The answer for me was seeing that little girl walking away with the tiny denim dress—probably the first dress she ever had. It gave me a satisfaction I would never have found at the beach. Maybe we didn't change much in Honduras, but Honduras sure changed us.

Jinny Pattison

[EDITORS' NOTE: *For information on Teen Missions International, Inc., contact 885 East Hall Rd., Merritt Island, FL 32953; 321-453-0350; fax: 321-452-7988; e-mail:* info@teenmissions.org; *Web site:* www.teenmissions.org.]

Reunion

I stood at the side of the stage and gazed out at the fifty men and women in their early twenties, all in the varied shapes, sizes and styles expected on any American college campus. I had been privileged to address many audiences as a professional speaker, but the anticipation of this presentation had my heart beating a new rhythm.

A hundred times I had told the story of how I "accidentally" became involved in the 1975 Vietnam Orphan Airlift. Countless times I told how I had volunteered to escort six babies to their adoptive homes in the United States, but then President Ford okayed a gigantic airlift and I helped bring out three hundred orphans as Saigon was falling. Thousands of people had heard me share life-lessons I'd learned from that adventure. But this audience was different—they were those orphans.

Dozens of times I had recounted being on the airstrip when the first planeload of orphans crashed after takeoff. But this audience was different—they were the survivors of that crash.

It was the twentieth reunion of the airlift. As I surveyed the audience of young adults, a few with their parents, my heart skipped a beat as it swelled. I looked at the young man filling the wide shoulders of his football jersey, and my mind asked, *Were you one of the babies we placed three to four in a cardboard box?* I glanced at a beautiful young woman with long black hair holding her baby. *Were you one of the older kids who cheerfully helped us feed and diaper three hundred squalling infants?* My eyes spanned the entire crowd and I mused, *You were all part of the diarrhea diaper drama!*

Almost reverently, I shared slides of Vietnam, of the airlift—my story, their story. Then came the questions they had saved for a lifetime.

"Where did we all come from?" one girl asked. Snickering trickled through the crowd. "You know what I mean!" she blushed.

"Most babies were abandoned at birth." I had always despised that phrase, but I went on to explain how women had their babies at birthing centers—huts, really—throughout the countryside. Knowing they could not care for their children, they relinquished them there, hoping to give them a better life.

A young man with spiked hair and an earring sneered, "She loved me so much, she gave me away."

"*The* greatest act of maternal love," I said. He nodded slowly.

Remembering a lesson I'd learned from a speaker there the day before, I repeated, "The Vietnamese believed in a God that cared for all children. They believed that if they left a child, even on the street side, God would send someone to care for it. So the mother was not abandoning the child, but relinquishing it to God. Only by giving her baby away, could she save its life."

Smiles glimmered one by one.

Then came the toughest question. "Why didn't someone get us a better plane—better accommodations?" The voice was shaky. So was my hand as I gripped the mike.

"Bombs were exploding three miles from the Saigon city

limits. Armed Vietnamese soldiers patrolled the streets. When President Thui finally okayed the airlift, we knew we had to get as many orphans out as fast as possible. The Vietnamese government had allotted only eleven cents per day per orphan. We knew any we left behind were at risk. And many of you were of mixed race. We feared you wouldn't survive if we left you."

"Thanks," came a soft voice from the back.

The smiles widened.

Then I told them my favorite part of the story. "My husband and I had expected to get our son from Vietnam in about two years. With the airlift, I was told I could enter a building housing one hundred babies and choose a son." I flashed the slide showing Mitchell sitting on my lap. "But I didn't choose him. He chose me."

I took a deep breath to keep my voice from quaking. "It is my absolute conviction that this child was created to be our son." I swallowed past the lump in my throat. "Just as you were created for your adoptive families."

The young man wiped tears with the sleeve of his jersey.

"I don't know why you were conceived in another womb in another country. I have lots of questions for our Creator someday." Then very slowly, deliberately I added, "But what I *do* know is this: You are where you are supposed to be."

Sniffles were drowned out by another young man shouting, "Yes!" He raised his hand and slapped the palm of his friend.

"I *am* where I'm supposed to be!" a young woman with almond eyes said tearfully as she hugged her blonde mother.

"I guess the rest doesn't matter," a young man in the front row gleamed. "We *are* where we're supposed to be!"

LeAnn Thieman

The Magic Key

What feeling is so nice as a child's hand in yours?

Marjorie Holmes

It was a cool September morning when we piled into a rusty blue university van and began our journey across one of the great divisions in our society: affordable housing. Our group of fifteen college students was heading to Milwaukee to help build homes in a poor inner-city neighborhood with Habitat for Humanity.

After passing through miles of farmland that slowly segued into subdivisions and strip malls, we were soon driving through city neighborhoods where the homes were older and packed tightly into plots protected by chain link fences. As we drove on, we saw many homes and businesses boarded up. That's also when our idle conversation boarded up into stunned silence.

Weaving through a maze of old row houses and empty lots, we knew we were near the Habitat site when we saw cars lining the streets, Dumpsters and a small knot of people armed with work gloves.

At the site, I told the construction supervisor we wanted the toughest job of the day. He smiled and led us to an enormous pile of debris.

"I figure this pile was here before any of you were born," he laughed, mostly to himself. "I'd like to chuck it all in the dumpster out front."

After dubbing the pile "Mount Habitat," we began our arduous task. About two hours into our work, several children walked over and became our kid corps of sidewalk superintendents. We invited them to join us in our mountain assault, and those munchkins enthusiastically agreed.

The smallest boy of the group hung back as the other children put on gloves and dug in. While I was working on a far corner of the pile, I smiled at him when he glanced my way. He strode up to me, puffed out his chest and stated, "My name's J. T., and I'm real strong."

"Well, I can see that," I replied. "My name is David, and I really need some help." I grabbed a shovel that was nearby and handed it to my small helper.

The shovel towered over him by a full two feet and his tiny hands couldn't even wrap around the handle. Without a moment's hesitation, he dug into the pile with great passion. Every few minutes he would stop, then look up at me and exclaim with pride, "I'm helping."

And each time I responded, "I don't know what we would do without you, J. T."

He was dressed much like the other kids: blue jeans rolled up at the bottom so he could grow into them, a T-shirt dirty from the day's adventures, and an unbuttoned well-worn red and white flannel shirt. He wore high-top basketball shoes that were purposely left untied, and upon closer inspection, I realized they were actually two different shoes.

But it was his beautiful brown eyes that set him apart. When he smiled, his eyes remained wide open, which forced his cheeks to bulge out like the cheeks of a cherub. I tried to imagine what this little boy would look like when the rest of his frail body caught up with his eyes.

To amuse each other, we took turns making up stories about items that we found in the pile. A rusted hubcap became a gear from a flying saucer that crashed many years ago. A beat-up old shoe and a broken cup were transformed into a priceless modern art exhibit. I found an old rusted skeleton key and created a story about a magic spaceship. When I finished telling the story, I gave J. T. the key and said, "Now you have the magic key that starts that spaceship."

He gazed at me with those huge brown eyes and ran over to his friends to show them his new treasure.

J. T. and I worked side by side the entire day. I had to give up my shovel a few times when some of the adult volunteers needed one, but I always made sure my new friend had his orange-handled shovel.

And then, as we were getting ready to quit for the day, a well-dressed elderly man walking with a cane called one of the children over. The man then began to yell, "Unless you're gettin' paid, you git away from there and go home right now. I mean it, right now."

All of the children dropped their shovels and quickly dispersed. A woman from our group approached the man and tried to explain Habitat for Humanity's philosophy to him. He was unfamiliar with Habitat's work and refused to believe that people would volunteer their time and then sell the home for no profit. He turned away and continued to shout to the children.

I watched J. T. as he scurried off. He slowed and seemed suspended between the urgings of his peers, the commands of the elderly man and our group. I stood silently clutching my shovel. He turned and his eyes found mine. We shared a mutual smile. Again, he ran toward his friends, but then he stopped, turned around and ran back toward me.

He grasped my hand and pulled me down so that we were eye to eye. Standing on his tiptoes, he whispered in my ear, "You'll always be my friend." Then he pressed something into my hand and ran off with the other children.

I never saw J. T. again, but I will always treasure the gift he gave me, the old rusty key to his magic spaceship.

David "Goose" Guzzetta

[EDITORS' NOTE: *For information on Habitat for Humanity International, contact 121 Habitat St., Americus, GA 31709; 229-924-6935, ext. 2551 or 2552; e-mail:* publicinfo@hfhi.org; *Web site:* www.habitat.org. *For information on the Jimmy Carter Work Project, visit the Web site:* www.habitat.org/jcwp/2000/friny.html.]

The Reluctant Den Leader

When the best leader's work is done, the people say, "We did it ourselves."

Lao Tzu

Running late again, I rushed into the Cub Scouts parents' meeting. With windblown hair, as a result of my brief dash from the car to the church basement, I hurriedly took a seat, noting the surplus of empty chairs. *At least, I wasn't the only one running behind,* I told myself with ample relief.

The Cubmaster checked his watch, and with a barely audible sigh, started the meeting. I continued to look around, stunned to count only five or six other parents present, despite the fact that our pack had at least fifty boys. As the Cubmaster explained the challenges that the group faced in the coming year, he pointed out that the empty chairs, which should have been filled with parent volunteers, were our biggest obstacles.

Several of the dens were lacking parent leaders and with the summer coming to a close, it became unlikely that someone would step in and commit an entire year of Tuesday nights to help guide a group of young boys through the requirements needed to earn their badges.

As he spoke, I felt a rising sense of guilt mounting within me. After all, even I had tried to evade helping out with the Tiger Cubs the previous year. *Wasn't I looking forward to leaving my seven-year-old in the care of a competent adult while I ran errands? Wasn't I the one who conveniently "forgot" to bake a couple of cakes for the annual fund-raiser and found excuses not to man the yard sale table?* I quickly came to realize that the problem wasn't just about empty chairs; it was also about people like me who were unwilling to sacrifice some of their time to a worthy cause.

Before I could change my mind, I raised my hand to volunteer as den leader to guide the Wolf den through its first formal year of scouting. Although I knew next to nothing about teaching a group of noisy, exuberant and restless second-graders, I was determined to make it work.

My first den meeting was as chaotic and noisy as the first day of a county fair. The boys were too excited to sit still. The craft I had chosen was too complicated and ran over the allotted time. I spent a great deal of my time apologizing to the parents for my ineptitude as a den leader. *What have I gotten myself into?* I wondered, composing a letter of resignation in my head.

Much to my surprise, the boys actually enjoyed themselves. They even invited their friends to join our den, and before long, our ranks swelled from four boys to ten. My son was thrilled to have his mom as den leader; it gave him bragging rights on the playground. I was having as much fun as the boys and had no idea that I'd be so popular.

As I walked through the school's parking lot, it was rare when one of "my" boys didn't call out a greeting or stop me for a quick hug and a story to share. It almost became a contest among them to see who would spot me first. They would talk with me about the little things going on in their lives—whether it was a loose tooth ready to wiggle its way out or a special event coming up. They'd tell me about their homework and their latest Playstation victories. They'd complain about little brothers, sisters and neighborhood bullies. I'd ruffle their hair, ask questions and listen to their answers before hugging them as they scampered back to their teachers or parents.

As I watched them dash away with that curious half-run, half-skip gait that little boys are notorious for, I thought of the empty chairs at that meeting and those who would never know this joy. I thought of those who wouldn't receive quick, warm hugs from little boys with peanut-butter breath, and those who would miss out on gap-toothed smiles and long-winded stories full of little joys and mini-tragedies. After all, I gave those boys only one hour of my time every week, but they rewarded me with their hearts.

Françoise Inman

[EDITORS' NOTE: *For information on the Cub Scouts, contact The National Council of the Boy Scouts of America, 1325 West Walnut Hill Lane, P.O. Box 152079, Irving, TX 75015-2079; 972-580-2000; fax: 972-580-2502; Web site: www.bsa.scouting.org.*]

The Deep End by Matt Matteo

Volunteer's Lament

As a stay-at-home mother and devoted wife,
I've volunteered my entire adult life.

A Sunday school teacher and Girl Scout leader,
Library worker and story-time reader.

Involved in every organization around,
Kept me running all over town.

Secretary, treasurer and sometimes chair,
Often it seemed I served everywhere.

I scheduled fund-raisers, baked cakes and pies,
Planned school picnics, then prayed for blue skies.

In a desperate pinch, a substitute teacher,
And at every ball game, I cheered from a bleacher.

I carpooled the kids of working mothers,
Served snacks to countless sisters and brothers.

When a teacher said, "Whose mother can?"
Up in the air went my daughter's hand.

In fifteen years of public school,
"My-mom-will-do-it" became the rule.

Now my daughters are away and grown,
With work and schedules of their own.

Yet even today I hear the call,
And volunteer to help one and all.

Someday, I'll leave this mortal Earth,
To stand and be counted, for what it's worth.

And when St. Peter looks my way,
I think I know just what he'll say.

"To give out the harps and halos here,
I'll need a willing ... VOLUNTEER!"

Mary Drew Adams

Swinging for Respect

The great pleasure in life is doing what people say you cannot do.

Walter Bagehot

Down the hospital corridor, screams of delight could be heard as children eagerly awaited their turn to hit the brightly colored tennis balls. With each smash, another child's laughter was heard as it echoed against the sterile walls.

On this particular day, our volunteer staff at Tennis with a Different Swing, Inc.® in Orlando, Florida, had traveled to a local Children's Hospital to work with children with prosthetic devices and those confined to wheelchairs. This unique rehabilitative program does not teach tennis but teaches essential life skills such as eye tracking and eye-to-hand coordination to people with disabilities.

Like many previous sessions, volunteers paired off individually with each of the children. After receiving some minimal instruction on how to hold a racquet, our participants were then allowed to hit the ball. With each mighty swing, the children became more confident.

Then the inevitable happened.

As we handed out racquets, I heard a small boy's voice behind me.

"May I play, too?" he asked from somewhere. I never looked around to see who was speaking to me and just reached for another racquet, while assuring the child that everyone would be given the opportunity to participate.

Suddenly, I was facing an eight-year-old boy named Joey. Each volunteer stopped what they were doing and gazed at me wondering how I'd handle this situation. While I turned in the direction of the racquet bag pretending to get a racquet, that was not my intention. Near the bag was a physical therapist from the hospital. "What do I do?" I mouthed to her like a mime in shock. "Should I give him a racquet?"

The physical therapist shrugged and whispered to me, "I don't know. Joey has never asked to participate in any of the sporting activities since he's been here."

All the volunteers were stunned because I had just promised Joey—a boy in a wheelchair with no arms or legs, only small stumps where there should have been limbs—a chance to participate. Another staff member asked a nurse where his prosthetic devices were and was promptly told, "Joey doesn't use them because he doesn't like them."

This precocious eight-year-old now embarked on teaching our staff a lesson in courage that we will never, ever forget. He was telling us that he counts. And never ever say that a child can't.

Joey promptly rolled his wheelchair over to me. He politely, but firmly, asked for the racquet. Before I could speak, he grabbed the racquet with the stub of his right arm and placed the handle under his armpit. With the stub of his left arm, he rolled the wheelchair to a far corner of the room. He placed his two leg stumps apart in the wheelchair to balance himself and ordered me to throw the ball to him. I immediately did what I was told. Everyone in the room looked on in absolute amazement as this fierce competitor firmly struck the ball.

However, I threw the ball in a wimpy way, trying not to hit Joey, and this did not sit well with him.

"THROW THE BALL HARD!" he hollered at me. A big grin emerged from his face as he commanded, "Throw it again!" Once more, this incredible eight-year-old boy hit the ball down the length of the room.

From that moment on, the philosophy of our organization was born. Volunteers routinely replace any child's "I can't" with Joey's "I can!"

Sheila A. Bolin

[EDITORS' NOTE: *For more information on Tennis with a Different Swing, Inc.*, *contact Orange Lake Resort & Country Club, 8505 West Irlo Bronson Parkway, Kissimmee, FL 34747; 407-239-2292; fax: 407-239-5192. Among her awards, Sheila has earned a "Point of Light" for her volunteering from the Points of Light Foundation & Volunteer Center National Network, 1400 I Street, N.W., Suite 900, Washington, DC 20005; 800-VOLUNTEER; fax: 202-729-8100; e-mail:* Info@Pointsof Light.org; *Web site:* www.pointsoflight.org.]

Just Obedience

We are here on Earth for a purpose. Yes, even in prison and beyond, God uses us for his glory and kingdom if we remain in accordance with his will and obey his commandments.

George Castillo

It was Christmas 1985, and I was scheduled to preach in several prisons in Raleigh, North Carolina. Arriving late on Christmas Eve, I checked into a hotel and, while preparing for bed, flipped on CNN to catch the late news. On the screen was Mother Teresa. The little nun with the love-lined face had her arms around two emaciated young men, advanced AIDS sufferers who had been released that very day from a New York state prison to enter a home established by Mother Teresa's order.

When a reporter demanded to know "why we should care about criminals with AIDS," Mother Teresa explained that these young men had been created in God's image and deserved to know of his love.

I sat on the side of the bed staring at the picture on the screen. How could she do it? Embrace those men who were dying of that deadly virus? I had to admit to myself that I wouldn't have the courage to do what this little ninety-pound woman was doing.

I went to sleep that night thinking about Mother Teresa, and at the same time thanking God that I didn't have to deal with AIDS patients.

The next morning I preached to several hundred women prisoners. As I was getting ready to leave, the warden asked if I would visit Bessie Shipp.

"Who is Bessie Shipp?" I asked.

"Bessie has AIDS," said the warden. "She's in an isolation cell. It's Christmas and nobody has visited her."

I reacted instinctively with, "I'm running late for the men's prison." *Besides,* I thought to myself, *I don't want to take the chance.* Much less was known then about how the virus was transmitted, and, frankly, I was afraid. Then the face of Mother Teresa flashed before me, and I heard her words: *These boys deserve to know of God's love. . . . Have this mind in you . . .*

"Well, all right," I said, "take me to Bessie Shipp."

As the chaplain escorted me through two secured areas, he explained that a petition had been presented to the governor for Bessie's release, that it hadn't been acted upon, and that she was feeling particularly depressed. The doctors had given her only a few weeks to live.

A chill came over me as we swung open the gate to the isolation cell, where a petite young woman sat bundled up in a bathrobe, reading a Bible. She looked up, and her eyes brightened as the chaplain said, "I promised I'd bring you a Christmas present, Bessie."

We chatted for a few moments, and since there wasn't much time for either of us, I decided I had better get to the point.

"Bessie, do you know Jesus?" I asked.

"No," she said. "I try to. I read this book. I want to know him, but I haven't been able to find him."

"We can settle it right now," I said, taking her hand. The chaplain took her other hand, and together we led Bessie in prayer. When we finished, she looked at us with tears flowing down her cheeks. It was a life-changing moment for Bessie—and for me.

Outside the prison, television crews were waiting to cover the "Christmas in Prison" story. Instead of my planned words, I made a plea for the governor to release Bessie Shipp, and that night on the plane flying back to Washington, I dictated a long letter to him. But the letter never had to be mailed. Two days later, Governor Jim Martin released Bessie, and she went home to Winston-Salem.

There Bessie studied the Bible, was baptized into a local church, and was visited regularly by Al Lawrence, our Prison Fellowship area director at the time. She told Al that those were the happiest days of her life because she knew that God loved her and God's people loved her as well.

Three weeks after her release, Bessie joined the Savior she had so recently come to know.

I shuddered later when I thought how close I had come to avoiding that visit. And since that day I have never hesitated to walk into an AIDS ward and embrace dying men and women. No heroics or courage on my part—just obedience. And in this case, through Mother Teresa's example, he took away the unholy fear that had gripped me.

Charles W. Colson

[EDITORS' NOTE: *For information on Prison Fellowship Ministries, contact P.O. Box 17500, Washington, DC 20041-0500; e-mail:* correspondence@pfm.org; *Web site:* www.prisonfellowship.org.]

The Deep End   by Matt Matteo

Reprinted by permission of Matt Matteo.

5

LOVE AND KINDNESS

Let no one ever come to you without leaving better and happier. Be the living expression of God's kindness: kindness in your face, kindness in your eyes, kindness in your smile.

Mother Teresa

You Got Another One, Joey!

All the gold in the world cannot buy a dying man one more breath—so what does that make today worth?

Og Mandino

I couldn't believe it. Of all the times for this to happen— a flat tire! But when is a good time? Not when you are wearing a suit and you have been traveling for nearly five hours, and, added to this bleak picture, nightfall is approaching. Wait! Did I mention I was on a country road?

There was only one thing to do. Call the local automobile association. Yeah, right. The cell phone I bought, for security and protection from moments like these, wasn't in range to call anyone. "No service," it said. *No kidding!* I thought.

I sat for a few minutes moaning and complaining. Then I began emptying my trunk so I could get at the tire and tools needed to get the job done. I carry a large, plastic container filled with what I call "just-in-case stuff." When I am training or speaking, I love to have props with me. I hate leaving anything home so I bring everything ... "just in case."

Cars buzzed by me. A few beeped sarcastically. It was as if the horns were saying, "Ha, ha."

Darkness began to settle in, and it became more difficult to see. Thank goodness it was the tire on the passenger's side, away from the traffic—but that only made it more impossible to benefit from the headlights of passing cars.

Suddenly, a car pulled off the road behind me. In the blinding light, I saw a male figure approaching me.

"Hey, do you need any help?"

"Well, it certainly isn't easy doing this with a white dress shirt and suit on," I said sarcastically.

Then he stepped into the light. I was literally frightened. This young guy was dressed in black. Nearly everything imaginable was pierced and tattooed. His hair was cropped and poorly cut, and he wore leather bracelets with spikes on each wrist.

"How about I give you a hand?" he said.

"Well, I don't know . . . I think I can . . ."

"Come on, it will only take me a few minutes."

He took right over. While I watched him, I happened to look back at his car and noticed, for the first time, someone sitting in the passenger seat. That concerned me. I suddenly felt outnumbered. Thoughts of carjackings and robberies flashed through my mind. I really just wanted to get this over and survive the ordeal.

Then, without warning, it began to pour. The night sky had hidden the approaching clouds. It hit like a waterfall and made it impossible to finish changing the tire.

"Look, my friend, just stop what you're doing. I appreciate all your help. You'd better get going. I'll finish after the rain stops," I said.

"Let me help you put your stuff back in the trunk. It will get ruined," he insisted. "Then get in my car. We'll wait with you."

"No, really. I'll take care of everything," I said.

"You can't get in your car with the jack up like that. It will fall. Come on. Get in!" He grabbed my arm and pulled me toward the car. Crack! Boom! Lightning and thunder roared like a freight train. I jumped into his car. *Oh, God, protect me,* I prayed to myself.

Wet and tired, I settled into the back seat. Suddenly, a kindly, frail voice came from the front seat. "Are you all right?" a petite old woman asked as she turned around to face me.

"Yes, I am," I replied, greatly relieved at seeing the old woman there. I suspected she was his mom.

"My name is Beatrice, and this is my neighbor, Joey," she said. "He insisted on stopping when he saw you struggling with the tire."

"I am grateful for his help," I responded.

"Me, too," Beatrice laughed. "Joey takes me to visit my husband. We had to place him in a nursing home, and it's about thirty minutes away from my residence. So, every Monday, Wednesday and Friday, Joey and I have a date." With a childish grin she looked at Joey.

Joey's whimsical remark, "We're the remake of *The Odd Couple,*" gave us all a good laugh.

"Joey, that's incredible what you do for her. I would never have guessed, well, you know . . . ," I stumbled with the words.

"I know. People who look like me don't do nice things," he said.

I was silent. I really felt uncomfortable. I never judge people by the way they dress, and I was angry with myself for being so foolish.

"Joey is a great kid. I'm not the only one he helps—he's also a volunteer at our church. He also works with the kids in the learning center at the low-income housing unit in our town," Beatrice added.

"I'm a tutor," Joey said modestly as he stared at my car.

I reflected for a few moments on what Joey said. He was right. What he wore on the outside was a reflection of the world as he saw it. What he wore on the inside was the spirit of giving, caring and loving the world from his point of view.

When the rain stopped, Joey and I changed the tire. I tried to offer him money, and he refused.

As we shook hands, I began to apologize for my stupidity. He said, "I experience that same reaction all the time. I actually thought about changing the way I look, but then I saw this as an opportunity to make a point. So I'll leave you with the same question that I ask everyone who takes time to know me. If Jesus returned tomorrow and walked among us again, would you recognize him by what he *wore* or by what he *did*?"

Joey walked back to his car. As they drove off, Beatrice was smiling and waving as she began to laugh again. I could almost hear her saying, "You got another one, Joey. You got another one."

Bob Perks

A Hug and a Kiss

*Kindness is more than deeds. It is an attitude,
an expression, a look, a touch. It is anything that
lifts another person.*

C. Neil Strait

Mary, a recent widow and devoted "fifty-something"
grandmother, worked as a nursing-attendant. Her triumph
over a heart attack and by-pass surgery was remarkable,
undoubtedly because of the deep love she held for her
grandchildren.

But this time, Mary's hospital stay was different. Afflicted
with a noncontagious form of pneumonia, she was
stunned to learn of her diagnosis—full-blown AIDS.

As part of a hospital volunteer visitation team, I call on
each assigned AIDS patient at least once a day. In my role
as patient-advocate, I let each person know that someone
else cares about them—aside from their family and the
medical staff. Once we become better acquainted, I greet
most patients with a gentle hug and a kiss on the cheek. I
can usually sense whether or not a patient is comfortable
with this gesture.

After my third visit with Mary, I asked politely, "Would you like a hug and a kiss on the cheek?"

Mary smiled, holding out two waiting arms, and whispered a barely audible, "Yes, I'd love one."

As I drew back, I noticed a tear working its way down one cheek. "What's wrong?" I asked.

"That's the first time anyone has touched me, since I was diagnosed with AIDS. The medical staff touch me, but . . ." Mary turned onto her side, placing both hands over her face. "My sons won't even allow me to see my grandchildren," she said between sobs. "When my family visits, they sit clear across the room, as far away from me as possible."

I simply sat by her bedside and listened in silence—handing her tissues and trying to understand.

A few days later, when I stopped to see Mary again, one of her sons and his wife were visiting. "Good evening, Mary. I see that you have guests, so I'll stop back later," I said, giving her a gentle hug and a kiss on the cheek.

Mary grabbed my right wrist as I turned to leave. "Wait a minute, Mack. I want you to meet my son, John, and daughter-in-law, Sarah." During the introductions, her anxious family sat clear across the room from Mary's bed.

Later, when I looked in on her, her visitors were still maintaining their safe distance. I respected Mary's time with her family and didn't intrude.

The following evening, John and Sarah were back again, and the scenario repeated itself like a familiar rerun on television. I went in, gave Mary a gentle hug and a kiss, promising to come back later.

When I returned, something had miraculously changed. John and Sarah were seated in chairs—one on each side of Mary's bed—and they were holding hands.

Obviously choked with emotion, John said, "I guess if

some stranger can hug and kiss my mother, we have nothing to be afraid of."

Fortunately, Mary became well enough to return home and continue her loving relationship with her family, including her cherished grandchildren—in spite of her illness.

Mack Emmert
As told to Tom Lagana

[EDITORS' NOTE: *For more information on HIV/AIDS, contact Project Inform, 205 13th Street, #2001, San Francisco, CA 94103; 415-558-8669; fax: 415-558-0684; Web site: www.projinf.org.*]

The Sign of the Rabbit

What we learn with pleasure, we never forget.

Alfred Mercier

Eighty-seven-year-old Lucia had the hands of a twenty-year-old woman. Soft and graceful, they would move through the air as if in a dance. Watching her fingers lightly tickling an imaginary stage in front of her, one could barely resist being drawn into her lyrical movements. Those hands always delivered an insightful message. Deaf since the age of three, Lucia was particularly energetic and adept with sign language, her only form of communication.

I visited Lucia at a local nursing home with my pet dwarf rabbit named Cadberi. Pet therapy was a new concept in nursing homes. But Cadberi was a "ham" and loved his "job." His animal magnetism stemmed from his gifts of compassion and cuteness that radiated through his soft brown eyes, long whiskers and briskly bobbing nose.

Cadberi understood visitors and instinctively knew their innermost desire to be needed and touched. He inspired even the most confused residents who, during

Cadberi's visits, sometimes even spoke or responded lucidly. His job benefits included endless caresses from the residents as well as all the carrots and kale he could eat in a day. While he lay in many residents' arms or stretched out on their beds, Cadberi had a special bond with Lucia. She was definitely his favorite.

I did not know how to speak sign language. But after a few days, I realized that even if I didn't know the words, our smiles and laughter communicated volumes. I increasingly became more interested in learning and purchased an American Sign Language dictionary. Goodness knows what Lucia was thinking as I clumsily tried to sign back to her. But her bright-eyed smile and fighting spirit always encouraged me even if she had to guide my hands physically until I got the big "Aha!"

We quickly bonded as student and teacher as well as friends and companions. Our visits became the melding of two worlds far apart in time, yet precious in all the knowledge she was giving me. I wasn't sure who looked forward more to the visits—Cadberi or me. Whenever it came to "that time," he would willingly jump into his carrier labeled "Have Bunny—Will Travel." Arriving at the nursing home, he perked his ears up expecting his first "client" meeting. Yet when Lucia rolled around the corner while flashing me the sign meaning "cute rabbit," Cadberi would begin squirming in my arms, preparing to leap into her lap. She was the only person with whom he'd ride on a wheelchair.

"Cute Rabbit" was the first sign I ever learned, as it was the most repeated in our conversations. This sign of the rabbit became our hello and good-bye, and as time went on, it also became my name.

After three years of continuous visits, Lucia never gave up on me nor I on her. Yet I couldn't help but notice the Alzheimer's disease catching up on her bit-by-bit. It broke my heart to see her struggle and sign back the same questions to me with a deeply bewildered effect. Sadly she would grimace in pain from her increasingly tight and throbbing arthritic hands. I knew the time was coming when Lucia would no longer be guiding my hands in speech, but I would be holding hers in support.

One day I came to visit and found every nursing home volunteer's worst discovery—a stripped empty bed. Seeing no personal effects, I thought the worst. I felt the tears gathering in my eyes. I could see the disappointment in Cadberi's eyes as well. Minutes felt like hours until a nurse filled me in.

Lucia was still alive but had been transferred to a "step-down" nursing home. This was a smaller center that specialized in caring for the more seriously ill, and it was near her daughter's residence. Lucia was now in a center that was ninety minutes from my home. I thought I would never get to see her again, and worse, not get the chance to say good-bye.

After a few weeks, I couldn't go on without seeing Lucia. Impulsively, I called the center. I was told Lucia was unable to leave her bed and could barely recognize family members. Still I asked if Cadberi and I could come by for one more visit.

During the long ride to the center, Cadberi got restless in his carrier. He shook with nervousness from the drive as he was only accustomed to "short hops" in the car. Arriving at the center, I was greeted in the hallway by Lucia's daughter.

"It's not one of her good days," she said. "She won't recognize you and can barely sit up."

"That's okay," I replied. "I just want to give them one more chance to visit."

We walked quietly into Lucia's room. She lay still, sleeping in her bed. She was drawn and pale. Only wearing a hospital gown, she didn't resemble the vibrant woman who taught me so much on survival. Yet Cadberi knew. He knew immediately who she was and began his light kicking, trying to let me know where he wanted to go.

In one quick leap, Cadberi lay comforted by her side. Awakening to find Cadberi's warm brown eyes gazing into her own, she smiled. It was the first smile her daughter had seen all week. Their bond was still there. Then amazingly, Lucia raised her hand and curled her fingers into rabbit ears. She wiggled them in an upward curve . . . "Rabbit."

"Yes, Lucia," I returned the sign "Cute Rabbit." Lucia smiled again after signing what would be her final words to me. I continued to hold her hand while petting Cadberi with the other until she fell asleep. Two weeks later, Lucia died.

My bond with Lucia was more than a volunteer experience as we connected much deeper than teacher and student, or volunteer and patient. It was the melding of two souls. We had a language of our own with the sign of the rabbit.

Cadberi passed away quietly one afternoon, after eight years of service to those he loved. But he never forgot the sign, always nuzzling up close to my hands. Maybe in remembrance. Maybe in understanding. But mostly, reminding me that language doesn't have to be a barrier to love.

Pamela B. Silberman

Grandmother's Gift

Mace was an independent, frail wisp of a woman with terminal cancer. But there was nothing fragile about her mental outlook. Her ill health had not hindered her vitality. The last three years had been a battleground, fighting her disease with a determination and strength that would have brought others to their knees. Mace, accompanied by a God-inspired appreciation for life and a spirit that won our praise and admiration, knew she was losing ground.

Hospice offers a team of people to care for those whose life expectancy is less than six months. Mace had less than six weeks. I was one of her new volunteers. This lady, so loved by many, could be sharp-tongued, but she was a priceless friend, and her friends drifted in and out of her home at will. Since she was so uncomfortably close to death, we were all looking for ways to make her last days special.

One day I asked, "Mace, what could I do for you that no one else is doing?"

"Well," she quipped with an Irish twinkle still visible in her eyes, "tell me what you're good for."

I rattled off a few accomplishments that didn't seem to

impress her until I said, "Oh, and I do needlepoint."

"Thank God!" she almost hollered her response. "I've been wondering what I'd ever do. No one I know could do this for me. I thought I might be finished before it was . . . look in that basket."

Among other things, Mace was an artist. She'd designed and painted the composition for this particular needle-point picture, working her layout on the incredibly small eighteen-inch mesh canvas. It was breathtaking. The scene of sand, sea and sky was in muted colors ranging from cream to gold, pale blues to turquoise and all shades of beige to white. A small Native American child stood in the midst of it as though awestruck. It was to be a gift for her long-awaited great-grandchild expected in June. Since this was February, Mace had accepted the fact that the child would never know her. Her strongest yearning was to be some part of the child's life. This exquisite artwork was only part of her plan.

Because time was extremely short, I started immediately, delighted to be an instrumental part of her gift. As I stitched for hours at her bedside, we became fast friends. She was a treasure to know—sharing with me insights into her life, her beliefs about God and her attitude about approaching death. In a terminal illness, trust and love must develop fast—everything becomes now and today.

"Both of my grandmothers died when I was a very young child. I developed a hunger for the loving connection of 'grannies' that some of my little friends had. I did so want to be a great-granny," she sighed. "Don't you remember how grandparents made such an impact on a child's life? You'd hear someone say, 'my grandma says,' and what followed were usually words to live by. That's what I wanted to be," and her weakened voice trailed off.

But Mace had already put into action a marvelous plan of future contact with her great-granddaughter. She would share her life with the girl by way of special writings. She'd set up a series of letters for the girl's future celebrations, covering all the important events in a woman's life. There were letters for special birthdays like sweet sixteen, graduations, her wedding day and even the possible arrival of babies. Her clever grandmother would be a part of these events, though not in person.

A few of her letters were to be attached to personal items: an ancient and intricate lace handkerchief belonging to her grandmother for 'something old,' and a porcelain cross and white leather Bible for a sweet-sixteen birthday with an inscription that would break her heart but acknowledge her faith. Also included was a silk baby cap made by Mace's hands years before while she'd waited for another grandbaby who never arrived.

Mace's vivid, well-written letters with pictures and memorabilia were historic, humorous and revealing, and in each letter, Mace brought God into the child's world in ways that were acceptable for her age. There were invaluable bits and pieces of information remembering celebrations of another era. She allowed me to read them, and they were jewels—just as she was. Although her life had been filled with love, sadness and sacrifice, she had many personal accomplishments.

"I even took up flying," she smirked. "My husband and I were into golf and bridge, and I wanted to learn to fly—this was in the 1930s . . . not considered right for women. His response had been an absolute, 'No!' So pleading boredom, I quietly gave up golf and bridge and sneaked out to take flying lessons. The plane was a puddle jumper, and I loved it. But I don't have time to tell you all that. I didn't tell him until he was on his way overseas in World War II, and when he got back, it no longer seemed important."

It was important to Mace that the needlepoint picture she hoped would hang in the child's room would serve as a constant reminder of "great-granny." Mace felt compelled to leave a lasting gift that spoke of her artistic talents and would perhaps convey without words some of her great-grandmother's attitudes about the beauty of the world and God's hand in its creation.

On one of her more difficult and painful days I said, "Mace, pull the needle on this stitch for me."

"Oh, Ruth, not today, I just can't," she moaned.

"Mace," I insisted. "Please, just pull this one stitch." She looked at me like a good friend looks at another when her patience is being tested. We were used to that with Mace, so I knew I had to be insistent. "Hey, lady, just help me with this one stitch."

And with a frustrated yank, she did.

Then grabbing her hand and holding on to it, I said, "Mace, you put the first stitch in here months ago, and just now you put in the last one. It's finished!" And we both cried.

As Mace gazed at her finished canvas, I knew it was the grandchild she visualized in the scene. She wanted her to see and appreciate the beauty of the world around her and to value it, just as her greatest granny had.

Mace died just days later. The picture was framed and ready in time to welcome a much-loved great-granddaughter who would have a lifetime of reminders of this special woman's love.

Ruth Hancock

[EDITORS' NOTE: *For information on Hospice Association of America, contact 228 Seventh Street, S.E., Washington, DC 20003; 202-546-4759; fax: 202-547-9559; Web site: www.hospice-america.org.*]

Her Spirit Lives On

When you extend yourself in kindness and spirit, one to another, that comes back to you.

Oprah Winfrey

Our family was hit hard by the news of Mom's diagnosis. Always a paragon of health, Mom lived a textbook life. At the age of eighty, she still had the figure, skin and energy of a much younger woman. Her physical well-being was equally matched by her youthful outlook, serenity and spirituality. Mom was a doll in every sense of the word.

She died of liver cancer on November 17, 1992. Mom's passing left us feeling devastated and alone. We felt the overpowering emptiness of our first holiday without a vital member of the family who had always been there to share in the festivities.

Our college- and high-school–aged children were home for Thanksgiving, as well as my sister. We tried to mask the gloom that was in our hearts, but the sadness remained as our memories of Mom continued to surface.

During all of our family dinners, Mom always offered to be the "cleanup" person. She worked right along beside me as I cooked the feast, joyfully peeling potatoes, washing the dishes and wiping up spills with a smile and a song. When dinner was over, Mom would swirl into the kitchen and begin scraping plates. With a spirited laugh, she would glance over at me, raise her right eyebrow, and say, "Just sit and rest, dear. I'll put this mess in order."

As Christmas approached, I wondered how we would manage that holiday—one of Mom's favorites. While Dad was still alive, the two of them always spent Christmas Eve with us, and after he passed away, Mom continued the tradition. She delighted in watching her beloved grandchildren squeal with delight as they opened each present from Santa on Christmas morning.

On impulse, I grabbed the phone and called our local soup kitchen. "Could you use some volunteers to help prepare and serve the noon meal on Christmas morning?" I asked.

The secretary sighed, sounding relieved and a bit flustered. "Oh my . . . Yes! Every other holiday of the year is no problem, but Christmas is especially tough to fill. Can you come at 8:00 A.M.?" She signed us up as I eagerly volunteered the five of us.

When I sheepishly told my family what I had done, they were in total agreement. They weren't relishing that first Christmas morn without Grandma either. That year, we started a new tradition—opening our presents on Christmas Eve and rising bright and early on Christmas morning to head for the soup kitchen.

After being officially welcomed by the regulars and chefs, we donned our aprons and began peeling potatoes, washing pans and wiping up spills. Later, as we served a wonderful banquet of turkey and all the trimmings to the needy, I thanked God for my blessings—a wonderful husband and children, and our comfortable life together.

As we wiped off tables, scraped plates and restored the

kitchen to order, I realized that there could be no better tribute to my mother than what we were doing. Mother's idea of a joyful way to celebrate the holidays was doing the same menial chores, year after year, with love and enthusiasm for the family she held so dear.

Although we continued to volunteer at the soup kitchen for several more years, until the children moved away, it never held as much meaning as that first Christmas morning. That year, we masked our heartache by serving others in a kitchen—a place where Mom's love and generosity lives on.

Santina Lonergan

A Child's Gift

About a year ago, as I prepared to leave the house, the telephone rang. For a fleeting moment I toyed with the idea of not answering it, but I ran back to the kitchen anyway.

My husband called and said, "Sorry, honey, but I have to work overtime. Guess you'll have to pick up Taylor at school today. I'll be home as soon as I can."

Each week I set aside several hours to bring a little joy into the lives of the women at a nearby home. On this particular day, I was bringing freshly cut red and yellow snapdragons and mammoth zinnias.

Accompanied by my unexpected companion, we started our rounds with bundles of blossoms in my arms and Taylor at my side. After we visited the third or fourth room, I noticed that, just as we were ready to leave each room, my son would hug each woman and then whisper something into her ear. Because I wanted to make sure that we had enough time to visit all of the residents, I didn't ask him what he was whispering, but he elicited a smile from every lady.

Later that evening, during dinner, my husband asked how my volunteer job worked out with our son in tow.

"It was actually lots of fun," I said. "We were quite a pair. Whatever Taylor said to the ladies, it definitely made them happy." Puzzled, I stopped and glanced across the table at our son. "What was it that you whispered?"

Looking at both his dad and me with an angelic face, he responded, "All I said was 'I love you, Grandma. You look soooo beautiful today.' I wanted to make them feel good."

Pamela Strome-Merewether

One Step Ahead

*Character cannot be developed in ease and
quiet. Only through experiences of trial and
suffering can the soul be strengthened, vision
cleared, ambition inspired and success achieved.*

Helen Keller

As I prepared dinner, my twelve-year-old daughter,
Ashley, ran into the kitchen and shouted, "Mom, have you
seen the news today?"

"Yes, dear. Why do you ask?" That began a week I will
never forget.

The news revolved around a flood that hit Elba,
Alabama, a small town to our south. A low area already
prone to flooding, Elba relied on a levee system to hold
back the waters of the Pea River. Heavy rains created
excessive pressure on the levee, causing it to give way.
The entire town was suddenly engulfed in water.
Everything in its path was gone, and several families were
left with nothing.

"Mom, can I help?" Ashley asked with compassionate
concern. Her idea was to start a nonperishable food drive

for the people of this small town. Knowing that food was of major importance, she was especially concerned for the babies. Having a baby brother herself, she knew there would also be a critical need for other items, such as diapers.

Ashley asked, "Can I help get things for these people?"

"Yes . . . but how will you deliver these items, dear?"

"That is where you come in, Mom. Will you help me?" Knowing full well what my answer would be, our work began. As Ashley planned how to collect the items, I helped her find a way to transport them.

She placed boxes in the school and local businesses to collect what she could. Ashley made flyers on the computer, announcing the food drive and posted them throughout the neighborhood. I called the Salvation Army and arranged for them to deliver the food to Elba. Since they had already been there with desperately needed supplies, some of the items would remain with our local Salvation Army for use in future disaster relief efforts. Because their supplies were dwindling rapidly from the recent flood in Elba, they helped us set the date, and our collection began.

Everything went well until one week into our food drive. On April 8, 1998, a tornado struck Birmingham, Alabama, and completely destroyed everything in its path, killing more than thirty people and leaving little behind.

The major with the Salvation Army phoned me and said, "If it's all right with you and Ashley, we'd like to send the majority of the items you collected to the tornado victims in Birmingham." Since efforts were already underway in Elba and the people in Birmingham were in such dire need, naturally we agreed.

Already one step ahead of the rest of us, Ashley updated the flyers. She was in the midst of planning a door-to-door collection in our community when she had the idea of calling area businesses to request donations. Upon calling the local Wal-Mart store first, she received an immediate offer from the manager. He invited her to set up a drive-by drop-off at his store that Friday. It would be challenging, but she enthusiastically agreed.

After calling her school to explain our beneficent plans, the principal granted her permission to be excused for that day. We were all set to begin the collection at eight o'clock Friday morning.

Then, the night before the collection was to begin, the unthinkable happened again. Another major storm, moving across Southern Tennessee, spawned a tornado that hit a small town just across our state line. It destroyed several homes and injured many. Once again, people were in need of assistance.

Arriving at the Wal-Mart store on Friday, around seven, we began setting up the collection. The Salvation Army truck arrived shortly before eight. Wal-Mart's manager had even arranged for the local radio stations and newspaper to cover the story, and the collection took off. I have never seen a twelve-year-old work so hard.

With a poster labeled, "COLLECTING ITEMS FOR THE TORNADO VICTIMS" in hand, Ashley walked the pavement in front of Wal-Mart for twelve uninterrupted hours. She managed to collect a truckload of items and nine hundred dollars in cash for the Salvation Army and the victims of the 1998 spring storms.

As she closed the door of the truck, Ashley turned and smiled. "I worked hard, and I'm tired, but I feel great inside!"

As we stood and watched the truck drive away, she looked at me in tears. "Thanks, Mom, for helping to make this happen. If it weren't for you, I couldn't have pulled it off."

Wiping the tears from her cheeks, I replied, "No. Thank

you for teaching me about reaching out and helping people in need."

Denise Peebles

[EDITORS' NOTE: *For information, contact The Salvation Army Headquarters, P.O. Box 269, Alexandria, VA 22302; 703-684-5500; fax: 703-684-3478; Web site: www.salvationarmy.usa.org.*]

Thank Gawd fo' Y'all

I'll never make the mistake of being seventy again.

Casey Stengel

I'll never forget Percy Tabb.

My first year out of college was 1993, and I was living in Selma, Alabama. I had just started a year of service with the Edmundite Mission Corps, a Catholic lay missions program where my friend Chris and I spent our time building and rehabilitating homes for people in need.

One day in October, Father Steve, the director of our program, asked if the two of us could assist Mr. Percival Tabb, a man of ninety-plus years living alone some thirty miles west of Selma. Mr. Tabb lived in what is commonly called a "shotgun shack," a long, narrow, rectangular house with three small rooms lined up one behind the other. The house had suffered some structural damage in a storm and needed repairs to make it safe again.

The three of us drove out to take a look at Mr. Tabb's home. After winding down a sparsely populated dirt road, we found his house and pulled slowly into his driveway.

The greeting committee consisted of a family of cats scattering in all directions and a big, black, scary-looking dog barking from a doghouse where he was chained. Calling out to Mr. Tabb, we walked up the makeshift stairs to the small porch. He answered from inside and slowly shuffled to the door, ambling from one supporting object to another.

The old man who appeared before us was a heartbreaking sight. When he came closer, I noticed his sad eyes, slightly glazed and yellowish. He appeared to have only one tooth left in his mouth, hanging alone at the center of his upper gums. His hands were lined and leathery, and he looked apprehensive about the three white men standing at his door.

"We've come to look at your house and see if we can repair it for you," Father Steve told him. Mr. Tabb then seemed to relax and told us to go around back and look at the damage.

The house stood eighteen inches off the ground on cinder block pylons. We found that heavy rains and strong winds had caused some of the pylons to lean over. If they weren't repaired, they might collapse completely and bring the house down.

When we went inside to look at his chimney, we were struck by the squalid conditions. Clothes and junk were strewn all over the place. The sheetrock on the walls was filthy and crumbling in places. Cockroaches were rioting everywhere. The pungent smell of years of kerosene fumes permeated the entire house and Mr. Tabb as well.

Taking all this in, I slowly narrowed my focus on the wood-burning stove which, when burning, spilled smoke into a brick chimney. The stove stood in the center of his house, and the chimney rose through his roof.

Mr. Tabb told us the insurance adjustor had assessed 'amage and said not to use the wood-burning stove until repairs had been made. When the house leaned over, the pressure had caused a crack in the chimney. The adjustor was afraid the concrete flue might also be cracked, causing a smoke or fire hazard.

Through the holes in the sheetrock, we could see the house had no insulation either. So at night it was about as cold inside as it was outside. To fix it, the insurance company had given him five hundred dollars for repairs. Mr. Tabb had hired some laborers and paid them upfront. Big mistake. The men fixed one corner of the house and never returned.

Sitting on the edge of his bed, he shook his head and began to cry. "It's just too cold at night for this old man," he muttered tearfully.

We told him we'd be back in an hour with some blankets and warm clothes, and then return in the morning to begin the repairs. The three of us drove home in silence, too disturbed to speak.

The next day Chris and I drove back to Mr. Tabb's residence to start work. We went inside and found him sitting on the edge of his bed. He was happy to see us as he had a good night's sleep from his new blankets. "Thank Gawd fo' y'all," he kept repeating in his singsong voice. "I asked the Lawd to send someone to keep me warm, and the next day y'all came. Thank Gawd fo' y'all."

That day and the next we managed to jack up the house and set it back down on new pylons. We lit a fire in his stove to make sure the smoke went out where it was supposed to go, and it did. As we prepared to leave, Mr. Tabb sat us down and gave us a pretty stern lecture about why we should never do drugs.

During those two days, he laughed a lot which was great to see after how depressed he'd been when we first met him. As we left, he peppered us with a few more "Thank Gawd fo' y'all's" and hugged us.

Throughout that year, we continued to visit Mr. Tabb and built a great relationship with him. We kind of adopted him as a grandfather, or maybe he adopted us as grandchildren.

Over the next few months, we brought visiting volunteer groups out to work on different projects. We painted his house, installed a flush toilet, insulated, sheetrocked, painted his bedroom and planted a garden. We'd bring groups to meet him even when we didn't have a project to do. When the volunteers reflected on their time in Selma, they always mentioned Mr. Tabb. He was truly unforgettable and had a strange impact on everyone who met him.

As our year in Alabama was coming to an end, Chris and I went to visit Mr. Tabb for the last time. He always hugged us when we said good-bye, but that day he held us a lot longer than usual. He didn't want to let us go. Over and over, he repeated ever so sadly, "I hate to see ya go. I hate to see ya go."

Less than a year later, he suffered a stroke and passed away at the home of a relative. Today, his picture hangs in my bedroom and every time I look up at Mr. Tabb, I can hear that Southern drawl voice of his saying, "Thank Gawd fo' y'all. Ah LOVE ya!"

Chris Bibbo

The Children of Russia

Everywhere we went, the Russian Rotarians were so honored by our visit they rolled out the red carpet. As a member of a group from the United States, Canada and Australia, we were traveling together to present official charters to four new Rotary clubs in Western Siberia in 1997.

They showed us their cities. They dined us, and they fed us an obscene amount of vodka. When we arrived in Tomsk, I expected no more and no less. I was wrong. That visit literally changed my life.

"Carolyn, would you take fifteen minutes out of your schedule," asked Savely Volfson, my Rotary host. "I would like to show you the first humanitarian project the new Rotary Club of Tomsk wants to sponsor. I want to take you to the children's cancer ward at our hospital."

Thinking like a good Rotarian, I agreed but was not eager.

In the nearby city of Seversk, there is a nuclear plant. Radiation had leaked. Although the size of the leak was not dramatic enough to be reported on television, the effect was the same. The doctors were seeing more and more children coming into the hospital with leukemia and other forms of cancer of the blood.

Although the doctors had a fine chemotherapy program with an 80 percent success rate in May 1997, the hospital had gone a year without receiving its government funding. The doctors, who had often used their own salaries to help purchase the medicine, had gone unpaid for a year. Families were left to beg or borrow the money to buy the chemo medicine so their children would live.

Be strong, Carolyn, I kept telling myself as I rode in the car to the hospital. *These children have already suffered enough. The last thing they need is to see a grown woman cry.*

I walked through the big, wooden double-doors to the hospital. I met the doctors and listened to them explain how they treated the children. They took me along the hospital corridors, downstairs, upstairs and finally to the children's cancer ward.

The ward accommodated ten children in little tiny cubbyholes that were smaller than some American bathrooms. There were seven children—and their mothers—there that day. Because most hospitals were short on staffing, the mothers had all moved into the hospital to be with their children.

The kids went on instant alert. They looked. They sat up. They came to the doorway of their cubbyholes. *Who was this person?*

They were weak. They were pale. They were thin. They were bald. I wished I had brought presents. Something. Anything. The only thing I could find in my purse was my Rotary business card with a picture of me in my red jacket. I gave a card to each child. Each kid looked at the card, looked at me, then held the card to his or her heart and smiled. I knew right then and there that I was a Rotary trading card, and I was worth a lot!

Well, I did not cry. I thought I had satisfied Savely's request and that I would get out of the hospital without disgracing myself. I was wrong again.

Each mother came out of a room. Through the translator, each mother said the same thing to me: "Thank you for taking time out of your busy schedule. Thank you for coming."

Then it hit me. My visit was not just a visit to the mothers. They thought my visit meant something. They thought I would take their stories outside the four walls of the hospital. They thought I would help. They thought their children would live. They had so much faith in me.

I knew their faith was misplaced. I had not come to save their children. In fact, I was already thinking ahead to the evening's festivities, to curling my hair and shaking the wrinkles out of my dress. Savely had asked a favor, and I was done. Wrong again.

After that meeting, I learned more about the children of Russia. I learned that, throughout Russia, the children were in crisis—dying, abandoned, orphaned, abused, suicidal, hungry, cold and uneducated.

Looking back, I now understand that meeting the children in Tomsk was no accident. It was destiny—theirs and mine. They had the courage to fight and to live. I had to find the will and the ways to help them.

It was a defining moment in my life. I am so accustomed to carefully mapping out my life and eliminating the risks. This time fate took charge of my life. Lightning struck and got my attention. I never stood a chance. I was committed and took a risk.

Just one month after that fifteen-minute time-out in Tomsk, it couldn't have been a coincidence that I began serving as an officer of Rotary International. My new position automatically gave me many opportunities to tell the story of the children of Russia. And a year after visiting the kids with cancer, Rotarians worldwide had raised $620,000—enough to finance thirty humanitarian projects for children in twenty-two communities in Siberia and Far East Russia.

Raising the money was breathtaking. But I never forgot the seven children who were the inspiration for the "Children of Russia" project. Would they still be alive by the time the money was raised, the grant application approved and the money transferred to the hospital?

I went back to Tomsk in November 1998 and revisited the children's cancer ward. This time I remembered to take presents. I brought a supply of baseball caps, the perfect fashion accessory for a bald head.

The doctors reported that all seven children were still alive and doing well. That's the happy part. The sad part is that I met eight new children who had leukemia. One little boy was less than two years old.

You wonder how these kids endure chemotherapy treatment, hair loss, nausea and all the side effects. Yet when you come to visit, they can still smile, pose for pictures and speak softly to their moms. Cancer is definitely not for sissies.

Every day those children do what they must do in order to live. I only have to try not to cry.

Carolyn E. Jones

[EDITORS' NOTE: *For more information on Rotary International, contact One Rotary Center, 1560 Sherman Ave., Evanston, IL 60201; 847-866-3000; fax: 847-328-8554; e-mail:* pr@rotary intl.org; *Web site:* www.rotary.org.]

Find That Child!

*Life is a flame that is always burning itself out,
but it catches fire again every time a child is born.*
George Bernard Shaw

On that day in May when my daughter was born, I held her in my arms and memorized every detail. Leigh Ann was beautiful, perfect in every way. Except one. She was stillborn. Her death came as a complete shock. I had a wonderful pregnancy, and everyone was eagerly awaiting her arrival. Especially our four-year-old son, John. But four days before my due date, I noticed something was wrong; the baby wasn't moving.

When my supportive husband and I saw how perfect she was at birth, how much she looked like our son, we both felt as though our world had come to an end. As I held my baby, I looked up at the nurse and made a vow, *Something good will come out of this. I don't know how or when, but I will not let this be the final moment of her life.*

With the help of family and friends, we planned a simple memorial service. On the Saturday before Mother's Day, we stood beside her grave and said good-bye to our daughter.

When reality settled in, it was difficult to be in public. Every time I saw a baby or a little girl, my heart broke. I altered my lifestyle to avoid pain. I learned to shop at the all-night grocery store where there were no young mothers or babies at 11:00 P.M.

The following May, I knew I was pregnant again. Heidi was born a few days before Christmas. At last, we had our baby girl. She was strong, healthy and another mirror image of our son! We brought her home on Christmas Eve, the night of miracles.

The following spring, I learned our church needed volunteers for a special program called Respite. The name of the program came from its mission. Once a week, during the school year, volunteers went to the homes of young mothers and gave them a respite from childcare.

Volunteers took the children to our church, played with them, sang with them, gave them a snack and then returned the children to their homes three hours later. During their break, young mothers could rest, run errands in town, clean house or just enjoy a few "child-free moments."

These children lived in extreme poverty. Sometimes they lived in homes where abuse had been reported or was suspected. Yet for a few hours each week, they could play in a safe, warm environment surrounded by loving volunteers.

Besides needing new volunteers, the Respite program also needed someone to serve as director. When I told the ladies I would be interested in serving, one of them immediately turned and ran up the stairs to tell the minister their prayers had been answered!

On my first morning, we rode into neighborhoods the average American cannot imagine. The children we picked up lived in homes without indoor plumbing or glass in their windows.

Most of my time was spent planning activities, coordinating volunteers and keeping our classroom bright and cheerful. Usually the only contact I had with the children was during our rides to and from the church. But these wonderful kids found a way into my heart. As the months went by, I found myself spending more and more time with them in the classroom.

One day, I noticed a three-year-old boy who was always hungry. So I decided to make some pancakes for the children. The other volunteers marveled as the little boy ate six huge pancakes. Another time, we baked chocolate chip cookies. A four-year-old girl spilled some flour, and I watched her body brace for the beating she was conditioned to expect from such a mistake. I took her in my arms, and with a smile on my face, quickly and quietly cleaned up the small mess. When the cookies came out of the oven, I gave one to each child. That same little girl held the cookie as if it were gold. She had never had a freshly baked cookie before!

When I agreed to serve as the Respite director, I thought I had something to give each of these children. But I did not realize how much I would get in return. I gave them love, and they helped my heart to heal. They helped my love for Leigh Ann to live on.

As grieving parents, we have a choice. We can always mourn the loss of our own child, always long for the time with them that death cheated us. But somewhere out there is a little child who can return our love. Find that child!

Tammie L. Failmezger

A Friend for All Seasons

*F*riendship with oneself is all-important because
without it one cannot be friends with anyone
else in the world.

Eleanor Roosevelt

"David, are you frightened of big dogs?" asked Sue, a volunteer coordinator for elderly services in my hometown.

"No, Sue, I love dogs. How about you?" I asked.

"Well, actually they frighten me to death," she replied.
"But one of my clients needs someone to walk her dog.
She'd probably enjoy a short visit with you, too. Her name
is Alice," she hesitated and then added, ". . . and her dog's
name is Thor. Could you help us out?"

"Sure. When do you need me?"

"How's tomorrow morning at 8:30?"

"See you then," I replied enthusiastically.

As we knocked on Alice's door, a ferocious roar greeted
us followed by a frightening crash against the door panel.
"That's Thor," Sue exclaimed as she nervously retrieved a
dog biscuit from her coat.

A small, frail woman slowly opened the door and stared at us with an unfocused gaze. A huge German shepherd had wedged himself between the woman and us.

"Sit, Thor, sit!" Alice commanded in a quiet but stern voice.

Sue was ready to retreat, but I decided to bite the bullet. "Nice boy . . . nice Thor," I said, reaching out to pet his long, majestic head—he was beautiful.

Thor sniffed me a bit and, as I had hoped, backed off. We followed Alice into the apartment, Sue still gripping the biscuit as if to ward off evil dog spirits. Alice explained, "I'm not seeing too well today." Later I came to realize this was her way of acknowledging her deteriorating vision.

Sue and I had previously agreed that if things went well, she would leave and I would stay on for a bit, perhaps taking Thor for a short walk.

After a relieved Sue made her exit, Alice said, "The trouble with that young woman is that she doesn't understand dogs!" I guess she thought I did.

From that moment, the three of us—Alice, Thor and I—became friends. I walked Thor that day and many mornings thereafter. I generally visited with Alice twice a week, and she always served tea. She reminded me of my grandmother—frail but full of life. I was always nervous when Alice insisted on getting up in the middle of a story to totter off and retrieve an interesting memento. Thor would follow closely at her heels.

At twelve, Thor was also showing his age, most noticeably in his hip joints. Medicine wasn't helping, but once launched on his morning walk, he became young again.

I loved it when Thor rolled around like a puppy. One November morning after the first snowfall of the season, I watched him frolic and snort. I was reminded of Gertrude Stein's sage observation: "Inside we are always the same age." No one had told Thor he was an old fellow.

Alice and Thor were a close pair. Once I heard Alice talking to Thor in words I didn't understand. She stopped as soon as she realized I was close by. I guess she had a secret language she used with him. I respected their bond and never asked about it.

I walked Thor in all seasons—on rainy summer days, on brisk leaf-crackling autumn mornings and on frigid winter afternoons—even when his ever-worsening hip dysplasia made climbing up and down the porch steps a painful ordeal.

One day in February, Thor suddenly whimpered and stumbled as I was walking him. He slowly slumped over on the snow-covered path, moaning in pain. I managed to carry him home with the assistance of a neighbor. We carefully settled him on a rug at Alice's feet. I called the vet who promised to make a special trip over later in the day.

"David, you can leave now, I'm fine," a concerned Alice assured me as she leaned over her beloved Thor.

"I can stay with you until the doctor comes, Alice. "

"I'm sure you have other things to do, dear. Besides, I'd rather be alone with Thor. Please . . . do go."

Reluctantly, I put on my coat and leaned down to say good-bye to Thor. He usually walked me to the door, but that morning he only raised his head and slowly licked my hand. I reached over, patted Alice's arm and left.

When I made the dreaded telephone call to Alice later that day, she told me that Thor was gone. "They took him away on a stretcher," she said sadly, her voice quivering. Then she added, "He never made a sound. He was in such pain, and I wouldn't want him to suffer. He knew it, too."

I told Alice I would be over the next day. "Only if it fits your schedule, dear. There's no Thor to walk anymore," she replied.

As I entered the big hallway outside Alice's apartment the following morning, I was acutely aware of the silence—the absence of the familiar barking and frantic banging against the door.

"I didn't expect you today, David," Alice said. "I don't imagine you'll be coming around anymore. Sue already called me." I had telephoned the agency that morning to tell Sue about Thor's death. Alice must have thought I was giving my notice as a volunteer.

"Of course I'll be coming . . . if you'll let me. You're important to me, too."

Suddenly, Alice turned her face from me and began to weep. I let her have what my grandmother used to call "a good cry," and then I went over and knelt beside her. Alice dried her eyes, managed a smile, and said, "Well, I guess Thor made sure I'd be well taken care of."

"Yes, Thor knew how important we all are to one other," I replied.

Alice reached out her right hand, placing it squarely on my left shoulder. "Let's have a nice cup of tea," she said.

David Garnes

"That's my beeper. I volunteer down at
the fire department."

My Brother, My Hero

In 1975, at the age of twenty-eight, my older brother John drove off a cliff during a monsoon rainstorm. The accident occurred in Borneo, where he was working. He was in a coma for almost three months before regaining consciousness and sufficient strength to be flown back to his hometown.

Three years later, John moved to Los Angeles to live with my husband and me on a one-year trial basis. Although John was only one year older than I was, I always looked up to him as being my older and wiser *big* brother.

Our trial year was an emotional roller-coaster ride. John took two steps forward and one back. He had daily temper tantrums, which frequently included putting his head through a wall, ripping his clothes or throwing something. I had to juggle my time between our graphic-design business and taking him to physical therapy, speech therapy, the podiatrist and the ophthalmologist.

This put a tremendous strain on my marriage, not to mention our business. As difficult as it was, I wasn't about to relinquish John to some unknown institution. I knew in my heart that would be the end of his spirit, his competitive nature and his essence.

We were fortunate to find a pilot program for the disabled at our local community college. This would give John a place to go on a daily basis, and we prayed it would also help him relearn some basic work skills.

What we thought would take one year turned into several. We watched and assisted John as he relearned everything necessary to become whole again and eventually independent. That meant having his own place to live, and something to do during the day.

Since John had a background in physical education prior to his accident, he was given the opportunity to assist people who were more severely disabled, as part of a pilot program. This was the first time since his accident that he had the opportunity to give to others.

This was a major step forward for John. Helping someone else made him feel his life had purpose. After six years, John completed the pilot program at the City College. It was time for him to move into his own place.

John's first volunteer job was at a hospital. There, he learned how to sort the mail, distribute it to the different floors and get outgoing mail ready for postal pickup. Several years later, when the hospital closed, John needed to find another position.

His next volunteer job gave him the opportunity to work in a print shop. Once again, the people with whom he worked, especially his boss, were like angels, compassionate and patient with his mood swings and occasional bursts of temper and depression. When he got depressed, they gave him the time away from work he needed to regain his balance. When he finally settled into his job, John marched proudly off to work, never expecting compensation.

It had been more than twenty-three years since his accident. Thanks to his volunteer positions, some very special people and John's natural tenacity, his life was full once again. His work gave him a reason to get up in the morning. He had a place to go every day where he knew his contributions were making a difference.

On numerous occasions, John was given the Volunteer of the Year award. The doctors who had tested him several years earlier were stunned at how vastly his skills had improved when he was reevaluated. They acknowledged that no one really understands how the mind heals or what role love and support play in one's recovery. When he left the Los Angeles area to move back to his hometown, there was a special ceremony acknowledging him for his years of service.

After his return to Santa Barbara, John found another volunteer job, working at the American Red Cross. And, the best news of all, twenty-five years after his accident, John moved one more step toward total independence when he got his driver's license in October 2000.

Volunteering has played a major role in his ongoing recovery. His struggles have been monumental, and yet he has shown that life can still be about love, perseverance and giving to others, even while experiencing personal pain.

Having a place to go every day, where you can make a contribution and be with people who really care, is what continues to give his life value. John was, still is and always will be, my hero.

Nansie Chapman

[EDITORS' NOTE: *For information on the American Red Cross, contact your local Red Cross chapter or visit their Web site:* www.redcross.org.]

Without a Word

Words are sacred. They deserve respect. If you get the right ones, in the right order, you can nudge the world a little.

Tom Stoppard

As a young girl with a disability, I know firsthand that growing up can be very challenging. Like many teenagers, my perception of the future was a bleak one. I had envisioned myself in "sheltered workshop" situations, living a life of isolation. However, I found my refuge in volunteering, as it offered me a safe place to discover my wings.

In my early days of volunteering, my path crossed with a little eight-year-old girl named Sara. She was full of life and had a great love for nature and animals. Sara lived on a farm and spent endless hours with her rabbits and horses. One bright summer day, something spooked one of the horses. It bolted out of control. In the mayhem, Sara was crushed against a fence post causing extensive injuries.

As a result Sara lapsed into what is called a "locked-in" coma. In this state, people are aware of their surroundings.

They can recognize voices. They can hear the world but cannot reach out to it.

I was asked to be a member of the volunteer team working with Sara. The team would work with Sara to help her use her senses as a means of reaching her. Each visit I would chat with Sara and her mother, who rarely left her side. With scented markers and textured toys we worked with her each day. I would talk about the aromas she smelled and the tactile objects we put in her hands. Although her eyes remained closed all the time, Sara gradually learned to communicate "yes" or "no" through the movement of her eyelids. These small steps in communicating with Sara were greatly celebrated.

Using her love for animals, we introduced Sara to the Pet Therapy Program at the hospital. One day as Sara reclined in her wheelchair, I placed a rabbit on her lap. I described the rabbit to her, talking about the softness of his fur and the twitching of his nose. Suddenly, Sara began stroking the rabbit and feeling his fur. Oh, how excited everyone was. We danced with joy that day.

Many times at our team meetings, we would speculate about whether we thought we were getting through to Sara. We wondered if she was really hearing us. It was like seeing someone you loved and had known all your life trapped behind a wall of dark glass. You know they are in there, but you aren't sure they realize you are out here and near them. At times, this would not only break my heart but also touch my soul.

As summer drew to an end, I was getting ready for a vacation to Australia—a trip that was planned long before I met Sara. As is true for most people, I find good-byes very difficult. Sara had woven her way into the very fabric of my world.

Even though she would be in good hands, leaving was the hardest thing I had to do. As a good-bye gift, I bought a koala bear to give to Sara, so she could hold onto and love it while I was gone. I kissed her cheek, told her I would miss her and started for the door.

My emotions began to get the best of me. I stopped with my hand on the doorknob and looked at the very dear mother and daughter who had come to mean so much to me. I glanced again at Sara, and I could see there were tears running down her face—real tears and real feelings. Suddenly, it hit me: We can deeply touch each other's lives without ever sharing a word. The sound of a voice, the gentle touch of a hand, a soft furry koala bear and a kiss on the cheek carries a loving message that can help heal the wounds of life.

Nancy Blain

6

DEFINING MOMENTS

*When we quit thinking primarily about
ourselves and our own self-preservation,
we undergo a truly heroic transformation
of consciousness.*

Joseph Campbell

Reprinted by permission of Christian Snyder.

Forgive Me, Davey

It is very easy to forgive others their mistakes; it takes more grit and gumption to forgive them for having witnessed your own.

Jessamyn West

My curiosity grew to mammoth proportions as I stood at Dr. Rayburn Matthews'* doorstep and rang the bell.

I was a member of the volunteer team for the Public Health Awareness Campaign, to create general awareness among the townspeople. We had invited Dr. Matthews for a guest lecture on how people could work toward taking care of their personal well-being, despite being busy with their family, homes and careers. The doctor had accepted our request, and here I was, at his doorstep, waiting to give him a formal invitation.

The man was regarded as some sort of a local legend, since he moved into town fifteen years ago. He was in his sixties and had retired after a distinguished career as a general physician. In the early years, he had a busy practice with a huge patient list. Despite that, he donated several

_____
Names have been changed.

hours a week at the local hospital. Twice a week he also
ran a clinic in the not-so-affluent part of town. All through
the years, despite a hectic schedule, he managed to spend
time with children at a local orphanage—a sort of unoffi-
cial counseling session. Not many people knew that he
also had a degree in applied psychology.

Now that age had caught up with him, he didn't practice
medicine anymore, but he still spent a lot of time in other
support activities. He now counseled in two orphanages,
working with the welfare department to help children
under state care. He also visited the local hospital and spent
time with patients, especially the elderly ones who had no
one to visit them. His wife had been active in her own way.
Even now, she spent three days a week at a maternity center volunteering to care for premature babies. The couple
had donated a lot of money over the years, but it was their
commitment in terms of time and tireless effort that stood
as a shining example of community help.

I stepped into their home and enjoyed my meeting
with Dr. and Mrs. Matthews. After my formal agenda was
over, they graciously invited me to have tea. Our conversation led us through many areas of common interest.
Then I asked him something that I'd wanted to know for
a long time.

"Doctor," I said, "when did you get started in community support? I mean, what inspired or drove you?"

Everyone, no matter how good, has his or her spot of
vanity, and I suspected that this would be his. I waited for
a lofty statement about an inspiration to do a greater good
beyond medicine or the driving need to help the less fortunate—but he said nothing of the sort.

Instead, before my eyes, the man seemed to shrivel
within himself. His eyes turned misty and sorrowful with
a faraway look in them.

I flushed, acutely aware of having intruded in something

very personal. I tried to salvage the situation as best as I could. "I'm sorry . . . I didn't mean . . . it's not necessary," I concluded rather inadequately.

But he seemed not to have heard me. He turned toward his wife, and they shared a long look of understanding that only comes with a lifetime of togetherness. I don't know what he asked, but Sheila Matthews gave him an imperceptible nod and a smile.

He turned toward me. "Over the years, I've been asked a lot of things," he said after a brief silence, "but you're the first one to ask me this." He sat up straighter in his chair. "Let me tell you a story, young lady."

"It happened seventeen years ago. There was this young man. That day he was . . ."

The story went . . .

He was driving home with his wife after a good game of golf. The weather was pleasant, a breezy evening with the possibility of rain later. The radio was playing John Denver hits, and he felt a pleasant sense of well-being.

He knew he was a good doctor—the practice was thriving. It had grown over the years, and he had a large number of patients. He had already paid off the mortgage of their beautiful house in a quiet neighborhood. He drove a late-model BMW, and they planned to buy a small boat later that year. Materially they were not wanting, and their bankbook was as healthy as ever.

He looked at his wife sitting next to him. She was a gentle, supportive woman who had always encouraged him over the years, and together they had Davey. The doctor's heart warmed when he thought of Davey—how he loved the boy. Over the years, he had felt an occasional pang when they didn't have any more children, but they'd been blessed with this one. He had been a sweet, loving child and had now grown into a young man whom any parent could be proud of.

Yes, life was good to him.

A fleeting imp of doubt nagged him that all his pursuits in life had been more material than humane, but he banished it. There were plenty of people for that. Surely, the world wouldn't suffer if he didn't do a good deed.

He turned onto Carter Street on the last leg home. Within a few minutes, he realized that something was wrong. The street was too crowded for a Saturday evening—the traffic wasn't moving at all and there seemed to be some sort of a commotion up ahead. From years of experience, he guessed what the problem was, when an obliging pedestrian confirmed it for them.

"An accident. Happened a few minutes ago. Nasty crash."

He cursed silently. *The street would be blocked for a long time.* As he prepared to get them out of the traffic mess, his wife looked at him in surprise. "Don't you want to see what happened? Someone may be injured."

"Forget it," he muttered. "The police and the paramedics will be here soon. They will do what's needed."

"But . . . "

"If I get involved, it will take me ages to get away," he told her decisively. "Too much of a hassle. Let's just go home. Davey should be back by now. It's not every day that your child has an eighteenth birthday. Besides it may rain any minute."

She fell silent as he reversed slightly and maneuvered the car into a side street.

"Thank goodness, we got out of that mess," he said as they pulled into the driveway of their home.

Davey was not back yet, so he sank into an easy chair in the living room, looking forward to a comfortable evening, when their son came home. The ringing phone was not a pleasant intrusion, but he answered it anyway.

"Dr. Matthews speaking," he said into the phone.

"Doctor, it's me, Malcolm."

"Hi, Malcolm," he told the Detective Sergeant of Police. "What's up?"

"Can you get to the North Valley General Hospital immediately?"

He groaned. Obviously, this wasn't meant to be his day. Aloud, he only said, "Sure thing. Is there any medical emergency?"

Malcolm hesitated. "I'm afraid it's worse than that." He added gently, "It's your son."

"My son?"

"Yes, Doctor. David had an accident on Carter Street."

"Carter Street?" Dr. Matthews thought of the accident scene he had left a little while ago, and his blood ran cold.

"Is Davey all right?" his voice was trembling.

Malcolm was silent. Finally, he said, "When they brought him in, he was bleeding profusely." There was another uncomfortable pause. "I'm sorry, but he . . . died a few minutes ago."

Rayburn Matthews stood frozen, feeling his entire world shatter around him, when Malcolm said, "I'm really sorry, Doc, but there was nothing anyone could have done."

Pooja Krishna

One Whale of a Volunteer

My oldest son Perry was different from other kids. He was bigger and got that way early. He was six feet, four inches tall and 230 pounds by the time he was fifteen.

His brother Mike, two years younger, was considered tall at six feet but almost one hundred pounds lighter. Mike was an easygoing kid, but Perry was troubled and in trouble for most of his teen years.

Perry had what you might call an "attitude." It eventually got him expelled from high school—permanently. However, he had this longing within him to do good and slowly realized that this was a part of his being.

When we were on a family trip, he always wanted us to pull over when someone needed help on the side of the road. He wanted to rush to someone's aid when there was an accident. He was attracted to the Wharton, Texas Volunteer Fire Department, and a better lot of people we could not have asked for.

As parents, we were concerned when Perry didn't come home one night. We imagined all sorts of scenarios. When the phone rang about two in the morning, I just knew it was bad news, that our son was involved in some tragedy.

Instead it was a volunteer firefighter who knew me. He identified himself and said, "Doc, I know you're worried about your son, but I wanted you to know where he is and that he is okay. We're all working with him. He's staying here at the fire station and learning the ropes as a volunteer. He has a place to sleep and plenty to eat. He's a good kid at heart." I slept well that night knowing that my son was in good hands.

In the days that followed, Perry gradually found something meaningful to do with his muscle and brawn. As a volunteer, he answered emergency calls, dragged hoses and freed trapped victims in automobile wrecks.

Perry even got a job and earned the equivalent of a high school diploma by studying for and taking the GED exam. But it was his role as a volunteer that breathed life into his soul. He took the next step and studied for the EMT (Emergency Medical Technician) designation. More than once, he was credited with saving a life through EMT techniques.

Once at a local football game for the very school that had expelled him (with good reason, I might add), a man in the stands had a heart attack and appeared to be dead. Perry, dressed in his usual cowboy hat and boots, rushed into the stands to give the necessary compressions and mouth-to-mouth resuscitation that brought the man back from the depths of darkness. Every time I saw that man thereafter, he would always point at me and say, "Your son saved my life. He's one whale of a volunteer."

One day Perry startled all of us when he announced that he had just volunteered again—for the Marine Corps. Frankly, given his inability to take orders in the past, I feared that this might result in the first court martial in the Blakely family history.

The Marine Corps turned him down because he was twenty pounds overweight. Perry calmly said, "I'll lose twenty pounds and be back in a couple of months."

He did exactly that. In boot camp at San Diego, he quickly became a leader and graduated number two in his platoon. I asked how he felt about losing the top spot. He smiled and said, "I gave him a run for his money. We battled for that position every week. About half the time I was number one and half the time he was, but in the end he beat me fair and square. He deserves the honor."

Perry was then 190 pounds and stood tall with an inner peace that I had never seen before. I asked, "What did the Marine Corps do for you to bring about this transformation?"

He replied with startling quickness, "They taught me how to make a decision. And once it's made, to never look back."

I secretly wished I had volunteered for the Marines instead of getting drafted by the Army. I still have splinters under my fingernails where they dragged me off the back porch.

After boot camp, Perry was sent to the Naval Air Station, Whidbey Island, Washington, where he continued volunteering as a firefighter and EMT.

His most glorious moment in our eyes was when he was honored as the most outstanding person of the year among the thirty thousand sailors and marines.

One fine spring day in April, Perry and several other sailors and marines, all of them EMTs, were practicing rappelling off a sheer-faced cliff on the beach at Deception Pass. They were all off-duty, but as volunteers they were spending their own time to practice a skill sometimes needed to rescue people from burning buildings. It was a lot of fun and good practice as well. They had been jumping all day, using two ropes in the rappelling rings—the prescribed and safest method, I understand.

Later in the day they decided to switch to single ropes so they could jump two at a time. But first, the new system had to be tested. One of the others was supposed to have his turn, but Perry volunteered to check out the new system since he had the most experience. This is logging country, and a large log had washed up under the cliff and had been left high and dry by the tide—too large to move. It was in the jump area, but the guys merely joked about the hazard.

Something happened. Nobody is sure just what, but about twenty feet from the ground, the system failed and Perry, still in the harness, fell. The back of his head struck the log. He never cried out or moved. On the beach and in the ambulance, his buddies, the best EMTs one could ask for, worked frantically over him. His heart stopped twice, and twice they revived him.

He was airlifted to Seattle but to no avail. Perry was twenty-two years old and destined never to become older. But what a life he lived, and what a spirit he left behind. In our eyes, he was the ultimate volunteer.

Perry's brother, Mike, and I perform a musical-comedy program with fiddle and guitar, the Swing Riders Show. Mike wears his brother's cowboy hat on those occasions when we perform—and only then—to honor his memory. Only a few people know this, but it's symbolically important and comforting to us.

And back where his real development started, at the Wharton Texas Volunteer Fire Department, there is a solitary plaque dedicated to his memory. On it is a photo of Perry wearing his favorite cowboy hat. Fittingly, under the photo are names of other volunteers who have served and passed on. The inscription is appropriate for all volunteers. It reads: "Taking the first step in good thought, the second in good word and the third in good deed, I enter paradise."

Doc Blakely

Residuals from Roger

You can't do anything about the length of your life, but you can do something about its width and depth.

Evan Esar

It was a beautiful Southern California day in the summer of 1988. It was the kind of day that makes you feel everything's right with the world.

My oldest son, Wally, who has dyslexia and visual difficulties, called to say he'd enrolled at a local university. Fourteen-year-old David, who has learning disabilities, was on a plane to Canada where his chorus was on tour. And my daughter Angela, twenty, had just arrived in Iceland with a teenage missionary group that planned to build a Bible school. With her severe visual impairment, she felt honored to be on the team.

For the next month, the only child at home would be eighteen-year-old Roger. His fine voice and upbeat attitude overshadowed his learning and attention disorders. He was elated at being accepted in his high school's elite choir and at landing a summer job.

As a single parent for eleven years, I couldn't ask for more loving children. Money was tight, but thankfully I taught Spanish that summer and had signed my teaching contract for the fall. Yes, all was right with the world!

... Up until eleven o'clock that warm Saturday night.

Roger should have been home from work hours before. When the phone rang, I prayed it would be him.

"Your son is in a coma, critically injured," the administrator from a hospital trauma center crisply informed me. "Come quickly."

Roger had been riding on the back of a friend's motorcycle when it collided with a van. Doctors said if he lived, which wasn't likely, he probably wouldn't regain consciousness.

"One thing is clear," a neurologist stated. "He will never be a candidate for rehabilitation."

But Roger triumphed over all their predictions when, fourteen months later, he was able to come home. With some support, he walked right through the front door. And while he was thrilled to return to his high school, he had to be placed in a different area: a special-education program.

Ironically, although he had trouble seeing, speaking, walking and using his right hand, he became extraordinarily concerned about other people. With all his challenges, everyone found his extrasensory caring absolutely amazing.

His memory and thinking skills were poor, and violent seizures sometimes caused even more cognitive loss. Nevertheless he'd still remember to buy a birthday card for an elderly neighbor or to bring extra food for a school friend who frequently forgot his lunch. Teachers greatly appreciated Roger's voluntary help with students who had more severe disabilities than his own.

One day, a newspaper reporter who was writing about Roger's miraculous milestones asked him, "What kind of job do you want to strive for?"

Although Roger often stuttered and took inordinate time to cobble together a sentence, this time he spoke clearly and succinctly.

"All I want is to somehow really and truly help mankind," he smoothly answered. "That's what I want to accomplish."

But Roger's seizures were getting more severe, requiring frequent ambulance rides to emergency rooms. Now, four years after his accident, he needed to have someone with him at all times. One day, I had to fly out of town for a convention. I felt secure leaving Roger with Angela, David and a paid caregiver in the house.

But when I arrived at the hotel and the clerk told me I had an urgent call from home, my hands trembled dialing the number. The voice that answered was my oldest, Wally.

"Mom, Roger had a seizure . . . and he aspirated . . . fluid got in his lungs . . . and . . . he . . . he's gone . . . he died."

The grief was overwhelming; I prayed for guidance and understanding.

A few months later, in my sleep one night, God's message ignited every cell in my brain and body. I jumped from the bed, ran to the kitchen, picked up a notepad and began writing. The noise awakened my daughter.

"Mom! Are you okay? It's three in the morning," Angela shouted.

"I know what I must do," I answered quickly. "Remember Roger's ambition, his dream of doing something that will 'help mankind'?" Angela nodded.

"Roger didn't know that he had already begun," I continued. "I've received dozens of letters and phone calls from people telling me how he made a difference in their lives. One of his friends had a lonely, grumpy grandpa who hardly ever talked. Apparently, Roger spent many hours with Gramps, listening to his war stories and laughing at his anecdotes. He made the grandfather feel important and cheerful. The family was very grateful.

"And the school-bus driver told me how Roger volunteered to help him every day, assisting students in wheelchairs on and off the bus, even though Roger himself limped and had poor vision."

More of Roger's acts of spontaneous kindness and assistance had been related by teachers and parents of his friends with disabilities. After reading some of them to Angela, I said, "What better way is there to honor Roger than to continue his work, carrying out his goal, his dream?"

No, I couldn't help "mankind," but certainly I could reach thousands of people.

During twenty-six years dealing with my children's disabilities, I knew firsthand the frustrations of getting accessible transportation, housing and hotel rooms . . . the red tape involved in getting healthcare and insurance . . . the exasperating discussions to get appropriate educational services.

And I understood the challenge shared by disabled people everywhere: being treated with dignity and equality. I'd met and conquered many of these obstacles on behalf of my own children with disabilities—now, it was time to help others.

"Angela," I said finally, "I'm going to start a newspaper column with information and inspiration that will help people with disabilities to achieve their goals, become more independent and achieve a higher quality of life.

"And I'll volunteer to help people personally, in the same way that I've helped you children; our experiences will serve to help others with similar situations."

Angela nodded. "You're going to dedicate your life to this, aren't you?" she asked, knowing the answer.

"Yes," I answered. "It will take time, research, patience and all my energy to make it work. But I guess I'm committed to this challenge."

A few months later, I started a weekly column, "Challenger," in Southern California's *Orange County Register*. Upbeat and positive, it covers disability-related topics about social, educational, healthcare and legal issues, sports, recreation, products, events, resources, caregiving and volunteer opportunities that benefit people with disabilities.

Readers call and e-mail requests for help; often, it is overwhelming. Kyle is in jail and fears he has schizophrenia; he wants to be evaluated. Will I help find a doctor? Mike is seeking a support group for single fathers of special-needs kids. Can I recommend one or help him start one? Kim's apartment manager won't put in another disabled parking space. Will I talk to him? Mrs. Schmidt wonders if there's a religious education class for her daughter with Down's syndrome.

With each volunteer mission, I thank God for the opportunity to continue my son's dream to "help mankind." Surely, Roger is smiling.

Diane Rodecker

An Armful of Love

*Those who bring sunshine to the lives of others
cannot keep it from themselves.*

Sir James Barrie

Sally was devastated when she learned that she and
Josh would never have children.

Since Josh had a well-paying job, Sally didn't have to
work, but the days dragged on. The fun of tennis, swimming lessons and afternoon movies wore thin after a
while. She drifted away from her friends; they were all
having babies and caught up in motherhood.

Finally, Sally decided to spend her time helping others.
Just as long as she didn't have to be near babies. It was too
painful a reminder.

In her desire to be very busy, Sally chose to volunteer in
a local hospital. She tried working all the different floors,
but finally asked to be assigned to the emergency room. It
was always busy: Time passed quickly, and Sally believed
that was where she was needed most.

When she finally got up the nerve to tell Josh, he was furi-
ous. "You'll expose yourself to all sorts of danger," he said.

"But I want to be occupied with something other than playing all day," she said.

"So volunteer for a reading program or making meals or something. Something safe," he added.

"I don't want to be just *safe*. I want to be interesting and useful, too."

He finally gave in. But when Sally came home each night, morose and tired, he tried again. "Do something else," he pleaded.

But she refused to give up.

One day, as Sally was scurrying down the hall to tell one of the doctors, who hadn't answered his page, that his wife was on the phone, the ambulance pulled up. This in itself was nothing new. However, this time one of the paramedics wheeled around frantically, his eyes searching the crowded noisy room. He spotted Sally and thrust a tiny bundle into her arms. "Hold her and don't move," he said as he ran after the gurney his partner was maneuvering into a waiting cubicle.

Sally stared down at the tiny infant in her arms. Just then the doctor, whose wife was on the phone, walked past. Sally told him of the call and explained how she came to be holding the child.

"I'm sure the paramedics checked her out or they wouldn't have handed her to you, but let's just make certain," he said. He then took her from Sally who followed him into an empty room where he examined the little girl. "She's fine," he said with a smile and handed her back.

Sally followed him from the room, but before she could protest, the paramedic, who had given the child to her, walked over. "I don't work here as a nurse, I'm just a volunteer," she said.

"I know, I've seen you here before. Please take care of the baby until it frees up a bit in here and someone can take over. They're aware you have the infant."

"But . . . ," she said. With a wave of his hand, he turned and was gone.

The baby started to cry. Rocking her gently until she fell asleep, Sally realized how wonderful it felt to have a baby fall asleep in your arms. This was one of the things she was missing by shutting herself off from her friends' and relatives' children.

A few minutes later, one of the nurses came and took the child. "Her mom and dad were in a car accident. They'll be fine. Thanks for taking such good care of her," she said.

But it was Sally who was thankful. This tiny baby opened Sally's eyes like nothing else had. For the first time in ages, she went home to Josh happy and full of plans.

She made his day when she told him she'd discovered a new place to help out.

"Good, you've left the hospital," he said.

"Nope," Sally answered with a smile. "I just found a different area to volunteer. They need someone to hold and love the abandoned babies. I start tomorrow."

Josh smiled.

Elaine L. Galit

Conversation with a Wise Guy

The real art of conversation is not only to say the right thing at the right place, but to leave unsaid the wrong thing at the tempting moment.

Dorothy Nevill

As a sixty-eight-year-old, bored retiree, I was dissatisfied with just about everything. This wasn't what I envisioned. Commercials touting the "golden years" made me laugh. I had plenty of time, but my income was about a quarter of what I earned at the top of my profession.

So when my neighbors heard I was going to be a Foster Grandparent in an old inner-city elementary school, many felt I was taking on too much. They asked, "Why would anyone want to tie themselves down to that kind of schedule and responsibility?"

A spokesperson for the Foster Grandparent Program came to our senior citizen meeting to give a presentation. The speaker reminded us that the kids we would be working with had learning and behavioral problems resulting from a chaotic childhood. Most were poor minority students who came from single-parent homes or had no parent at all. The free lunch program provided them with, in all probability, the only nutritious meal of the day.

I envisioned myself in the role of kindly grandma, guiding small children through the intricacies of multiplication tables, reading, writing and everyday skills they would need to develop into "productive" citizens. I had a feeling my days of boredom were over and so began my volunteer career.

What a perfect day, I thought, as I walked briskly to the portable classroom in the old elementary school. I was eager, as always, to see "my kids." They made such a difference in my life. Although it was exhausting, I felt good at the end of a long, hard day. For the first time in years, I was sleeping soundly, and without idle time to sit around and snack all day, I was slimming down.

After greeting the kids, I went to my table at the back of the room and waited for the teacher to send me a student who was struggling with reading, spelling or math. Suddenly, the classroom door opened with a thundering crash. I watched in dismay as an angry young man was escorted to my table. I thought to myself, *Why do I always get the tough ones?*

The teacher handed the newcomer a worksheet and pencil, both of which he sent flying across the room. With jaw firmly set, the teacher placed the items on his desk again and asked me, "Would you work with him?"

Pulling my chair up to his desk, I greeted him calmly, "Good morning, may I help you with your math?"

"I ain't doin' nothin'!" he growled, throwing the paper to the floor. He crossed his arms in protest and stuck his chin out.

"Well," I said, retrieving the worksheet, "if this paper gets any dirtier, we won't be able to see the problems. Let's see now."

"I said, I ain't doin' nothin'!" he repeated vehemently with more volume. Only this time the paper and the pencil remained on the desk.

Pinning the paper down with my elbow, I picked up the pencil and began to look over the problems. "Looks like I'm going to need a little help."

"Why do I have to do this stuff?"

"When you get older, and you have to make choices about what you want to do with your life, the more information you have, the easier it will be to choose the path you want to follow."

He mumbled, "I ain't gonna get older," and slumped down under his desk.

I maintained a calm, even demeanor and smiled as he scowled at me and promptly looked away.

"Why does there have to be police?" he shouted in a sudden outburst. "Why can't they mind their own business?"

"When we stop hurting one another and ourselves, we won't need the police," I responded, curious about his question.

"These police came and stopped me from shooting myself. I had the gun pointed at my chest and was going to kill myself. They took my gun away and then they took me away." He stared at me, as if to see whether or not I was shocked.

"You must have been very sad if you wanted to kill yourself," I replied, choosing my words carefully.

He was clearly in pain. I didn't ask questions. *Should I tell his teacher about the incident?* I wondered. I placed my hand on his and was saddened when he tried to reject my touch. Then, as I continued to maintain contact, the bravado seemed to leave him like air from a balloon.

"You know what?" he said. "People should mind their own business. They say they love children, and they only want to help. Why can't they just stay home and love their own children instead of messin' around with other people's children?"

"Maybe we're not all fortunate enough to have our own children," I said softly, praying that I didn't say the wrong thing.

"What you talkin' about? You're a grandma. You got children, " he argued.

"Well," I answered, "I'm not a real grandma. I'm a foster grandma. See, it says so right here on my badge." As he looked closely at the badge I wore so proudly, I continued, "I've never had any children, so I know what it feels like to be sad."

He laughed scornfully, "You're sad because you have no kids?"

"I'm not as sad as I used to be," I replied.

"Are you happy? I mean, about not having kids?"

I thought for a moment before answering. "I'm not happy about having no kids, but, yes, I am happy."

"When you were sad, did you want to die?"

Careful now, I said to myself. *How can I expect him to talk about his pain if I couldn't be honest with mine?* I prayed for the wisdom to say the right words, without being maudlin, or worse, sounding like a phony. "Yes, there were times when I was that sad."

"Did you ever try to kill yourself?" he probed.

"Yes!"

"Why didn't you?"

I knew I had to continue. *Please God, help me!* I prayed. "Well, a little voice inside my head said not to do it."

"What did the voice say?"

"It said I was being saved for something very *special*."

"You were?" he asked in amazement. "Did you ever find out what that *special* thing was?"

Tears filled his eyes and mine as we continued to hold

hands. I could barely get the words out, "Well now, what do you think?"

Elizabeth T. Verbaas

[EDITORS' NOTE: *For more information on the Corporation for National and Community Service, visit their Web site:* www.seniorcorps.org. *The Foster Grandparent Program can be reached at 800-424-8867.*]

Volunteer 101

It was my last semester in college, and I was interested in some easy classes to breeze through. My roommate, Tom, overheard my dilemma as I tried unsuccessfully to line up "Basketweaving 101" or "The Films of Stephen King" on our state university's Tele-Registration system.

"I got a gig as a teacher's aide for my last semester," Tom bragged, combing his perfect hair in our mirror. "It's an afternoon class, twice a week. You can zip off to happy hour afterward."

I nodded eagerly, hearing only the words "afternoon" and "happy hour," watching as Tom took over my phone registration procedure and punched in the code for the class successfully. Smiling triumphantly, he hung up the phone. *Happy hour, here I come!*

Later that week, Tom offered to walk me to the first class.

"Why?" I asked. We weren't exactly buddies.

"Oh, I dunno," he mused, zipping his backpack. "Just seemed like the roommate thing to do."

"Yeah, right," I grumbled, following him across campus to the Health and Science building. "You just want to make sure I show up."

Minutes later, oozing sweat after a cross-campus hike

and six flights of stairs, I stared at an odd assembly of female protestor types and skinny men milling around our classroom. I finally wondered aloud, "Just what have I gotten myself into?"

Tom smiled. "Didn't I tell you?" he asked. "Why, it's Introduction to HIV."

Naturally, this was not going to be an easy class. It wasn't just the explicit nature of the nightly documentaries we were forced to endure: thin men covered in sores and women tearfully receiving the news that they'd just passed on their condition to their newborn babies. It wasn't even the sensitivity exercises we engaged in frequently, role-playing as homosexuals or IV drug-users and then reversing roles to face our own prejudices head on.

For me the hardest part of Introduction to HIV was the volunteer requirement. As part of our grade, we were required to volunteer at one of the local HIV charities in our spare time.

Somehow, each week, I managed to skip out on my volunteer hours. Before I knew it, we were taking our final exam, and I was selling my four-thousand-page *History of HIV* textbook for beer and pizza money and getting measured for my cap and gown. Easy "A," here I come!

Several days after the exam, my friends and I were anxiously planning our graduation party festivities. Kegs had been ordered, the forty-foot sub was being prepared and designated drivers were being, well, designated.

Then the phone rang. It was Tom. "You never satisfied your volunteer hours," he grumbled, like something out of a bad nightmare. "I can't possibly pass you. If I don't have your volunteer form signed by tomorrow afternoon, you'll fail the class."

"Tom," I stammered, "I'm planning my graduation party. It's tomorrow. How can you fail me?"

"This is important," said Tom as I dropped the forty-foot

sub brochure to the ground. "If you don't volunteer, the class will be wasted. I left the form on your bed. You can go tonight—the requirement is only five hours—and have your stupid party tomorrow after all."

The sun was setting as I consulted an address in my class syllabus and pulled onto a sad side street on the wrong side of town later that night. Idling up the road in my battered Datsun, I saw a welcoming sign: HIV House. Underneath, an asterisk explained that HIV stood for Helping Individuals who are Very special!

I parked, gulped, approached a screened-in patio, and was greeted by a blind man in a bathrobe.

"May I help you," he asked cheerfully.

"Y-y-yes," I stammered. "I'm from the university, ummm, here to volunteer."

The man smiled. "Ah, yes," he nodded. "We've had quite a few of you here today." I was thankful that he couldn't see me blush.

With expert hands, the man led me to a battered couch in a living room straight out of 1972. I sat, and the man, who introduced himself as Ben, asked me what I thought I could contribute.

"Well," I said, eyeing a candy dish full of condoms in the middle of a coffee table loaded with safe-sex pamphlets. "I'm a really good typist, and I can handle my way around a computer fairly well."

"Splendid," said Ben. "We've been looking for someone to update our volunteer files. If you'll just follow me, I'll show you to the office and you can get started. I'd say there's at least five hours of work for you."

I blushed again, realizing that Ben knew exactly how long I would stay, and worse, why. As he showed me a stack of three-by-five cards and an old Apple IIe computer, I realized that there were five days worth of work here, let alone five hours.

He sat in a cozy wicker rocking chair while I typed, seemingly lost in thought. While I found an old file marked "voluntears," obviously written by yet another soon-to-be college grad in a hurry, I fixed the name and began to clean things up.

"Ben," I said after an hour or so. "Is it just you here?"

"Not usually," he explained. "But there's a big rally in the state capital tomorrow, and all of my housemates are attending."

Moments later, the phone rang. Ben answered it, his face growing concerned as he listened.

"Oh dear," he said. "I see. Yes, yes, I understand. No, certainly. Please don't apologize. And thanks again for calling."

Ben sighed and rubbed his temples.

"Is something wrong?" I asked, looking up from my keyboard.

"No, no," he said quietly. "It's just that one of our dear friends has finally given up the struggle, and his partner has no one to help with the funeral."

"I'm sorry," I found myself saying, turning from the computer and facing Ben. "Is there something I can do?"

He seemed surprised by the question. "Oh no," he said, somber yet not hysterical. "It's a relief, after his suffering. It's just that, well, the local churches usually help us out, but their offices are all closed now. And tomorrow . . . I've managed to fend quite well for myself since I lost my vision, but reading the yellow pages is still one feat I haven't quite mastered yet!"

I regarded Ben as he frittered idly with a loose seam on his threadbare robe. I saw the promise of an empty house and an unpleasant and sobering task ahead of him the next day.

"I can call churches for you," I blurted out, almost as if my heart wanted to beat my brain to the punch.

"You don't understand," he said, almost impatiently.

"The church offices are closed tonight. I know your volunteer hours are important to you, but . . ."

"I heard you the first time," I said forcefully. "You'll have to call them tomorrow. That's what I'm offering. To come tomorrow and help you call churches."

Ben sighed, almost as if he didn't want to deliver the bad news: "But that's not all," he confessed. "The churches always want someone to accompany them to the funeral home and handle the necessary details. I'll need a ride there, and a ride back, and there are other details, too."

"I understand," I said, more slowly this time. "I have all the time in the world."

Ben smiled, and pulled a pad from his robe pocket and began jotting notes for his big day tomorrow. I thought of my graduation party and hoped they would have fun. Perhaps, with one less person in attendance, there would be enough of that forty-foot sub to bring back to HIV House.

Rusty Fischer

[EDITORS' NOTE: *For more information on HIV/AIDS, contact Project Inform, 205 13th Street, #2001, San Francisco, CA 94103; 415-558-8669; fax: 415-558-0684; Web site:* www.projinf.org.]

Reprinted by permission of Christian Snyder.

Sap to Seedling

When twelve-year-old Ryan showed up at our office at Tree Musketeers, he said he "just wanted to help out" as a volunteer for our youth environmental and leadership organization.

Then his principal spilled the beans on him.

Big-boned and tall for his age, Ryan was there as a last-resort punishment for chronic misbehavior in school and was ordered to perform ten hours of "volunteer" service. The huge bully chip on Ryan's shoulder told us that this kid's problems were layered deeper than that. He also had floundering grades and feelings of depression and isolation. His terrible social skills with people made him generally unpleasant to be around.

Ten hours isn't enough time to take on an environmental project, so we gave him a list of little tasks to keep him busy. After one hour a day for ten days, Ryan was done. Let's just say we didn't mourn his departure.

Then we got another call from his dad. Ryan was being punished with five more volunteer hours for bad grades. "Okay, okay," we sighed, "send him back." This time, Tree Musketeers was gearing up to launch a community-wide, recycling program here in my hometown of El Segundo, California.

So we assigned Ryan to work with a sixteen-year-old volunteer supervisor and gave the reluctant older boy a bonus: two hours of volunteer time for every hour with Ryan since he was such a handful.

During those five hours, Ryan talked with residents about recycling and worked as a team member with other kids. Together they had a task to accomplish and had to report back on their success.

Much to our surprise, Ryan began to enjoy working at Tree Musketeers. He felt he was contributing something meaningful to the world and promptly announced, "I want to come back."

My mother, Gail (our executive director), and I collectively said, "Sure, Ryan, come back whenever you want," but doubted we'd see him again.

Sure enough, a week later, he was on our doorstep.

Proud of his persistence, we sat down with Ryan and drew up a schedule for him to volunteer at tree plantings and public education. Miraculously, he stuck to it and proved to be an enthusiastic worker. Quickly, he adopted a desk as his own and never wanted to leave the office!

I think that for the first time in his life he felt like a responsible adult. Maybe it was because at Tree Musketeers, an organization founded by eight-year-olds in 1987, we believe that kids have the power to do anything they set their minds to. Ryan became an asset to us and, in return, we gave him autonomy and responsibility.

Ryan dug in. He helped care for our forest of trees, became a tree planting supervisor, did data entry, ran errands, responded to children's letters and even assisted us with fundraising.

When we applied for a grant from the California Department of Conservation, Ryan wrote the "cover letter" in support of it. When we got the grant for sixty-three thousand dollars, Ryan reminded us that it was probably his letter that clinched it. With that major accomplishment under his belt, he had a new conception of his role at Tree Musketeers. Nothing seemed impossible.

As part of our grant, we made plans to organize a Youth Management Team charged with promoting projects to encourage recycling with the residents of El Segundo. Ryan became the Project Manager and in a few months recruited twelve other kids to volunteer by using skills he didn't know he had.

His new position as chair of the Youth Management Team led to his first speaking engagement. Ryan and I rehearsed for three weeks for his speech before the El Segundo City Council announcing Earth Day, 1998.

When he got up to speak, I could feel his nervousness. He faltered at first, but then as he found his confidence a tremendous sense of admiration and pride washed over me. He was so wonderful! When he finished, everyone cheered, and the mayor lauded him as the "future Mayor of El Segundo." Ryan looked at me, his eyes aglow and face beaming.

At the end of the year, he was elected President of Tree Musketeers and even flew to Seattle to present a workshop at a national conference.

Before he tried volunteering, Ryan didn't think he was good at anything, and he acted like it. But then, what began as drudge work for a troublemaker turned into 787 hours of volunteer service that changed not only a community, but also a life.

Tara Church

[EDITORS' NOTE: *For more information on Tree Musketeers, contact 136 Main St., Suite A, El Segundo, CA 90245; 310-322-0263; fax: 310-322-4482; e-mail: Info@TreeMusketeers.org; Web site: www.TreeMusketeers.org.*]

Saving Grace

It was cold out, and I needed new shoes. That's really how it all started. I had moved far away from home to take a new job, but I still didn't have enough vacation days to return for Thanksgiving. I thought if I spent a lot of time outside walking, it might make me feel less lonely and depressed.

There was a rundown shopping center close to where I worked. It had a no-name grocery store, a dollar store, one of those places that cashes checks, a pet shop and a discount shoe store all lined up in a row. I went there after work on the Wednesday before Thanksgiving.

The day was cold and gray, and I was feeling three shades of blue. I had nothing but time to kill before I returned to my lonely one-bedroom apartment. I walked over to the grocery store for a hot cup of coffee to cheer me up.

"How ya doing, brother?" came a booming voice as I approached the rundown store. A huge man in a too-tight coat embraced my hand in a grip that could have easily swallowed me up to my elbows.

"No sir, I'm not selling a single solitary thing," he insisted. "I'm just spreading the good word about 'Harvest House,' a simple little place me and nine other down-on-our-luck gentleman like to call . . . home."

As he let go of my hand, I felt an inexpensive, folded pamphlet remain in my palm. "Would you care to make a donation and help our holiday be a little more thankful?"

I looked up at his warm, green eyes and broad, bright smile. Something about his gentle, though booming, voice kindled something deep inside of me. His weathered coat and face made me appreciate the life I led, and I reached quickly for my wallet.

There was change in my pocket for coffee, and I could always charge the shoes and a couple of pizzas over the long weekend ahead, so I gave him what little money I had. His eyes lit up as I dropped two fives and a single dollar bill into a grimy jar full of dull pennies and bright quarters.

"Now that's what I'm talking 'bout," he shouted as he clapped me on the back and sent me sprawling into the warm grocery store. "Happy Thanksgiving, brother."

As I waited for the listless teenager behind the deli counter to brew up a fresh pot of "gourmet" coffee, I perused the cheaply printed brochure.

There was a picture of Harvest House on the cover. It looked barely big enough to hold the gentle giant outside, let alone nine other weary, downtrodden men.

I read of the morning scripture classes those men enjoyed. Of their daily work program and how they pooled the money they made for such necessities as toothpaste and milk. Their curfew was 8:00 P.M. and lights-out was at ten—every night.

I don't know why that flimsy brochure calmed me. Yet it was strangely comforting. A cup of coffee in the morning and hard, honest work during the day. A roof over your head and a comforting Bible passage to start your day.

By the time I paid for my steaming cup of "Mocha Java," I was so warm inside I didn't even need it.

"Now this is *too* much," shouted the friendly giant as I handed him the steaming Styrofoam cup. "I can't accept this." Sneaking a peek back at him a few steps away, I saw him taking his first tentative sip.

Inside the shoe store, they were already playing Christmas carols. I found a stack of decent walking shoes marked "Clearance" and on sale for $9.99 each. I tried on a pair in my size and looked at the ridiculous blue racing stripes in the ankle-high mirror bolted to the floor.

How comfortable they were. How firm and solid on my tired feet. If they felt like that to me, I thought, how much more comforting and welcome would they be on a pair of feet just starting out a new life?

I quickly said a short prayer that my credit card company had already processed my last payment. Then I tried a quick calculation of what size the mountainous man outside the grocery store might wear.

"Do you have these in a size fourteen? Extra-wide?"

I had just enough quarters in my car ashtray for a drive-thru, Thanksgiving Eve dinner at Taco Bell. As it sat there in the back seat among the towering boxes full of ten brand-new pairs of shoes, the fast-food smells made my empty stomach rumble while I slowly made my way to the address on the Harvest House brochure.

Stopping at a dimly lit gas station for directions, I took a pit stop in the restroom first. Then the old man behind the counter proceeded to spend nearly ten minutes recounting the history of the street I was on and ten minutes more drawing me a map that resembled nothing less than Bluebeard's guide to lost treasure.

By the time I got back out to my car, it was so dark out that I didn't even notice the shattered glass of my rear window until it crunched beneath the soles of my brand new shoes. Whoever had so stealthily broken it had also taken every single pair of shoes I'd bought on my maxed-out credit card. They even stole my spicy soft tacos.

I thought of the men at Harvest House and their ratty, old shoes and wondered what I would tell them when I finally got there. I needn't have worried . . .

"There he is," said the mountainous man when I knocked on their flimsy front door, thankfully remembering me from earlier in the afternoon. "Mr. Big Spender. What a nice surprise and just in time for dinner."

Before I could explain my miserable failure, his oak-solid arm had whisked me into a warm, inviting dining room full of smiling faces and hands clasped in preparation for saying grace.

"We've got a visitor," the big man said, as the room full of men waited for me to speak.

But I couldn't. I grunted something that might have sounded like "shoes," but it was quickly lost in the silent stream of tears that leaked from my lonely, tired eyes. How could I tell them about their shoes and what I thought they might have meant to them? How could I tell them it would be another month before I could save up the money to buy them new ones? How could I tell them that I didn't even have enough money for dinner that night or anyone to share it with even if I had?

In a few moments, ten pairs of gentle arms surrounded me. They patted my back and said reassuring things like, "We know, man . . ." and "We've all been there, son . . ." I sniffled and tried to explain, but they wouldn't hear of it.

Instead they welcomed me to their table as if they'd been expecting me. There was only one catch. "The new guy has to say grace."

"Dear God," I began softly as I tried to cover my new shoes beneath their humble table, "thank you not only for the food we are about to eat, but also for the new friends we are about to share it with. . . ."

Rusty Fischer

The Silent Breakthrough

The less one seems able to say, the more ways one finds of saying it.

Jeffrey Burke

Having just joined the Charleswood Rotaract Club in Winnipeg, Canada, I wasn't sure what I was getting into. We were there early to greet parents who were dropping off their kids for the afternoon.

The young boys arrived slowly at the Big Brothers Big Sisters office for a special one-day outing. Then suddenly they poured in until we had fifty of them crammed into a small room. These were the Little Brothers not yet matched with Big Brothers, of which there is a constant shortage.

Despite our twenty-something energy and enthusiasm, how were the ten of us Rotaractors ever going to manage these kids at the pool? This thought turned over and over in my head as I watched them pile into the room.

Most of the boys were your typical eight-year-olds. Socks rarely matched; jokes about body functions pro-duced hysterical laughter; and they turned into giggling fools once their parents departed.

Amidst all this mayhem, I noticed one little boy cowering in the corner. Noticeably smaller than the rest, he was not comfortable in this group. He wrapped both his arms around his towel roll and silently stared at the floor. He was even more fearful of this crowd than I was so I made my way toward him.

Just then, the announcement was made to form smaller groups. Since I was halfway there, he automatically fell into my group.

Although the pool was only a couple blocks away, we had to cross a busy street. As the signal changed, I was about to step off the curb when I felt a little hand brush my palm then grasp it. It was the forlorn little boy. He was still staring at the ground and clutching his towel with his other arm.

When we hit the other curb, I expected him to release my hand but he didn't. He held it the rest of the way to the pool.

The next couple hours were a blur—kids splashing in the pool, whistles blowing, plastic balls flying in all directions. The high-pitched screeches of fifty, sugar-driven, rambunctious boys free of parents and teachers reverberated off the pool walls.

In the middle of all this joyous confusion, I eventually noticed the small boy again. He was still cowering in a corner. This time, a corner of the pool.

As I moved closer, I could see his eyes occasionally lift up from staring at the glaring water to catch a glimpse of a passing ball. When one of the balls landed near me, I threw it toward him. But I purposely threw it short for fear of konking him in the head as he stared at the water.

It startled him. As he reached for it, another boy dove in from the pool's edge and snatched it away. But it got his attention as he looked for the source of the thrower. He caught my eyes looking back. I gave a little grin, and to my surprise, he returned it with a crooked smile and started wading out of the corner.

I instinctively grabbed another ball and threw it to him. As he caught it and threw it back, his sheepish grin grew into a smile.

Just as I was getting used to the chaos, the whistle blew one last time. In a flash, all the boys ran through the locker with a high sense of urgency: Pizza and sodas waited for them back at the Big Brothers office.

When we organized for our groups to walk back, this time the little boy reached for my hand even before we started walking. He was much different than a few hours earlier.

Although he hadn't spoken yet, he was bright-eyed, smiling and no longer interested in studying his feet. As we approached the corner where he first took my hand, I was beaming with pride at the day's accomplishment. By taking just a few moments to share with this little boy by my side, he opened up and had a great time.

He'll probably cherish this day for months to come, I mused.

A slight tug on the arm broke my cheery visualization. As I looked down at the little boy, I saw he was looking straight into my eyes. He then said the only words I heard from him all day, "Would you be my Big Brother?"

Rod Delisle

[EDITORS' NOTE: *For more information, contact Big Brothers Big Sisters of Canada, 3228 S. Service Rd., Suite 113E, Burlington, Ontario L7N 3H8; 800-263-9133; fax: 905-639-0124; e-mail: BBSCMaster@aol.com; Web site: www.bbsc.ca. For more information on Rotary International, contact One Rotary Center, 1560 Sherman Ave., Evanston, IL 60201; 847-866-3000; fax: 847-328-8554; e-mail: pr@rotaryintl.org; Web site: www.rotary.org.*]

It Only Takes a Few

A group of ten cared about kids,
And had an idea that was very fine.
But one was asked to donate money,
And now there are only nine.

Nine caring people,
Thought helping kids would "be great!"
But one was asked to commit some spare time,
And now there are only eight.

Eight thought that a new youth center,
Would be a special gift from heaven.
But one was asked to join a committee,
And now there are only seven.

Seven concerned about juvenile crime,
Wished it was something that they could fix.
But one was asked to spend time with a teen,
And now there are only six.

Six were thankful for the gifts,
They had acquired in their lives.

But when asked about planned giving,
The six soon became five.

Five were frustrated,
Wishing for just a few more.
But one became tired of people leaving,
And suddenly there are four.

Four people asking themselves,
Will the next one be me?
One asked the question too many times,
Now they are down to three.

With only three remaining,
And so much work to do,
One decides to just give up on kids,
And now there are only two.

But the two that remain are leaders,
And to help kids they will find some more.
They each call up their own best friend,
And suddenly there are four!

Four friends who share a common thought,
Helping kids is great!
They each recruit their own personal banker,
And now their team is eight.

Soon these eight recruit eight more,
And I think you will begin to see,
That the number of people helping kids,
Can start with you and me.

Now you can be like the eight who left,
Or be more like the final two.
But when you make your decision,
Just please remember . . . It only takes a few.

Dave Krause

7

A MATTER OF PERSPECTIVE

We ourselves feel that what we are doing is just a drop in the ocean. But the ocean would be less because of that missing drop.

Mother Teresa

Smashing Potato Chips

*We can easily forgive a child who is afraid of
the dark; the real tragedy of life is when men are
afraid of the light.*

Plato

He looked like a pirate.

With his bandanna tied in a knot behind his little nine-
year-old head, he looked like a pirate, a sad pirate. The first
time little David came to the Hole in the Wall Gang Camp
in Ashford, Connecticut, he was bald and worn out from
chemotherapy treatments. He was also very angry.

Paul Newman's camp counselors were hoping to fill
David's days with fun and laughter. But David stayed
inside himself, wanting to be alone, or in a corner of the
cabin. At this camp for children with life-threatening illnesses, we had seen some pretty tough children worn out
by cancer rally and bounce back despite their illness. But
the destructive forces raging through little David seemed
to be winning no matter what we tried with him. Five
days into the eight-day session saw a quiet, sad little
pirate.

Then something happened on that fifth night. Something at camp that we would call "huge."

It was cabin night. That's the time when campers and counselors spend time together in each individual cabin instead of an all-camp activity. Campers love cabin nights because there's always a bedtime snack. On the cabin table that night were bags of Jays Ripple Potato Chips and cartons of Newman's Own Lemonade.

David slowly walked over to the table, leaving his corner to join the rest of us. He took one of the bags of potato chips and started smashing it with his little fists. As all the other campers looked on in disbelief, I wondered what the cabin counselor would do.

The college-age volunteer counselor positioned a bag of chips on the table in front of himself, and he, too, started smashing it with his fist. The campers went bonkers as everyone ran to the table to get in on the fun of smashing potato chips with their fists.

Somehow everyone knew, everyone sensed, that whatever anger held David captive within, was now being released.

For the last couple days of the session, David was a different kid. He was a little nine-year-old boy again, trying to fill the hours of each remaining day at camp with as much fun as could be possible.

When the session ended, David asked if he could come back again. Since so many children want to come to camp, it's rare that a child can come twice in one summer. Somehow the camp doctor saw the need to make an exception to this rule. So David, the little pirate, showed up a few days later with a smile as wide as a mile on his face.

This time, there wasn't anything he wouldn't try to fit into his day. He sure was having a great time at camp. David asked me if I needed an altar boy when I celebrated Mass at the gazebo in the woods. Sure enough, he was my altar boy. I remembered how intently he listened to me when I talked about death. I said it's only a doorway. You walk through the door and there's the Lord God and behind God a whole line of people waiting to hug you.

After Mass, he said to me, "Hey Fatha, a door, huh?"

A couple more days of fun passed and tonight was the talent show. The tradition is that campers and counselors dress up in costumes, and everyone gets a standing ovation for singing and dancing or simply just acting like fools on stage.

The show had begun: lights, camera, action.

Unfortunately, the only action taking place in our row of seats was little David making his way from counselor to counselor to say an early good-bye to camp. He had become quite ill and had to go to the hospital because of this new crisis.

When this little nine-year-old pirate stood in front of me, he gave me a hug and a big wet kiss on my cheek. I was crying. He was crying. A whole row of counselors was in tears. After the hug and kiss, he put his hands on my shoulders, winked and with a gleam in his eyes said: "See you on the other side of the door, Fatha."

Father Domenic Jose Roscioli

Christmas Presence

It was the night before Christmas, and all through the evening I reminisced, fondly reliving past Christmases spent with my family. As a second-year nursing student, just nineteen, this was to be my first Christmas away from home. Although I knew that someday I'd be working on Christmas, I never expected to feel this lonely.

Secluded in my room, I yearned for the mouth-watering aromas of Mom's freshly baked cookies, hot chocolate and love. The absence of the usual giggling, slamming doors and ringing telephones made the dormitory seem cold and empty. The unappetizing smell of disinfectant replaced my visions of cookies and cocoa.

Standing in front of the mirror, I conversed with my reflection. "You wanted to be a nurse, didn't you? Well, you're almost a nurse. Here's your chance to find out what Christmas spirit really means." Determined to make the best of it, I turned in early.

I'll be home for Christmas. You can count on me. . . . My faithful clock radio announced reveille as I slowly dragged myself out of a toasty-warm bed. I trudged across the snow-filled street and grabbed a quick breakfast in the cafeteria before reporting for duty on the medical-surgical unit.

As I prepared to take vital signs on my first patient, I was startled by a robust voice that came from behind. "Merry Christmas to you. Want anything from the cafeteria? I'm headed that way, Missy."

I took the stethoscope out of my ears and turned around. From the dimly lit room I could see a gigantic, roly-poly elderly gentleman with long, curly hair, all decked out in a bright red, plaid shirt, tucked haphazardly into baggy red trousers. The trousers appeared to be held up by only two, wide, fire-engine-red suspenders that had long-since outlived their elasticity. This Santa Claus facsimile was standing in the doorway waiting patiently for an answer to his query. The only thing missing was a beard.

Looking toward the bright hallway lights from the darkened room, I thought for a moment that I was dreaming. "No thanks," I responded. "I just came on duty. I'll grab something at lunch."

Before disappearing down the hall, he added, "Name's George. Just let me know what I can do for you, Missy."

As I cared for my patients, George was right alongside. I watched him spread holiday cheer as he became a guest to the patients who had no visitors that day. When trays arrived, he knew who needed assistance and who needed to be fed. He read letters and cards to those whose eyes could no longer see the letters on a printed page. George's powerful body and tender hands were always ready to help hold, turn, pull-up or lift a patient. He was a gofer who made countless trips to the supply room for the "needs of the moment."

George also knew when to call for help. While reading a letter to Mr. Jenkins, George noticed that the patient suddenly started to "look funny" and instantly ran to the nurse's station to summon aid. Thanks to George's swift action, we managed to reverse the effects of an impending diabetic coma.

Jovial George clearly enjoyed helping others while he spread cheer and told jokes—the same jokes, over and over again, all day long, one patient at a time. We all enjoyed his presence that Christmas day.

When I finally took my lunch break, I was surprised to find the cafeteria elaborately decorated for the season. I sat down next to one of the staff nurses from the unit. During lunch with Andrea, I had the chance to ask a burning question. "Who is this George fellow? And why is he here on Christmas day?"

"About ten years ago, George's wife became seriously ill. He spent almost every waking moment by her side. Those two lovebirds were so devoted to one another. There was nothing he wouldn't do for her." Andrea stopped for a few moments, sipping her coffee in silence, before continuing.

"George started to visit other patients while his wife was sleeping or having treatments. He was here so much that he seemed to take naturally to helping out wherever he could."

My natural curiosity made me ask, "Does he have any family?"

A serious look came over Andrea's face as she continued. "They never had children, and as far as I know, there are no relatives. But you see, George watched his wife suffer for a very long time. He shared every second of her pain and anguish. On Christmas Eve night, after I prepared his wife for sleep, they prayed together. During the prayer, George promised his wife that if God would take away her misery that night, by taking her 'Home,' he would spend the rest of his life as a Christmas volunteer."

Andrea and I finished our lunch in silence.

Laura Lagana
Previously appeared in Chicken Soup for the Soul
Christmas Treasury

The Eyes Have It

It took me a long time not to judge myself through someone else's eyes.

Sally Field

The exhibit was entitled "Anne Frank in the World," a collection of photographs that depicted what life was like for Anne Frank and other persecuted Europeans during the Nazi regime.

Although I am fortunate enough not to have lost any relatives to the Holocaust, I was nonetheless reared in its specter. Even as a child I innately understood that, had my great-grandfather emigrated from Russia to western Europe instead of to America, my destiny may have been very different.

So it seemed natural to volunteer my services to Facing History and Ourselves, an educational organization committed to eradicating prejudice via classroom curricula. Their hope is that students will connect the lessons of the Holocaust and other examples of collective violence with the moral choices they face today.

My time was spent stuffing envelopes and answering

phones in the office. Though the staff was grateful for my help, I had doubts about my contribution's significance. *They also serve who sit and stuff*, I reminded myself. *Not all crusaders wield swords.*

When the call came for docents to lead groups through a touring photographic exhibit, I signed up immediately. This was the interactive role I craved, a chance to do something really useful. During our brief training period, we learned there would be no memorized text to reiterate; tours would consist of applicable information in whatever manner the docent chose to present it. The idea of ad-libbing turned my hands clammy. What if someone asked a question, and I didn't have the answer? I took a deep breath and plunged in.

After the first few knee-knocking tours, I became more at ease. Several children did ask questions that I couldn't answer immediately, but I realized it wasn't crucial that I know the answer. It was more important that the question had been *asked*.

The majority of students touring the exhibit were adolescents whose attention spans are not lengthy at best. For many of the kids, this excursion was a holiday from the classroom, nothing more. I quickly realized that I needed drastic measures to capture their attention at the start and sustain it throughout. I remembered hearing about an exercise that was used in the 1960s to show students how harmful the myth of white superiority is, and what, as a result of this myth, it meant to be black in America. I tried it first on a group of seventh-grade girls from a local Catholic school.

The students gathered around and looked at me expectantly. I gave them a warm smile.

"Would everyone with blue eyes please raise her hand?" I instructed without preamble.

A number of hands went up. "Good," I acknowledged.

"Please come to the front of the group. Those whose eyes are not blue, step to the back wall."

The girls complied, looking bewildered but intrigued.

"Okay, all you blue eyes, come with me. Everyone else, stay by the wall. You will not be taking the tour."

At this point, the group eyed me warily. Had this crazy lady gone off the deep end?

I turned to the pairs of brown and hazel eyes huddled in the back. "Tell me, what did you think of my announcement?"

"It's not fair," one girl proffered. "It doesn't make any sense."

"You're right," I replied. "But that's exactly the way the Nazis treated people they considered inferior: Gypsies, Jehovah's Witnesses, homosexuals . . . not only the Jews."

A blonde girl in the front group looked puzzled. "But how could they tell who was Jewish and who wasn't?"

Out of the mouths of babes . . . "They couldn't. That's why Jews were forced to wear identifying insignias on their clothing."

The girl pondered this, verbalizing her thoughts. "I've never met a Jew before."

"Well, now you can say you have," I smiled.

Understanding dawned, and the blue eyes widened in astonishment. Involuntarily, she backed a few steps away from me. "You're Jewish?"

"I'm Jewish. And you see? I'm no different from anyone else."

I was surprised at my own hurt feelings. Her reaction was completely devoid of malice, yet it spoke volumes. What had fostered this girl's impulse to physically distance herself from the unfamiliar?

In our progression through the exhibit, I noticed that the girl paid close attention to my commentary. She asked introspective questions and digested my replies with a thoroughness that drew giggles from her classmates. The final leg of the tour was a brief oral presentation by a Holocaust survivor. As I watched the plaid skirts and navy-blue blazers shuffle into the lecture hall, the blonde girl glanced back and gave me a shy smile.

During the ensuing weeks, I escorted hundreds of children through the exhibit, running the gamut from inner-city public schools to ultra-Orthodox Jewish day schools. Somewhere in between was a twelve-year-old Catholic girl who went home that evening and told her parents about her class trip to "Anne Frank in the World." Maybe she even told them about the Jewish tour guide who looked just like a regular person.

And if that girl was the only one I had reached with a life-changing message about tolerance and understanding, then I had done something worthwhile.

Cynthia Polansky Gallagher

[EDITORS' NOTE: *For information on Facing History and Ourselves, contact 16 Hurd Rd., Brookline, MA 02445; 617-232-1595; e-mail:* info@facing.org.]

African Eyes

The voyage of discovery is not in seeking new landscapes but in having new eyes.

Marcel Proust

Those eyes. I've seen them before. The pleading stare from the child on the TV screen is so familiar. Her swollen belly peeks out from beneath the tattered shirt that she has long outgrown. Her face is soiled with a mixture of dirt and remnants of food. The commercial begins to fade as I close my eyes. The emotions return, and I am again in Africa.

Those same eyes looked into mine just months earlier. It was our last night in Samburu, Kenya, and we had been working all day. We had spent the week in this village through the CHOICE Humanitarian program working alongside the villagers in building schoolrooms, making bricks, hauling dirt and teaching lessons in the schools. The preparation for the trip had begun almost a year before, however. It was an inaugural student trip. Sixteen students were chosen to travel to Africa. The program emphasized "helping locally to help globally," so each of us had chosen a place to render service throughout the year. We each completed one hundred hours of service. I had worked at a local elementary school helping tutor children and reading to them three times a week. So here I was, an admittedly sheltered girl from Utah, in the middle of Africa. In addition to helping with physical tasks in the village, we had also been involved in cultural exchange activities—learning about the Kenyan culture while they learned about ours. Since it was our last night, some of the villagers had invited us to their homes for dinner—a huge honor—and we accepted. As we reached the end of the long walk down the dirt road to their collection of huts, the sun was just setting on the African horizon. We stopped as we turned the corner to see all of the children of the village running toward us with wide smiles almost fighting to hold our hands. One young girl in particular stood out. She stood about waist high and looked at me smiling shyly. She reached up her hand and took mine. Wordlessly, we walked into the village together.

Some time passed as her mother prepared dinner. It had grown dark. We sat outside the mud-and-stick house that the little girl and her family called home. It was a one-bedroom hut that held the mother and her nine children. The little girl could only speak Swahili, and I could only speak English so she looked at me, studying my white skin and touching my straight, blonde hair. I set her on my lap and looked at her. Her tattered dress was hanging off of her body. She made no attempt to swat at the flies that constantly buzzed by her head frequently landing on her nose. Yet, as I looked at her, her eyes sparkled against her beautiful black skin. There was something there I had never seen before—a sort of genuine happiness. It puzzled me. This little girl lived in a house that barely kept out the elements. The other villagers often scraped together food for her family when their father who worked in the city to support them had not sent money, but when they invited us to eat, they offered to kill their last goat to make a huge meal for us. Of course, we refused and just told them to bring what they had, but it amazed me. This family was willing to give up everything they had to feed us and show their appreciation for what we had done for their village. They had nothing and were completely happy. I was on the verge of tears when the music began. The little girl slid from my lap, flashed me a smile, and pulled me from my chair onto the dirt floor outside the hut. Underneath the African moonlight with only a lantern to light the darkness, we danced. I held her little hand in mine as the music filled us both. We may have danced differently, but the feelings we felt were the same. We were one—me, the little girl, the music and Africa.

The music subsided, and I relaxed back into my chair. My new friend twirled my ring between her delicate fingers and laid her head on my lap as I stroked her soft, fluffy hair. Her mother announced dinner and we went into the hut cramped together but enjoying it all. They brought us all the food they had—a few chapatis and some sauce to dip it in. They denied us nothing and kept nothing for themselves. We politely ate and thanked them profusely for the dinner. I was touched and yet saddened. They had given up their dinner in feeding us. The children would most likely not get to eat, and I knew that this wasn't the first time it had happened. I also knew it wouldn't be the last. We sat in the hut talking as the light of the lantern began to grow dim. The villagers walked us back to the school where we stayed.

As I scooped up my little Kenyan friend when we said good-bye, I could see the sadness in her eyes. I felt the same. We had not spoken a word to each other, but I knew I was forever tied to this girl. Her wide eyes stared into mine, and I saw the dreams she held for what she could become. I had these same dreams when I was her age, yet

I knew my circumstances had been much different and the opportunities afforded to me much greater. Coming to Africa to live and work with the people that make the country so beautiful was priceless.

Through the hours of service it took to get there and the hours of service rendered while there, I had come to see what I could become with a little work. I had seen the hero inside of me—the best part that resides in each of us that just yearns to get out. I had looked at service, at Africa and at myself through those African eyes—eyes full of hope for a future that I may not see, eyes searching for whatever good may lie in things, eyes that see a need with arms that reach out to help, eyes that have seen sadness and boldly dared to hope against hope.

The commercial ends and I switch off the TV. If only everyone knew what I knew. If only I could show everyone else those eyes.

Stephanie Sheen

[EDITORS' NOTE: *For information on Choice Humanitarian, contact 7879 S. 1530 W. Suite 200, West Jordan, UT 84088; 801-474-1937; fax: 801-474-1919; e-mail:* ashton@choicehumani tarian.org; *Web site:* www.choicehumanitarian.org.]

No Batteries: No Survivors

Consciousness is the vital energy, which both gives life to the body and survives beyond the body in a different realm of existence.

David R. Hawkins, M.D., Ph.D.

"Oh, no. Not again," Kim mumbled sleepily to her husband as he rolled out of bed to silence the blaring pager. It was 3:23 A.M., January 3, 2001, and Wyatt hadn't been home from the previous call for more than an hour. "Can't you skip this one?" she asked from under the blanket.

"Sorry, Hon," he said, giving her shoulder a tender squeeze with his right hand as he grabbed for his jeans with his left. "House fire in Oak Orchard. Got to go. Be back as soon as I can." Before she could open her mouth to protest further, she heard his footsteps bound down the stairs, the storm door bang and the truck engine turn over.

Must be twenty degrees, Kim thought, *and he hasn't had more than two hours' sleep. How does he do it?* She buried her face in the pillow, snuggled deeper under the covers and drifted back into a restless sleep—grateful that their six-month-old son hadn't been awakened by the commotion.

Racing vehicles, mostly four-wheel-drives, pulled into the Millsboro Volunteer Fire Company from all directions simultaneously. Each firefighter donned protective gear and moved in sync like a well-oiled piece of machinery— the picture of efficiency that comes from years of training and well-rehearsed roles.

Wyatt took his place as engineer behind the wheel of the rescue truck as the fire engines pulled out with screaming sirens. He tuned them out, as usual, and estimated it would take six or seven minutes to get to Oak Orchard.

On first impression, except for clouds of billowing gray and white smoke mushrooming from every window, the ranch home with white siding didn't look too bad.

"At least it's not fully engulfed," Wyatt yelled with optimism to his dad, Lynn, as they yanked the heavy fire hose into position and adjusted the nozzle.

"Smoke inhalation," Lynn answered, "that's my fear for the people on this one. You know how it can kill in a matter of minutes." Turning to the left as they raced together toward the house, he called out over his shoulder, "Anybody know how many are in there?"

"No idea," another firefighter answered.

As they hurried through the front door and into the living room, a wall of thick black smoke and flames rose up as if to threaten, "Get out!" But Wyatt and the undaunted firefighters pressed on through the heat and breath-stealing smoke—and into the roaring flames. Their heavy boots kicked furniture and bumped into who-knows-what as they plowed forward in the eeriness of being able to see nothing but dense smoke.

Where are the people? Wyatt wondered. His palms and knees burned as he crawled on the floor. Smoke coiled around his head like an angry serpent ready to strike. The monster had taken over.

One by one, four adults and seven children were carried

from the blazing home into the yard and laid on frozen brown grass. Sounds of "CPR in progress" were heard over radios countywide—to no avail. Eighty-three-year-old Evelyn Shelton and ten members of her family died in that tragic, early morning blaze—Delaware's deadliest in more than one hundred years.

Exhausted and red-eyed, with seared lungs, drooping shoulders and a bruised heart, Wyatt returned home four hours later. Kim met him at the door in her terrycloth robe, with Kade in her arms.

"I heard it on the scanner," she said softly, her eyes brimming. Wyatt couldn't talk. He just stood there in the doorway and flung his arms around his little family, pulling them close to his chest and hugging them tight.

"One was a tiny baby," he choked out the words, "about the size of Kade." He drew in a deep breath and shook his head, "I tried and tried to resuscitate him, but they made me stop. They said it was no use," his voice cracked. "All I could think about was what if it were Kade?" He released his grip, looked deep into her eyes and continued, barely above a whisper, "Eleven people. We couldn't save *one*. Not one."

Kim steered Wyatt to the kitchen table, and he held the baby while she started breakfast.

"The worst part," he continued, "is that it could have been prevented. They had smoke detectors in the house, but none of them had batteries. Seems so senseless. Which reminds me of the Simmons' place. Did I ever tell you about that?"

"No, what happened?"

"The day of her fire, I was really down. Discouraged with firefighting. Grappling with my faith. Struggling with what to believe and wondering why I do this. Because my dad is a firefighter? And his father before him? And my brother? We got Mrs. Simmons out safe. But it was what we found in her living room that helps me work through tough times like today.

"Everything was destroyed. Everything. The walls were barely standing, and anything recognizable was either charred to a crisp or smoke or water-damaged. Except for one thing. We went back into the house to check once more for sparks and smoldering wood, and on the far wall was a picture of Jesus—you know, the one they have in Sunday school where he's dressed like a shepherd carrying a staff and holding a little lamb?"

Kim nodded.

"If three of us hadn't seen it at the same time, I wouldn't have believed my eyes. That picture was as clean as if it were brand-new. Not a smudge of smoke or speck of soot. Nobody could talk. We just stood there, staring.

"It was as though Jesus himself, holy and invisible, stood there with us as we looked at it. But more than the picture, it was the caption that gripped me. From that day on, I've never questioned God or doubted why I fight fire."

"What did it say?" Kim asked.

Wyatt lifted Kade high above his head, and the baby smiled down in innocent delight as he answered, "For this one I will lay down my life."

"Hey, little man, what do you say we go check our batteries?"

Candace F. Abbott

Coming Full Circle

"Man, this is just more of the s-a-a-a-m-e old garbage!" The sneering wisecrack reverberated from the back of the classroom, putting an end to my preplanned opening remarks. I had been sufficiently warned about the skepticism of these students, but it still caught me by surprise.

While developing a new training seminar, the thought had occurred to me that the same techniques could be applied to job interviews. Since I had done volunteer work for the Salvation Army in the past, I dropped them a note. I offered to teach a few skills to the students enrolled in their adult in-patient substance-abuse program—skills that would help guide them through a successful job interview.

Shortly afterward, the major in charge of the program met with me. After I proposed my idea, he rubbed his chin in silence for a few moments, before responding. "Trust doesn't come easily to these folks. But if your program will help, then let's try it." He smiled as we shook hands.

Addiction has no regard for social order or ethnicity—it preys on anyone. Sadly, many of those admitted to the Salvation Army rehab are therapy-wise from previous failed hospitalizations, and streetwise from years of feeding this insatiable predator. Given these circumstances, the Salvation Army has an excellent recovery program.

After chopping me off at the knees with his snide wise-crack, my detractor made no effort to conceal his contempt. Slouched low in his chair, he deliberately extended his long legs across the aisle. To further emphasize his defiance, he locked his arms firmly across his chest.

When my class of thirty students finally quieted down, I inquired in a casual tone, "Since you haven't heard what I'm going to say . . . how can you make a comment like that?" The room grew still.

Suddenly, he sat bolt upright with such force that I took a step backward, even though I stood twenty feet away.

Scowling he snapped, "Cuz, it's all the 'same-old, same-old'!" He gestured angrily toward the windows, "Same thing out there. It's about gettin' over!" As he raised his voice, his eyes narrowed. "You come in here, wearing your designer suit, with the idea that you can teach us your fancy way of gettin' over, so we can go out and get some kinda job? Well, it don't work." Angrily punching his chest with both fists, he said, "I *know* it don't work, my man. I've done nineteen rehabs . . . yet, here I am!" Leaning forward, he asked, "What do *you* know about *us*? What are you gonna say that we ain't already heard?" After his outburst, he retreated back to his slouched position. "Go ahead man, tell me!" he added, with a smirk.

Silently counting to ten, I forced a smile and said, "Excellent questions! And I will answer them . . . at the end of today's class."

As an experienced speaker, I understood that by conceding a battle I could sometimes win the war. Without pause, I moved directly into my presentation. During the following ninety minutes, few students showed interest.

Toward the end of our session, my unenthusiastic pupils began noisily shuffling papers. Taking the hint, I quickly summarized and gave them an assignment. "I promised to answer your questions." Their fidgeting ceased as they instantly became attentive.

Pointing toward the window, I said, "When you were out there, you made promises you couldn't keep. You lied and cheated . . . and you felt justified in doing it. *That's* 'getting over.' And you lost." As I slowly walked among the students, I continued, "If you think I'm here to teach you an easier way of 'getting over' . . . you lose again." Their silent stares met mine.

"Many years ago, I heard a speaker describe how he felt when he lost his job, his house and eventually his wife. Within the next few months, both of his parents died." The class still appeared unmoved.

With intentional sarcasm, I asked, "Did I mention that it was during the first nine months of his recovery . . . and that he stayed clean and sober through it all?" Their stiff features gradually softened as my revelation triggered whispers of awe and disbelief.

"That speaker finished by sharing the principles that helped him to deal with his problems, without relying on alcohol or drugs."

Clearing my throat nervously, I continued, "After that presentation, I leaned to the guy next to me and said, 'Y'know, pal, they pay speakers to come in here and make up this garbage . . . it's all just a con.'" I studied them quietly, looking for a reaction.

"Just twenty-four hours earlier, I had crawled into that place with everything I owned stuffed into a brown paper bag. My life was a mess, and the speaker was offering me a way to change it for the better—for free. But I was afraid, so I hid behind arrogance."

At this point, the Salvation Army drug counselor stepped quietly into the room. "Fortunately, a counselor exposed my arrogance for what it was. 'George,' he said, 'you're a pretty smart guy. But, if your way worked so well, what are you doing *here?*'" Finally, I seemed to be reaching them.

"By taking direction from people who had what I wanted, I learned how to trust." I turned toward my antagonistic pupil, and said, "And that was seventeen years ago. Today, I have a lovely wife, a successful business and, most importantly, I have earned respect." Extending my hand, I said, "So, my friend, thank you for expressing your fear." His angry eyes mellowed. "I can tell you're a pretty smart guy . . ."

Grinning sheepishly, he clasped my hand. "That's all right, my man. Say your thing. I'll listen."

The subsequent classes were no less challenging but far more positive. Each week they showed up, anxious to report the results of their job interviews. At one point, my "friend" in the back of the room proudly announced, "I got a job. I used what you taught us, George, and already negotiated a one-dollar-an-hour raise." As the students gave him a standing ovation, I think I applauded the loudest of all.

Many years ago, that volunteer speaker passed along a gift that he had also received from a volunteer—the gift of hope. Because that gentleman, whose name I never learned, willingly spoke to a room full of cynics, my journey through life began to take a more positive direction. I express my profound gratitude by passing the gift on through volunteer work. In doing so, I am reminded every day that my life has come full circle.

George M. Roth

[EDITORS' NOTE: *For information on The Salvation Army Headquarters, contact P.O. Box 269, Alexandria, VA 22302; 703-684-5500; fax: 703-684-3478; Web site:* www.salvationarmy.org.]

Gentle Words

He was another new face, handsome, wide smile and sparkling eyes. He wanted to volunteer his time in a new way. Brian had shared his time at the homeless shelter, providing transportation and assistance to people with disabilities and befriending those who were most isolated. Now he was ready for a different kind of challenge—he was interviewing for crisis-line volunteer training.

Brian was nervous about the interview, not knowing what to expect or even if he would be right for the job. He answered all the questions honestly. A positive attitude was one of the strengths he felt he would bring to the task. When asked why he wanted to do this type of work, he told the interviewer that he wanted to give back to the community. He had so many blessings in his life—a good job with a major insurance company, family, friends and great coworkers. He knew there were many people who didn't have someone to turn to when life became overwhelming. He wanted to be the voice that answered that two A.M. call. He wanted to be the heart that listened.

Brian was accepted into the eighty-hour training program. He couldn't believe how much work was involved.

He had reading assignments with written exercises that were graded every week. It was difficult. There was classroom training, role-playing and phone-room training. He learned about mental illness, addiction and suicide. Brian doubted that he could get through it. He questioned his abilities. *Could I be the one to help? Could I indeed make a difference?*

As a trainee, Brian monitored calls handled by experienced crisis line volunteers. He was highly nervous about one caller, Audrey, who had schizophrenia. With a serious mental illness, Audrey lived on the fringes of life. Medication didn't have much impact on her delusions and auditory hallucinations.

Audrey called the hotline frequently, and her mood was generally angry and unpredictable. She yelled at volunteers, accused them of bizarre actions and routinely berated everyone for being inept and decidedly useless. The volunteers, however, understood her illness and had a great appreciation for the fact that answering her calls was a form of support for Audrey that kept her in the community rather than in a state institution.

Brian dreaded his first call from Audrey. He wanted to do the best he could for her, but he wasn't sure he could handle her. When her call came in, even the trainers were surprised. Audrey was a lamb. Brian's gentle words and interaction both soothed and brightened her. After Brian passed his final tests and started on a regular weekly shift, the magic continued for the next four years.

Over time, Audrey figured out when Brian worked, and it was rare that she missed calling when he was on duty. Brian's shift-partners would say "hello" and receive an angry blast, and yet when Brian would answer in the same way, Audrey was charmed. No matter how psychotic she became, Brian could always interact with her in a positive and upbeat manner.

With Audrey and so many others, Brian brought a sense of hope, mixed with kindness, respect and abiding compassion for those facing crises of the spirit. The fears he held about his effectiveness were groundless. He was very successful in this venture, and he went on to train new crisis-line volunteers, teaching the skills that were second nature to him.

Brian died at age twenty-nine after battling cystic fibrosis his entire life. In the end, his body gave out, although his spirit remained strong. Audrey noted his absence while Brian was in the hospital for an extended time, and she called the staff at the crisis center to find out what was happening to her special friend.

When she was told about his disease and his fight for life, she became very quiet. "I will pray for him every day," she said slowly. With unmistakable concern she added, "In spite of my not-so-wonderful life, I believe in God. I believe because I know Brian." That powerful message and moment of clarity was indeed a gift from Brian.

The staff dreaded telling Audrey the news about Brian's death and letting her know that this gentle light had moved on. Several days after the funeral, the associate director, who had delivered the eulogy, called Audrey to deliver the somber message. She met the news bravely, thanked the director for keeping her informed and tried to say good-bye, but it was evident that she was struggling with her emotions. Seeking to comfort her, the staff person read part of the eulogy to her—an old Native American quotation: "On the day you were born you cried and the world rejoiced. Live your life in such a way that when you die the world cries and you rejoice."

After a long pause, Audrey whispered, "Amen."

Karen Zangerle

8

OVERCOMING OBSTACLES

*When you are inspired by some great
purpose, some extraordinary project, all
of your thoughts break their bonds: Your
mind transcends limitations, your
consciousness expands in every direction,
and you find yourself in a new, great
and wonderful world. Dormant forces,
faculties and talents become alive, and
you discover yourself to be a greater person
than you ever dreamed yourself to be.*

Indian Philosopher Patanjali

He Taught Us to Love

It's not what you do for your children, but what you have taught them to do for themselves that will make them successful human beings.

Ann Landers

Proudly I watched Russ, with his characteristic boyish grin, leave his seat to speak to a gathering of nearly two hundred people. Bursting with joy and triumph, a tear trickled softly down my cheek.

Russ was a lovable kid with a myriad of communication challenges—a speech impediment, dyslexia, auditory and large motor problems, mixed dominance and poor coordination to boot. But that day he was walking confidently, standing tall to make an acceptance speech for having been chosen one of the "Outstanding Young Citizens" in Ocean County, New Jersey, because of his phenomenal volunteer service in the tightly-knit town of Toms River.

As I listened, I closed my eyes. A few seconds later, I could hear his voice as a youth saying, "You know what I mean," when he couldn't pronounce a word. He struggled valiantly to learn what those words meant. I closed my eyes even tighter, remembering a cheerful fourth-grader telling me how he had to make a speech about his science project and how the very thought of it made his heart beat "really fast."

I found myself recalling other memorable moments. Like the days when I used to help out with Meals on Wheels. I'd run in and make the delivery while my volunteer partner stayed with Russ in the car. Or the times I directed a children's chorus and he'd be right there tugging on my leg. My mind was a blur of warm images of Russ as a loving, caring youth, a gentle soul, accepting his challenges. And now, as he stood at the lectern, I knew his heart must be racing.

As Russ continued his speech, I thought about the fateful day he was diagnosed with all those impairments and how proud his tutors would be if they could see him today. Here he was at twenty-nine, being honored for ten years of service as a volunteer fireman. Russ was responsible for organizing clothing drives for the homeless, teaching preschool children about fire safety, and for playing a sensitive Santa Claus for terminally ill children by driving up in a fire truck.

At the end of his speech, Russ thanked his parents for giving him a good life—for instilling him with self-esteem and for teaching him about morals and integrity. Then, pausing for a few seconds, he looked intently at his audience. He took us by surprise by touching lovingly on the loss of his nephew, Austin Lee Hanning. Austin was just three years old when he died from a rare and incurable disease.

At that moment, I had to close my eyes again before I unleashed a different set of tears. A hush fell over the room as Russ dedicated his volunteer award to Austin's memory. He concluded his speech by lifting the audience up with the compassionate warmth of these words, "Austin taught me how to love."

I was in awe as I saw this young man come full circle—from dreading the thought of learning and speaking words, to holding an audience spellbound by his inspired speech.

What made the occasion even more special was the fact that Russ, who never made it as the star of the football team, and who had never been voted "most likely to succeed," had risen to be a true "star" in his community.

Russ became a man of strong character by his unselfish dedication and service to others. Labeled perceptually impaired, Russ now sees and acts clearly with his heart. His words and deeds inspire everyone who knows him. It is Russ, our son, who "has taught us how to love."

This time, my heart was beating "really fast."

Arline McGraw Oberst

The Healing Power of Friendship

Friendship doubles our joy and divides our grief.

Cicero

Some twenty-eight years ago, an appealing ad in a local newsletter in Rochester, New York, caught my eye:

WANTED: Men and women to provide support and friendship to someone who is feeling lonely and isolated. Must be kind, gentle and patient. Previous experience with the mentally ill a plus. No pay. If you care, you qualify.

Since I considered myself to be qualified, I signed up to help. I had been thinking about pursuing a volunteer opportunity anyway, and I knew what it meant to be lonely.

My responsibility as a participant in the Compeer Program was to befriend a person diagnosed with a mental illness. I was to visit my newly assigned friend and provide nourishing support and encouragement for at least one hour a week, over a period of a year. Although it seemed like a modest investment of time, I wasn't thoroughly convinced one hour a week would make the slightest bit of difference. Nevertheless, I was determined to try.

A short time later, I went to visit my first new "friend," Millie. Hospitalized at the local psychiatric center for years, she had recently been released to a group home. In the beginning, I did most of the talking. "Good afternoon, Millie. My name is Barb, and I'm looking forward to spending some time with you as your friend."

Millie was extremely quiet and severely introverted, shyly sitting in the corner of the sofa finding it difficult to speak. Occasionally she would glance up to peek at me, being careful not to allow our eyes to meet. Over time, Millie gradually began to trust me. She became more comfortable in my presence but remained somewhat cautious. Our weekly get-togethers usually meant sharing a mug of piping hot coffee, going for long walks, window shopping at the mall or taking slow rides in the country.

As I learned more about Millie, I discovered others close to her had betrayed her trust and let her down. No stranger to adversity throughout her life, the stigma of having a mental illness only compounded her feelings of isolation.

Although I felt like I was a good role model, Millie continued to lack self-esteem and the ability to make decisions. Her progress was excruciatingly slow. For Millie, success was simply maintaining her current condition and staying out of the hospital.

Millie never discussed how she felt about our friendship, even after we completed our first year together. Just enjoying our time together seemed acceptable. Our friendship continued over the years, and Millie knew she could always depend on me.

Then one day I got a call from our volunteer coordinator. "Barb, would you and Millie like to be interviewed on a local TV news show?"

Astonished, I responded, "Wow! Let me discuss it with Millie and get back to you. Is tomorrow morning soon enough?"

Besides my own fears, I didn't think Millie would be comfortable going on "live" television. We discussed it, and to my amazement Millie wanted to be interviewed as long as I would be there, too. I said, "If you will, I will. Deal?"

"Deal!" Millie stated confidently.

On interview day, I picked Millie up. She had been ready and waiting for hours. On the way to the TV station, Millie declared enthusiastically, "If I can help other people understand how important our friendship is, and how it has helped me, maybe they'll volunteer, too. Then people on the waiting list can be matched with someone like you, Barb. Wouldn't that be great?"

"That would be magnificent," I rapidly agreed.

As I drove, tears flowed from my eyes and across the steering wheel. Millie had never let me know how much she valued our friendship until that moment. We smiled at one another in silence.

At the TV station, the interviewer prepped us on the questions she was going to ask. Our tension mounted as a troop of Boy Scouts, touring the studio, lined up to watch the pending interview. Trying to conceal our frazzled nerves, Millie and I were like two swans swimming on a tranquil lake: smooth on the surface but paddling furiously underneath.

Our interview proceeded flawlessly, better than we could have hoped for. Millie turned out to be the poised, confident and articulate one, 99 percent better than I. She spoke with sincerity and without a trace of nervousness. With impressive candor, she revealed her situation and the positive impact her "new friend" had on her life. What a day!

From then on, Millie never missed an opportunity to plant the seeds about the Compeer Program with others. Her face literally lit up whenever she talked about our special friendship. I was proud of my friend who had broken out of her shell at last. Millie proved that no matter what label society gives us, being labeled a friend is the most treasured of all.

Barb Mestler

[EDITORS' NOTE: *For more information on the Compeer Program, contact 259 Monroe Ave., Rochester, NY 14607; 800-836-0475; fax: 585-325-2558; e-mail:* compeerp@rochester.rr.com; *Web site:* www.compeer.org. *Among her awards, Barb has earned a "Point of Light" for her volunteering from the Points of Light Foundation & Volunteer Center National Network, 1400 I Street, N.W., Suite 900, Washington, DC 20005; 800-VOLUNTEER; fax: 202-729-8100; e-mail:* Info@Pointsof Light.org; *Web site:* www.pointsoflight.org.]

Let the Games Begin!

1984.

Memorial Coliseum.

Los Angeles, California.

The lighting of the Olympic Torch is the signature event of the Games. Since it appears on international television, the pressure to be flawless is immense.

Originally built to host the 1932 Olympic Games, the Coliseum had a torch spire that had not been used in at least twenty-five years.

Several weeks prior to the Opening Ceremonies, a company was selected to make the torch work. After examination, the entire torch spire and five-ring Olympic insignia had to be rebuilt. Yet, at ten days and counting, there was still no solution.

The company then phoned my dad, Ed Buckingham—a licensed engineer, flame-control expert and Olympic volunteer. With an engineering sketch that looked more like chicken scratch, Ed drew up a plan. It consisted of five flame-control devices placed strategically within the five rings. Plus he included three backup options for igniting those controls. With his plan in hand, Ed was given the go-ahead to make it work.

Fortunately, my dad had volunteered earlier in the year to work at the pentathlon event and had a security clearance. This was a stroke of volunteer luck because as the director of volunteers up until a few months before the Games, I was acutely aware of the intense security.

Now with just days before the Opening Ceremonies, Ed arrived with his tool chest of expertise, equipment and security clearance. A large man, he spent the next tension-filled days cramped in the operations cubicle at the base of the tower. Testing, rewiring and rechecking were tediously executed day-by-day to insure a perfect lighting of the symbolic torch that would be seen by more than a billion people.

On the day of the Opening Ceremony, with sharp-shooters rimming the top of the Coliseum, Ed cleared his access and reached the locked and guarded door to the control room. Switching on the lights, he found that ALL the wires had been cut!

Clearly, this was a bomb scare!

The USSR was boycotting these Olympic Games. The Los Angeles Raiders football team was in nasty negotiations with the Coliseum Commission. And terrorists of any ilk could gain the attention they craved if the flame exploded, or failed to ignite, on the world's stage.

After the federal bomb squad arrived, I got there as well. Feeling the real potential of danger, I asked Dad, "I'm your eldest daughter; do you think it's safe for me to be here?" He calmly reassured me that security felt it was not a bomb.

Shortly after I left, agents from the Secret Service, Army Demolitions and other members of the Torch Team arrived. Bomb-sniffing dogs were released to cover all the rooms and substructure of the torch base. After a couple hours, the area was declared safe.

Yet the Opening Ceremonies had already begun!

With another sketch and only one option to insure it would light, Dad began the rewiring. Hot and under unbearable pressure, he spent the next ninety minutes crouched in the control room rewiring the torch.

As Dad worked away, he relayed his progress by walkie-talkie to a Torch Team member outside the tower. He in turn relayed it to security that passed it to the people choreographing the ceremony down on the field. A television crew installed a monitor inside the control room. As Dad made the final adjustments, the dancers and Olympians stretched it out for an extra forty minutes.

Finally, he put the finishing touches on the rewiring and pronounced it, "Ready!"

The Olympians were herded into place. "Torch Lighter" Rafer Johnson emerged and trotted around the track. Pausing at the base of the steps, he lifted the torch high and began his ascent as I held my breath until I felt I was going to pass out. Rafer rose steadily to the top.

Inside the torch, Ed was watching the television monitor. The Torch Team member on the walkie-talkie outside the tower whispered, "Ed . . . he's lifting the torch. The flame is there!"

Insuring that the heat from Rafer's torch ignited the Olympic torch, Ed hit the first control button and the base of the torch flashed up in flame. Using his watch and the television, he synchronized a ring of flashes by pushing the second, third, fourth and fifth buttons. The Olympic Flame exploded at the top! The crowd erupted.

Dad was the perfect volunteer at the perfect place at the perfect time and saved the day.

"Let the Games begin!"

Margaret Buckingham

The Bread of Life

Life is an opportunity to contribute love in your own way.

Bernie Siegel

It had been hard for Binh to leave Vietnam in 1975, just days before the fall of Saigon. It was harder to think of leaving now. She'd come back as a volunteer interpreter for a group of doctors. She couldn't refuse their request for help. They'd worked so valiantly, if unsuccessfully, to save her baby.

What she saw when she returned to her homeland shocked and saddened her. Preteen prostitutes plied their bodies to earn enough to eat. Younger orphans slept in the street with the curb as their only pillow. They'd long ago stopped caring about the flies that covered their faces. These children, known as "dust of life," were considered worthless in the Vietnamese culture.

Binh remembered the son she'd lost. *Although my baby's death was not preventable,* Binh thought, *perhaps I can help keep these children from dying. But how can one person change anything?* It seemed hopeless.

Before she returned to the States, Binh wanted to fulfill a promise she'd made at her mother's deathbed—to look up her mother's old friend Sister Tan, a Franciscan nun. This was not an easy task. Christians weren't popular, and no one would share information about Sister's whereabouts for fear that Binh would tell the authorities.

While visiting a beautiful wooded area by the beach, Binh got lost. Hoping to find the way back to her car, she followed children's voices to an iron gate. Once inside she found Sister Tan and twenty-seven orphaned children, who in that culture should have been left to die. Though the children were being loved and cared for within the meager means of the nuns, it was obvious to Binh that this little underground orphanage desperately needed money for food and medicine. It was divine providence that brought Binh to Sister Tan.

Binh had one hundred American dollars in her purse. She offered it gladly to Sister Tan. But instead of thanks, Binh received a reprimand. "How could we spend it?" Sister asked harshly. "The authorities would know at once where we were hidden and that we were caring for unwanted children. You just want to go away from here without feeling guilty," scolded the old nun.

Binh returned to her hotel in the city. The money, which would have bought so much for Sister Tan and the children, was worthless. Binh just couldn't ignore their plight. She exchanged the American money for Vietnamese currency, but her problems were still not solved. People had seen her make the exchange. Surely she'd lead the authorities to Sister Tan if she tried to go there herself. *How can I get the bundle of money back to Sister?* Binh wondered.

As she was praying for a solution, a boy rode past the hotel. He was selling fresh French bread from a basket on his bike. Suddenly, Binh had an idea. She called to the boy, "Come up to my room, so I can pay you." Once they were inside the room, Binh sliced open a loaf of the bread. After pulling out the soft insides she stuffed the bread with Vietnamese bills. Hiding the loaf beneath the others in the basket, she gave the boy some coins and sent him off to deliver the "doctored" bread to the nuns.

The bread arrived safely so Binh faxed her husband sixteen more times for additional money. She used it to transport Sister Tan and her children to Saigon in two vegetable trucks, where they'd be safe in the city.

When she returned to the United States, Binh's support for the orphaned and handicapped children in Vietnam continued. Her "family" of more than five hundred homeless children is now housed in five orphanages funded by "Children of Peace"—the organization she started. Binh, which means "peace" in Vietnamese, is still bringing the bread of life to the children of Vietnam.

Ellen Javernick

[EDITORS' NOTE: *For information on Children of Peace, contact P.O. Box 2911, Loveland, CO 80538.*]

A Child's Voice

When a man is singing and cannot lift his voice, and another comes and sings with him, another who can lift his voice, the first will be able to lift his voice, too. That is the secret of the bond between spirits.

Josh Hinds

"Sss-uue," four-year-old Karen says as I hold up a flash card showing a shoe.

"Good," I respond. Placing my hand in front of my mouth, I enunciate and say the word loudly: "Shoe!" Frustration in her eyes, Karen silently pleads with me not to make her say the word again. But I do it to help her learn. With my hand blocking my mouth, I pronounce, "Shoe," emphasizing the "sh."

Karen gazes down at the floor and whispers, "Sss-uu." Lifting her soft chin with my fingers, I look her in the eyes and smile. "Good girl," I encourage, but tears of frustration are ready to spill out from her tiny blue eyes. Four years old and words are still so difficult for her.

Along with four other children in my class at the Speech

School, Karen is deaf. At age two, she had a cochlear implant surgically placed behind her ear. Through magnets and a processor, electrodes passing through tiny wires restore part of Karen's hearing. Even today's highest-powered hearing aids can't deliver more than that implant.

Yet Karen is savvy, more so than the other children with implants at the school. For a year and a half after the surgery, Karen figured out how to hide her processor. Ashamed and embarrassed by the little square computer she had to wear under her clothes, Karen adamantly refused to wear it. Even at the age of two, she was clever enough to tuck it away by moving it around her room so her mother could never find it.

After three and a half years of silence, Karen came to learn how to hear with her implant. As soon as she learned other children were wearing the same processor she loathed, Karen relaxed and felt more comfortable. Unfortunately, she was already behind the others. Not only was Karen learning how to hear, but she was also learning how to speak—and I was her teacher.

Inspired by two camp counselors who were majoring in deaf education, I was motivated to teach deaf children. After volunteering in my sophomore year of high school by teaching reading and phonic skills to five- and six-year-olds, I was eagerly anticipating a greater challenge in my junior year. But it was one that I had never imagined: teaching speech.

Wiping away tears and pulling Karen close to me for a hug, I notice Molly, the head teacher, walking by. "Keep working with her," she advised with a knowing smile. "She'll come around with time."

Yeah, right. How much time? I'm used to teaching kids how to read not how to speak!

On one occasion, as I enter the classroom, Karen pops

out of her chair and runs to me. Screeching to a halt just in front of my legs, she arches her back and gazes up at me with a smile. "Ready, Miss Karen?" I ask as I take her hand and walk toward the table in the corner.

We begin as I hold up a flashcard with a fish. "Fissss," Karen responds. I block my mouth and make the "sh" noise, hoping she will imitate me. "Sss," she replies.

At the end of the day, I look right at Karen and ask her, "What's my name?" I point to myself, and say, "Sarah." Karen looks at me silently and just sighs. I repeat, "Sarahh," in a sing-songy voice. She nods in more silence. I wish she were able to say my name, but in the back of my mind, I know it will never happen.

Every Monday and Wednesday during the next year, I go to the school and work with the class, but I spend most of my time with Karen. Week by week, she inches forward, but the improvements seem so minimal. One day, as we play a computer game together, Karen points to herself and proudly says, "Kawen!" I smile excitedly at her. Then, pointing to the screen, she calls out, "Fisshh!" Out of the corner of my eye, I see Molly's head perk up.

"Molly, did you hear that?" I shout. She comes over. With a Cheshire grin, Karen points to the fish on the screen and yells, "Fisshh!" Molly smiles taking note of the progress.

I begin to keep a journal, my Karen logbook of learning. Her cognitive abilities are already outstanding, and her speaking skills are rapidly improving. Although she advances to pronouncing "nose" and "Karen," she still is having trouble with my name. Nevertheless she continues and says "snow" as snowflakes start to fall on the computer screen. Moving on to opposites and mastering the letter "O," Karen is talking more than ever in just a little over a month of practice.

Then, I write a journal entry I never thought I'd make.

Leaving at the end of the day, the kids shout good-bye. Right before I shut the door, I hear one little voice cry out, "Bye, Sa-wah!" I swing the door wide open and scan the room to pinpoint the voice. Karen stands up and says it again, "Bye, Sa-wah!" I rush over and give her a huge bear hug. "Bye, Karen." Backing up toward the door, I feel a rush of tears welling up in my eyes. After two years of teaching, I have learned how to relish each small victory, how to value the simplest words and half-words, and to find the greatest reward in a little girl's voice.

Sarah Hawkins

The Real Treasure

Gratitude is the memory of the heart; therefore forget not to say often, I have all I ever enjoyed.
Lydia Child

Beaches, ideal for discovering great treasures, are miraculous places for unearthing natural gems. For me, volunteering is like a beach. It offers precious nuggets of life that beg to be examined, cradled in my hands and then tucked away to cherish.

One such nugget came into my life in the mid-1980s, when I volunteered at a summer camp for children with cancer aptly called "Camp Goodtimes." It was July, and the children had gathered at Camp Byng on the Sunshine Coast near Sechelt, British Columbia. Taking a week off work to be there, I imagined sessions of creative craft making, leading adventures with imagination packed in our back pockets and singing around a blazing campfire. When I learned I had been sanctioned to the kitchen as assistant camp cook, I was disappointed.

We made enough sandwiches to feed small villages and washed tons of dishes. I gained a new appreciation for people who served their tour of duty in the army peeling potatoes. I anxiously waited for mealtime to arrive so I could connect with the kids. Based on the noise level alone, they seemed to be having a wonderful time.

I looked forward to seeing their happy faces as they peeked curiously around the kitchen corner, begging for snacks. When they asked if they could do some baking, I thought, *Finally, an opportunity to interact with the children.*

The head cook, a robust woman who seemed more suited to institutional security work, roared in protest, "They are not coming into *my* kitchen." She placed her hands on her ample hips for emphasis. Feeling as if we were in prison instead of camp, we gave her the nickname "warden."

I welcomed any opportunity to escape from the "warden" and help with the kids. During breaks, I would cheer on the sidelines of their baseball games or paint with a group of aspiring artists. One glorious, sunny afternoon, I relinquished my kitchen duties and packed us off to the beach, where I assisted as a lifeguard.

One small girl in my group, Nicole, clung to the shore, staring at each gentle wave as it rolled in. Like a barnacle that attaches itself to the rocks, she seemed interested in joining us in the water, and yet hesitated each time I asked her to enter.

I splashed around in the water to show her what fun we were having. Still Nicole hung back and watched with curious, wanting eyes. She took a small step toward us, hesitated and then planted herself on a new patch of sand. I continued to play with the others, showing them how to make handstands under the water. Each time I resurfaced, Nicole stood motionless, watching from the shore.

Again I invited her to enter the ocean. Thinking that she was afraid of the water, I yelled, "Come on in, Nicole. I'll help you swim." Finally, my instinct told me to ease up and wait. She needed to battle whatever was holding her back, just like the illness that had invaded her body. The decision had to be her own.

Nicole's next move took courage, determination and trust. She pulled off her wig and revealed little remnants of hair. She threw the wig to the sand with defiance and ran full force into the water with a gallop. The other children welcomed her. Her eyes sparkled with happiness. Gone was the look of fear that had held her hostage on the shore.

Together, we played and laughed like boisterous, happy children. In the water, the children were set free from hospitals, needles, pain and uncertainty. There were no adults hovering over them with grim consternation. We splashed and rejoiced in the waves. While the sun's rays warmed us on the outside, I felt a radiant warmth deep inside my heart.

We played in the waves until we looked like limp seaweed that had been washed ashore. Bundled in towels, everyone shivered as we gathered clothes, caps and wigs and scurried to escape the cooling breeze. Back on land, they had no choice but to face whatever fate awaited them.

That summer, those children taught me to see beneath their fears and beyond my own. I gained a better understanding of the challenges they faced. They offered their small, courageous hands to hold during evening sharing circles and energetic voices at singsongs. Together we convinced the "warden" to permit them into the kitchen where dreams, in the shape of monster-sized cookies, were created and consumed.

When it came time for them to leave, the children reluctantly boarded the bus, clutching their painted handiwork and dressed in hand-crafted T-shirts decorated with pride. Tearfully, I waved good-bye, reflecting on the world that I had seen through their eyes. Like the beautiful soap bubbles we blew, we knew it would all be gone in a moment.

Holly Frederickson

One Determined Angel

Everyone has the power for greatness, not for fame but for greatness, because greatness is determined by service.

Martin Luther King, Jr.

She looked so fragile and helpless. I was told she didn't even speak English. Olga and her family had come from Puerto Rico to receive the expert medical care that was unavailable in her own country.

I was working in the intensive care unit of our local children's hospital, as one of Olga's nurses. I couldn't help but think how frightened this little girl must feel with all those scary tubes, machines and monitors around her. When she opened her eyes, she was incredibly beautiful. Smiling back at me with big brown eyes, she spoke a universal language.

When her mother arrived early the next morning, she said to me, "My husband must return to Puerto Rico. He needs to go back to work. I'll stay here, near Olga, with her sister and brother, so she can get the medical help she needs to stay alive." As we talked, I discovered that Olga's mother was the only one in her household who spoke English.

The family had been staying at the Ronald McDonald House but would soon need to move into more permanent housing. Since they didn't have anyone else to help them set up housekeeping, I volunteered.

As I attempted to help get an apartment for Olga's family, I was told, "It's impossible. The child's mother isn't working, and the father doesn't even live in this country."

After I told this story to some of my nurse-friends, one of them contacted our local newspaper. One columnist promised he would write their story, but added, "This will be my last column of this sort. These stories just don't sell papers anymore."

That's when Becky, our determined angel, arrived. She was a vibrant, talkative and charming volunteer. We talked, and immediately she had some excellent ideas. As we concluded our conversation, she said, "Oh, by the way, I have cancer, but I'm under treatment."

Despite her condition, Becky took charge. She not only found housing for Olga and her family, but also helped with everything else they needed. I asked myself, *How could this woman do so much when she has such difficulties of her own?*

Becky got the children enrolled in a bilingual program and was able to find the mother a job close to home. When winter set in, Becky would go home from work, start dinner, check on the children and then call Olga's mother to see if she had a ride home from the hospital. If she didn't, Becky would bring her home.

When Olga's father returned to stay in the United States, Becky enrolled the entire family in a bilingual program and was instrumental in obtaining a job for the father. Becky and her husband even obtained a dependable used car for the family, so they could become more self-reliant.

In December, Becky asked her coworkers to adopt Olga's family for Christmas. The generosity of many volunteers provided a wonderful Christmas that year. Her kindness didn't stop there; Becky continued to do wonderful things for this family.

In April 2000, I was invited to attend the annual Jefferson Awards luncheon. Five outstanding volunteers from each state are nominated, and one is selected to represent his or her state in the national competition in Washington, DC. Not only was Becky chosen, but she also won the top award. She not only helped this family in need, but she also helped many others fight their own battles with cancer.

In 1980, Becky was diagnosed with Stage III ovarian cancer. The doctors weren't optimistic, but she was strong-willed and determined. Today, she continues to share her experiences, heartaches and triumphs. She is constantly placing the concerns and care of others before her own.

Becky is living proof that the human spirit can be remarkable, even under the most adverse conditions. Olga and her family thrive, thanks to a determined, kind-hearted woman.

Dorothy Rose

[EDITORS' NOTE: *For information on the Ronald McDonald House Charities, contact One Kroc Drive, Oak Brook, IL 60523; Web site:* www.rmhc.com. *For information on The Jefferson Awards, contact the American Institute for Public Service, 100 West 10th St., Suite 215, Wilmington, DE 19801; 302-622-9101; fax: 302-622-9106; e-mail:* info@aips.org; *Web site:* www.aips.org.]

If I Can Move I Can Win

Pick battles big enough to matter, small enough to win.

Jonathan Kozol

As retreat leader for the staff of St. Vincent's Hospital in Indianapolis, we participated in a wonderful day-long workshop entitled, Creating Healing Communities. In the afterglow of the closing banquet, two nuns asked me to join them later that evening. After working all day, completing a four-course meal and sitting through after-dinner speeches and awards, I wasn't enthusiastic at all—but it's hard to say no to nuns.

Sitting knees to chest in their tiny car, I arrived at New Hope, a separate hospital-affiliated facility for the profoundly impaired. Sister Francine motioned for me to enter the sprawling 140-bed building from a side door so she could help a resident who managed to get his wheelchair stuck in a soft shoulder along the edge of the sidewalk.

"How ya doing, Eddie?" she called.

Eddie spoke slowly. "Reeeal gooooood, Sister."

Francine rolled him inside. As we continued down the hall she told me that Eddie was the third sibling in his family to suffer from Friedreich's ataxia. This disease of the nervous system reveals itself in late childhood, causing paralysis and affecting speech. About a decade earlier, before state-of-the-art genetic identification and testing, it was impossible to tell in advance who would get this disease. Eddie's three siblings, ranging in age from their early twenties to mid-thirties, all lived at New Hope.

As we walked down the hall, Sister Francine stopped to hold and address each person we passed. She greeted a severely retarded, hydrocephalic young woman who blew in Sister Francine's hair. Francine blew back. The patient held me and blew on me. I blew back, too. Next, Francine said hello to a young man who was profoundly impaired following a motorcycle accident. Nearby, a former rock musician silently moving his lips while tapping his head rhythmically, as if to an imagined tune, was the next recipient of Sister's salutation.

Sister Francine saw me shake my head, although I thought it was done imperceptibly. She said, "Whenever I go away, even for just a day, I see changes in them. Oh, they might be microscopic compared to the changes you see in *ordinary* people. When I see how they fight to keep moving, compared to the ease with which I do things, I feel as if I've accomplished nothing in comparison." She continued our conversation as we slowly made our way down the long hallway. "I look at what I start with and where I am. Then I look at them and how they've learned and moved, and it makes me humble."

I thought, *She sees with eyes of joy, and I look in horror and sadness.*

"Come meet the Hoosier of the Year," Sister said enthusiastically, introducing me to John, a thirty-two-year-old man with cerebral palsy. John had severely limited functional use of his body, and he couldn't walk or speak clearly. He had required the use of a wheelchair since the age of five. Seated in the wheelchair next to him was Susan, his wife of two years, who also had cerebral palsy. Every resident in the New Hope facility, their families and the entire St. Vincent's community attended their wedding ceremony.

The governor named John Hoosier of the Year for his contributions to the Muscular Dystrophy Association (MDA). After his closest friend at New Hope died of the disease, John decided to raise money for the organization. He inspired people to pledge pennies, nickels and dimes for every mile that he could "run."

John ran those miles the only way he knew how—backwards, in his wheelchair. Having regular rhythmic control of only his left foot, he moved inches at a time, pushing his wheelchair backward with his toes. He pushed himself through the streets of Indianapolis for hundreds of miles, raising more than thirty-six hundred dollars toward research into muscular dystrophy.

John may not be able to speak very well, but he does have the ability to move his finger across a custom-built alphabet board that attaches to his wheelchair like a tray. As I sat on his bed watching him briskly move one finger with amazing dexterity, he swiftly pointed to each letter that comprised the words he wanted to communicate.

He told me that one day, while he was out on the road, away from New Hope, without the message board on his racing chair, he met some people who thought he was running away. John became frantic because they wanted him to return to the home, but gesticulating uncontrollably in his desperate attempts to speak, he only frightened them even more. In the two years it had taken him to raise the money for MDA, that was the only time he failed to complete his mileage for the day.

As I continued to watch John form new words, his expression became suddenly serious as he said, "I . . . have . . . cancer."

I glanced over at Sister Francine. She nodded her head. "Yes, it's true, Carl. A month ago John was diagnosed as having Hodgkin's disease."

Well aware of the magnitude of his diagnosis, I sat in disbelief. *How much does a person have to deal with in one lifetime?*

John kept moving, but his biological limitations ambushed him once again. He would not be defeated. He intended to keep moving, through this new leg of his journey. Pointing to his arm to show me the site where they administered his chemotherapy, he laughed and said, "My crew cut is only partly from the barber."

"Are you going to complete this race, John?" I asked.

With his rapid-fire forefinger he smiled and responded emphatically, "If I can move, I can win!"

Carl Hammerschlag, M.D.

[EDITORS' NOTE: *For information on the Muscular Dystrophy Association—USA, contact 3300 E. Sunrise Drive, Tucson, AZ 85718; 800-572-1717; Web site:* www.mdausa.org.]

Ward C, Room 842

The gray building sat on a pile of dirty snow in front of a gray sky. I knew that the dismal exterior was a match for the interior. My illness had brought me here many times before as a patient, desperate and in despair. This hospital was supposed to bring hope to those who suffered. Some found that hope and went home again; some never did. They would lie in their beds living, yet lifeless, cut off from the world, waiting to die.

Yes, I know it's true everyone dies. Why some must die and yet remain here . . . I don't know. Day after day, year after year, lying in one spot, not doing, seeing, hearing, touching or loving.

When I was a patient here, sometimes very late at night I would hear the crying—long, low, wailing sounds, lonely and lost. Down the highly polished empty hallways they came and slid under the doors to be heard by those of us who slept lightly. How we prayed that we would never find ourselves on Ward C, waiting to finally, hopefully die.

Now I was going back not as a patient but to visit others as a volunteer. The Bible says: "He comforts us in all our afflictions and thus enables us to comfort those who are in trouble, with the same consolation we have received from him."

With determination I headed toward the door.

My wheelchair crunched and slid in the snow as I made my way down the ramp into the basement of the building. My hair, once thick, had thinned from the medication; it no longer offered protection from the cold. My hands burned as they pushed on the metal rims of my wheelchair now covered with snow. I reached for the door, and my wet hand stuck to the metal door handle as I struggled to get inside.

Usually I waited for someone to take me places, but I wanted to try to be more independent, more in control of my own life. Now coming here, I wasn't so sure. This wasn't easy, but I was here—I was already inside.

I found the volunteer office; I was a few minutes early so I waited in the hall, up against the wall, staying out of the way, as I had been taught to do when I lived here.

I said a prayer and asked God to give me the strength that I needed to do what I was asked, whatever I could. I whispered, "Your servant, my Lord, let me help. In your eyes I'm still whole; in my heart I'm still whole."

I could hear voices from behind the door. "She wants to volunteer to visit patients," one voice said.

"I really don't see how she could help," said another.

"Well, I don't think that we can put her with anyone who matters; she's not very strong. If she gets sick after starting with a patient, it could really mess up the schedule. Anyway, I doubt that she will stay with this very long; disabled people generally tend to be unreliable. Don't get me wrong, it's not their fault, but she's not just disabled, she's sick as well."

"I understand the problem," said the second voice. "I had a terrible flu all last week, but I guess we can't turn her away. How about we give her old Mr. Cramer—he has no one. I don't think he'll last too much longer, and no one else wants to visit him anyway. It wouldn't be kind of us to turn her away. You know she's fairly smart for someone in a wheelchair."

The door began to open. I grabbed a book from my bag and pretended to read. A gray skirt stood in front of me. I looked up; she looked down. I looked at her thick curly hair; she looked at my leg braces.

"Hello, Chris, how nice of you to come," she said sweetly, giving me her best patronizing smile. "I have someone very special for you to visit with—Mr. Cramer, a stroke patient. He hasn't exactly asked for a visitor because he can't talk, but he can make eye contact from time to time. It appears he has no family or friends. I know he'll just love having you visit. I'll leave the amount of time you wish to spend with him up to you; it's Ward C, Room 842. I've really got to run . . . bye for now dear . . . keep in touch." Her high heels clattered off down the hall, taking her with them.

I hadn't said a word. I put away my book. Frightened, I slowly started for Ward C.

I entered the ward to look for Mr. Cramer; his name was at the foot of his bed. The bed was pushed right into the corner. All the necessary hospital paraphernalia was there, nothing I hadn't seen before.

I looked at the man. His hair was a yellow-gray-white, his eyes pale gray, staring and unblinking. The stroke had decimated his face. Who would ever know what he once looked like? His mouth twisted and fell in. Either he had no false teeth, or they couldn't or wouldn't put them in. One contorted hand lay on the covers, frozen in a gesture of supplication, a stark reminder of an internal battle fought and lost. The other hand lay on his chest, beautiful and whole, untouched.

I knew there was not much chance of there being any of

life's awareness left in Mr. Cramer, but . . . perhaps . . . maybe . . .

I thought, *What if he is trapped in there all alone, living in a nightmare of despair? What if . . .*

"My Lord, your servant," I whispered, as I wheeled closer to the head of the bed. Gently I stroked his cheek. The words began to come, and softly I began to speak.

"Mr. Cramer, I'm Chris, and I'm here to love you. I am going to hold your hands, kiss your cheek and comb your hair. I'm going to tell you about everything I know, and when that's all used up, I'll make up what I don't know. Now that should be interesting. I will tell you about all my joys and all my sorrows. And when we get better, we'll climb to the top of the highest hill we can find and scatter wildflowers in the wind. Or how about we make passionate love in the flower bed right out in front of the hospital . . .

"Mr. Cramer, I know you're in there."

The pale gray eyes began to move. They slid sideways, found mine and held. I knew at that moment that Mr. Cramer was there. I could feel his sorrow. A tear ran down his cheek. I wiped it gently with my finger, and it ran into my hand. The eyes slowly closed; the breathing stopped. I felt a quiet and tender peacefulness. His soul passed through mine, and he was gone. I kissed the tear in my hand.

"Mr. Cramer," I said, "you are free now."

I slowly wheeled to the nurse's station and told them Mr. Cramer was dead. I would come back here tomorrow. I would try again.

"Dear God," I asked, "was I just in time or was I too late?"

Sarah Ainslie

"Do they need any help at Toys 'R' Us?"

Reprinted by permission of Steve Smeltzer.

The Cry of a Woman's Heart

Life is short and we have never too much time for gladdening the hearts of those who are traveling the dark journey with us. Oh, be swift to love; make haste to be kind.

Henri Frederic Amiel

The underprivileged children who attended our church-sponsored Christmas party feasted on Christmas goodies, enjoyed a puppet show and received gifts from Santa. When the last carload of children had gone, we breathed a collective sigh of relief, tinged with fatigue and gratitude.

Pointing to the extra gifts left in Santa's black bag, Jean asked, "What are we going to do with all these toys?"

As we deliberated, Bobbie said, "Remember the three sisters who were at the party? Why don't we deliver the toys to their house on Monday while the girls are in school?"

Everyone agreed. Since I lived closest to the three little girls, I volunteered to deliver the gifts. On Monday, I drove to their home, confident their mother would be there. As I got out of my car, a small dog appeared. He barked ferociously and followed dangerously close to my ankles as I hurried to the front porch. Keeping the dog at bay with one immense bag of toys, I knocked on the door. No one answered. I knocked repeatedly for several minutes. Still no answer.

Exasperated, I said under my breath, "Okay, now what am I supposed to do? I can't haul these presents around all day!"

Managing to stay a few steps ahead of the yapping dog, I returned to the safety of my car. After I calmed down a bit I remembered hearing one of the ladies at the church mention some needy children she had transported to the party. The children lived in a frame house not far from where I sat.

As I approached that location, I saw three run-down frame houses side by side. "Oh, no," I muttered. "How am I supposed to know which house is the right one?" I turned into the large dirt yard that was shared by all three families. As I unbuckled my seat belt, I sighed. "Oh, well, I'll try the middle one first."

I knocked on the door. As I prepared to knock again, the door opened halfway. "Yes?" A tired-looking young woman with reddened eyes stood in the doorway. My guess was she had been crying for some time.

Feeling embarrassed, but remembering my purpose, I proceeded. "Sorry for the intrusion. I'm Johnnie from Glen Forest on Old Alabama Road. We hosted a Christmas party on Saturday, and I wondered if your children attended?"

"No," she answered, shaking her head despondently.

"Well, I happen to have a trunk full of extra presents that I need to give to some willing recipients. If you have children who need toys, I'd be delighted to leave them with you."

The woman began to cry. After several minutes, she regained her composure. Between sobs she explained. "I was just sitting here crying ... wondering how I was going to buy gifts for my children this Christmas ... and here you are ... standing at my front door."

She helped me carry the gifts inside. As tears trickled down her cheeks, she smiled and said, "Thank you ... thank you so much."

"No need to thank me," I said gently. "I'm merely the delivery person. Your Heavenly Father arranged for you to have these gifts."

Now, more than twenty years later, I still cannot explain God's mysterious ways, but I can recount the joy of being the one he used to respond to the cry of the woman's heart.

Johnnie Ann Gaskill

Little Changes

Perhaps an all-wise God knew that if any family could inspire a child to face the challenges that lie ahead, it was the Tapley family. My friend was born with a rare genetic disorder that left her with sensory neuropathy as one of its side effects. During her childhood, Rilla's inability to feel pain allowed simple injuries to go unnoticed, often resulting in the partial amputation of a finger or toe caused by the onslaught of gangrene.

As a petite toddler, she struggled in vain to keep up with her cousins, but another manifestation of her condition had left Rilla with a lack of balance, which is vital when learning to walk. Despite these challenges, she eventually learned to ambulate by keeping her head steady and using her eyesight to maintain balance.

One day I asked, "Rilla, how did you ever find the strength to face life against such great obstacles?"

Giving me a pensive glance she responded, "While other children gained confidence and skill by participating in team sports, I learned these attributes by playing board games. Hour after endless hour, my Aunt Grace played games with me. Through these games I learned that although I may not be able to run like other children, I am proficient in other things." As a tiny smile illuminated her face, she added, "I think Aunt Grace sometimes lets me win."

From a very early age, Rilla decided that, since this was the only life she was going to have, she might as well make the best of it. She worked hard at school and upon graduation won academic honors that allowed her to pursue her love of knowledge at university. Years later, when she spoke of her youth she said, "I spent my childhood never knowing what the words 'I can't do that' really meant."

In the middle of her young adult years, the disease continued to progress, and after essential surgery she spent months in rehabilitation. During her convalescence, Rilla noticed that others could benefit from her teaching skills, so she volunteered to help tutor handicapped children. Later on, she volunteered her teaching skills in the adult literacy program, and eventually she began to tutor a new immigrant family.

Sadly, as the years passed, Rilla's disease continued to rob her of her already limited mobility. After several more corrective surgeries, hip replacements and finally a hip fusion, she had to finally face the fact that she would have to spend the rest of her life in a wheelchair.

In the past, the more her disease progressed, the angrier she became and the more determined to prove that her doctors were wrong. She had always taken the doctor's "no" and turned it into a "yes," only this time her body definitely said "No!"

Her body could fight back no longer. "Where is God? How much more do I have to take?" Rilla railed for the first few days after surgery.

But gradually, in the days that followed, my friend began to dream once more. Day after day her spirits soared to new heights. Her husband was largely responsible for her healing. Jim, a wonderful and patient man, smiled whenever Rilla shared her dreams with him, and he did all he could to help her achieve those dreams.

In one instance, Rilla dreamed of being a part of the opening ceremonies of the Confederation Bridge—a bridge that linked her home province with Canada's smallest province, Prince Edward Island. Jim pushed her wheelchair across the bridge and made her dream become a reality.

She also dreamed of helping others. From her wheelchair, Rilla chaired the Terry Fox Run in our small community. Because no one could say "no" to Rilla, she and her team of volunteers raised thirty thousand dollars for cancer research in the last ten years. Rilla also served in her church, on the hospital board and at the local historical society.

Whenever asked about her motivation, Rilla modestly responds, "I believe that making little changes always makes a community a better place."

Through the years that I've known her, my friend continues to make "little changes" wherever she goes.

In October 2000, Rilla was awarded the national prize presented by Canadian Airlines for demonstrating the true spirit of volunteerism.

Elaine Ingalls Hogg

[EDITORS' NOTE: *For more information on The Terry Fox Foundation for cancer research, contact 416-924-8252; Web site:* www.terryfoxrun.org. *For information on The American Cancer Society, contact 800-ACS-2345; Web site:* www.cancer.org.]

Hi, I'm Jane

Standing in the middle of the gymnasium, I faced the Special Olympics athletes—wall-to-wall bleachers filled with energy and excitement. The incessant chatter and constant movement was interrupted only occasionally when an athlete would break loose and dash across the room. Their enthusiasm could not be stifled—this was their special day.

I was an inexperienced high-school junior. When I signed up to volunteer as a team leader, I had no idea what it would entail. Standing there completely baffled, I surveyed the chaos, wondering how the Games could ever be organized.

As I waited anxiously for my team of girls to be called, a small mob of schoolgirls, wearing matching Special Olympics T-shirts, closed in on me. Each girl had a distinctive gait. Some moved as if they were going to attack me, while others had difficulty putting one foot in front of the other.

One young woman bounced clumsily toward me with such liveliness, gravity seemed to have no effect. Strands of brown hair swayed back and forth in front of her blue eyes with every step, and a huge smile warmed her full, freckled face.

I felt paralyzed as I realized she was headed directly toward me. She stood next to me, placed her arm on my shoulder, and said, "Hi, I'm Jane."

"Hi, I'm Sandy."

Then, moving even closer, she said, "Hi, Sandy. I'm Jane."

Smiling, I asked, "How are you, Jane?"

"Fine," she said, her gaze focused on my face.

Just then the whistle announced the first event— a basketball-dribbling relay. The girls lined up behind the starting line, ready to dribble the ball to the cone at the other end of the court, and back again.

At the sound of the bell, my first team member picked up the ball and put as much energy as she could into her task. Bounce . . . Catch . . . Step. Bounce . . . Catch . . . Step.

"Come on! You can do it!" I yelled. Bounce . . . Catch . . . Step . . . Smile. Crossing the finish line, she passed the ball to the next girl, who took off.

"Go! Go!" I screamed.

Handling the basketball with confidence as she zigzagged down the court and back, she passed the ball to Jane.

"Watch, Sandy. I can do this." As Jane attempted to dribble, her bouncing gait kept her from controlling the ball. With almost every step, Jane's foot would kick the ball, sending it flying across the gymnasium.

"You can do it, Jane!" I yelled.

Her smile never faded as she happily retrieved the ball and resumed where she had left off. As if the ball had a mind of its own, it took two more trips across the gymnasium before Jane was back at my side.

"I did good, didn't I, Sandy?" Jane asked proudly.

"Yes, you did fine."

Then, as if she needed reminding, Jane once again placed her arm on my shoulder and declared, "I'm Jane."

"Yes, you are Jane," I responded, with a reassuring smile. This game continued throughout the other events.

I admired Jane's zeal and her extraordinary attitude. She faced each challenge optimistically. Nothing fazed her. Nothing could erase the beautiful smile from her face. Each setback seemed to fuel her exuberant joy.

At the end of the day, each athlete received a ribbon. No one on my team came in first—it wasn't important. The only thing that mattered was a job well-done and contented hearts. These girls were no different than any Olympian in Barcelona or Sydney; they had given their all, and now they looked at their ribbons with as much pride as a gold medalist.

"See! I did good!" Jane announced as she proudly showed me her ribbons.

It was time to go. Jane stood by my side and propped her arm on my shoulder. "Bye, Sandy. I had fun. I did good, didn't I?"

"You did your best. I am so proud of you," I answered, looking into her distant eyes.

Digging a piece of folded paper and small pencil from the pocket of her shorts, Jane handed it to me. "Can I have your address, Sandy?" she asked graciously.

"Sure," I said, jotting it down.

"I could write you, and then you could write me, huh? That would be good."

"Yes, I would like that."

All but one of the girls walked out of my life. Jane and I continued to communicate through letters and phone calls. We talked about comic books and baby dolls—trivial things to me, but to her, prized possessions.

A year later, as the Special Olympics approached, Jane wrote, "Can you come watch me in the Special Olympics?"

That year, I went as an observer. I stood next to Jane's mother during the floor-hockey competition. Occasionally I shouted, "Good, Jane, good!"

"I'm glad you came," her mother said. "You mean so much to my daughter. She enjoys your letters. When she asked if she could invite you, I said yes, but I also told her I didn't think you would come."

Looking at her in disbelief, I thought, *Why would you assume such a thing?* I replied, "Jane and I have developed a close relationship this year. She is my friend, and I'm happy to come." Pausing for a moment, I smiled and added, "Besides, I love Jane."

"I know you do, dear," her mother said. "It's just that . . . she's been disappointed so many times before."

The game ended, and Jane ran over to me. "I did good, didn't I, Sandy?"

Hugging her, I said, "Yes you did, Jane!" We walked to lunch, arm in arm, and then said our good-byes. That was the last time I saw her. Although we corresponded during most of my college years, the letters eventually stopped.

A few years later, I sent a letter to my special friend. I wanted her to come to my wedding. I pictured her saying, "You did good, Sandy," cheering me on like I had done for her. Unfortunately, the letter was returned—"No such person at this address." I felt heartbroken.

Because of Jane, I now find joy in the little things. I know that winning isn't really all that important. When life sends me in an unexpected direction, I now get right back on course and start again.

Every once in a while, though, I can feel her arm rest on my shoulder as she says, "Hi, I'm Jane."

Sandra J. Bunch

[EDITORS' NOTE: *For information on the Special Olympics, Inc., contact 1325 G Street, N.W., Suite 500, Washington, DC 20005; 202-628-3630; fax: 202-824-0200; Web site:* www. specialolympics.org.]

THE FAMILY CIRCUS® By Bil Keane

© BKi

"My doll doesn't do anything.
She just soaks up love."

$\overline{9}$

ON WISDOM

Wisdom begins in wonder.

Socrates

Thanks, Mom

While undergoing treatment in 1991 for throat cancer, my mother had to have a tube inserted into her trachea in order to breathe. Instead of breathing through healthy, moist nasal passages, which filter and warm the air, Mom's tracheotomy was exposed to the cold, dry air of winter, causing her secretions to dry up and her breathing to become blocked. She was instructed to keep the area moist at all times.

One day Mom suddenly began clawing at her neck and chest. She couldn't breathe. Her hardened secretions caused a blockage in her chest. Although emergency help was summoned, she lost consciousness. Mom remained in a coma until she was taken off of life support a few days later.

The sudden death of a loved one is a devastating event. Questions of "why" are natural. I felt cheated, especially since I had given my mother her first grandchild only seven months before. I prayed constantly, asking God, *Why did this have to happen? What do you want me to learn from all this?*

Three years and another child later, I managed to keep myself busy with my kids and volunteer efforts. One of my favorite projects was delivering Meals on Wheels to shut-ins with another mom from the Junior Woman's Club. We had a smooth system—one mom stayed in the car with the kids and organized the meals for each delivery, while the other packed up the food from the coolers and brought it to the house.

January 1994 brought record snowfalls, and much of the snow was too frozen to be cleared away. Normally I curled up like a cat indoors during cold winter weather, but that day I looked forward to delivering meals.

As I prepared to leave, my partner called and told me she couldn't go with me because her child was sick. "Call them and tell them they need to find a substitute driver," she urged. "No," I responded, "I'll be okay."

When I arrived at the church kitchen, I faced my first dilemma. The parking lot was covered with ice, and I would have to bring my children downstairs with me to pick up the food, instead of having them wait in the car with my driving partner.

As I escorted my children, one at a time, we made it in safely. Then the second dilemma occurred. *How do I get two children, one who can't walk yet, and two heavy coolers up the stairs, across the icy parking lot and into the car?*

Within seconds I said, "C'mon, Karen. I'll hold Maggie, and you can push the cooler while I pull. You're the caboose, okay?" It took fifteen minutes, but we made it up the steps. After skating across the parking lot, I strapped each child into the car and loaded the coolers. As I finally slid behind the wheel, I let out a long, shuddering sigh of relief.

On the way to our first stop, I explained to Karen what the Meals on Wheels program was about. "These are people who can't get out and enjoy a good, hot meal at lunch time." As we pulled into the first driveway, a new house on our route, Karen asked, "Can I come in?"

Who will watch the children while I deliver the meal? I decided to leave them in the warm car, in sight of the door, and decline any invitations to come in. It was enjoyable visiting the folks, but I had to make it speedy. "No, Sweetie," I said, "you get to guard the food, okay?"

"Okay, Mommy."

Going as fast as I could, being careful not to slip on the ice, I knocked on the old wooden door. When the woman opened the door, I almost dropped the food. I couldn't believe my eyes.

"Come in," the woman croaked hoarsely as she held her hand over the tube in her throat.

At first, I stared at her, shaking my head in an attempt to clear my vision. "How are you today?" I asked cheerfully. I quickly looked away, avoiding eye contact. I didn't want her to see my tears.

"Well, I'm okay, but this weather doesn't help my throat. I wish I knew what to do for this old tube." Fumbling in her robe pocket for a handkerchief, she coughed—an all-too-familiar sandpaper-like cough.

"I know exactly what to do," I said. "Fill the teakettle with water and simmer it on your stove. Keep it going and keep breathing in the steam. Open the collar of your robe and let the moisture in about every five or ten minutes while you're awake."

Looking astonished, the woman inquired, "Do you think that will help?"

Tearfully I said, "Believe me . . . it will help you." Then I explained that my children were alone and waiting in the car for me.

"Wait!" she bellowed coarsely. With her free hand, she reached into a basket on the table and pulled out a small package of cookies. "Give these to your children. They're so good to let their Mommy do this work. I bet their grandma is real proud of them."

My face lit up. "Yes, she is."

I made my way back to the car and showed Karen the cookies. She was delighted with the gift, and I felt grateful for the encounter. My prayers had been answered.

Liz Murad

[EDITORS' NOTE: *For information on Meals-On-Wheels Association of America, contact 1414 Prince Street, Suite 302, Alexandria, VA 22314; Web site:* www.givemeals.com.]

"It's my latest and greatest invention!
I call it 'meals on wheels.'"

Twenty-One

The last golden rays of the afternoon sun filtered through the windows of Four West, the oncology wing of The Children's Hospital in Denver. Walking down the hall, I could hear cartoons on televisions, Disney videos, a baby crying and the constant beeping of IV machines pumping cancer-killing drugs into the children's veins.

Surely there must be something different and fun I can do with Danny to get his mind, and mine, off being sick, I thought. We had played at least a "zillion" games of Connect Four, knocked the Jenga tower over almost as often, and I didn't even want to think about how many games of tic-tac-toe we had played.

Our son, Danny, was diagnosed with Ewing's sarcoma, a form of bone cancer. He was in the hospital for his tenth round of chemo. It took most of the day to slowly drip into his arm. *What can I do to make the time pass faster?* I asked myself again.

"All right, turkey, come on, get out of bed. Bring your IV pole. You're wanted in the lounge."

Who was this barging into Danny's room? Couldn't they see he was sick? My maternal protective defense mechanism was ready to do battle with this intruder.

Opening the door, the little old gray-haired lady, who could have been anyone's grandmother, entered. Indeed, I learned that Miss Sally, a volunteer, viewed all of the children on the ward as her grandchildren. She seemed so petite and almost frail. *Where did she get such a commanding voice? I wondered. Why does she see the need to use it on these poor sick children?*

"Come on, Danny. Your buddies are waiting. There's a hot game of Twenty-One going on in the teen lounge. They need you to join them." Miss Sally didn't give Danny a chance to protest. She ushered him out the door and down the hall they went, her pink jacket flapping in the breeze. Turning back to me, she added with a wink, "This is a 'guys only' game, but you can watch from the window."

A group of ten- to twelve-year-olds had finished a round of pool and were starting a game of blackjack just as Danny arrived. As they sat around the table, Robby's prized collection of baseball cards spilled around his feet. Joe described winning the midget car race last weekend. Danny told tales of tracking wild animals through the woods. Meanwhile, Jason (his friends called him the "Gambler") raked in all the poker chips. He reigned as the undisputed Twenty-One Champion.

All the boys faced similar challenges as Danny. Robby had ALL (acute lymphocytic leukemia); Joe, Hodgkin's disease; and Jason wore a patch over the eye he had lost to a neuroblastoma. Computerized IV pumps fed each of them a wide assortment of chemotherapeutic drugs. They sported the same hairdo—the "chemo cut."

Miss Sally approached me in the hall. Laying her hand upon my shoulder, she apologized, "I hope you will forgive me for being so brusque back there." Sighing deeply, she continued, "Sometimes you just have to 'play the heavy' to get these kids going. Once together, they start having fun. That somehow gives them the inner strength to fight their disease."

Looking back into the lounge, I saw a group of once-active, tree-climbing boys suddenly thrust into a grown-up world of facing a life-threatening illness chronicled with frightening tests, painful procedures, isolation from friends and arduous rehabilitation. Through the commanding efforts of Miss Sally, the "Pink Lady," they were unconsciously learning to face their illnesses by playing games and having fun.

Most adults set boundaries on what is fun and what is not. Cancer and having fun are not compatible for many people on this planet. Miss Sally was teaching these boys how to boost their immune systems by making the most of their time together and overcoming their grueling circumstances by having fun.

I wish I could say my medical background equipped me to teach Danny and his friends about dealing with their illnesses. Far from it. Miss Sally touched my life. She taught me, a mother and registered nurse, more about life and dealing with illness than anything I studied in nursing school.

Today, twelve years later, Joe still races cars, and Danny just graduated from college with a degree in biology. Sadly, Robby and Jason never survived their illnesses.

Whenever I see a group of guys playing cards together, I think back over that scene in the teen lounge at The Children's Hospital. Once again I hear Miss Sally proclaim, "Come on, turkey, get out of bed. There's a hot game of Twenty-One going on in the teen lounge."

Donna McDonnall

Bless Every Evelyn!

Most say that as you get old, you have to give up things. I think you get old because you give up things.

Senator Theodore Green

Evelyn was ninety-two when I came to know her. As the new accountant for a museum in Fresno, California, I inherited a cadre of volunteers assigned to "office functions."

Evelyn was the queen of these devoted ladies, leaving the rest in the dust, not only in volunteer years, but life years. Although frail and tiny, she had a feistiness that was legendary. Every Tuesday, without fail, she would steer her ancient Plymouth through the streets of Fresno to the museum for her weekly dose of culture.

I was hard-pressed to find tasks to keep Evelyn busy. Math skills were not her forte. She could not operate a calculator, and the numbers on accounting ledger sheets were too small for her to read. She couldn't type on an electric typewriter, let alone a word processor, and her lack of coordination and deteriorating eyesight prevented her from putting labels on file folders. Alphabetizing invoices seemed like a good assignment for her, but her concept of the alphabet varied from the rest of us. Most any task I assigned was either too difficult or had to be redone by another volunteer.

I'm all business. Museums might be nonprofit enterprises, but they still should be run with an eye toward the bottom line. I saw the volunteers as nonhuman assets, pairs of hands waiting to perform useful work at no cost to the organization. Evelyn taught me how wrong I was.

Before I learned that lesson, her weekly arrival frustrated me. She'd show up for her three-hour shift, unable to perform "useful" work, taking up space, chattering constantly with the staff and other volunteers, making extra work for others by not getting her assignment done correctly. I would give her a box of pennies from the donation box and ask her to wrap them into fifty-cent rolls. Even with a counter, her rolls contained forty-seven, forty-nine, fifty-three, whatever, number of pennies. As she left each Tuesday, I would dump out rolls and save the pennies for the next shift.

"Busy work," I fumed in my office. "What a waste!" Each Tuesday afternoon, Evelyn rolled up in that blue wreck of a car, and I'd feel a headache coming on. I began to dread Tuesdays.

Then one week, Evelyn didn't show up for her shift. Oftentimes, volunteers didn't call in to let us know they weren't coming. But when the following Tuesday arrived without Evelyn, someone called her home to check on her.

Evelyn had been in a car accident. It was her fault, and she was okay but still stiff and sore. She lost her driver's license. No one realized what a psychological blow this was to her. She saw the museum as family, like a church almost, a major social outlet in her life. None of us, especially "business me," realized this.

She became depressed, called us frequently to continue

the contact, but eventually even the calls dropped off. Finally, a few staffers went to her home and were shocked at what they found.

As a tiny person, Evelyn could ill afford to lose the amount of weight she had lost. She had cloistered herself in her small, modest home. Since she couldn't drive any longer, she rarely got out. Her only child, a daughter, lived in another state. She made a brief visit after the accident but returned to her home weeks before. Evelyn was fading fast.

That's when the museum folks went into action.

We connected Evelyn to various social services for other assistance. But every Tuesday, without fail, we took turns bringing her over for her volunteer shift. She was always dressed in her volunteer outfits, ready and waiting for the outing, the focus of her life. I let go of my drive for productivity and gave her tasks that made her feel useful and needed, regardless of their impact on the museum's operation. She thrived as the center of attention.

It was then I realized volunteers aren't mere cogs in wheels. They're there because they want to be, not because they have to be. Their sense of belonging and contributing is equally, if not more, important than the actual work that needs to be done.

After Evelyn died at the age of ninety-seven, the museum closed up operations while our staff attended her funeral. She taught us all, and particularly me, that volunteers are the soul of an organization, and the body of an institution is just an empty shell without the soul. Bless every Evelyn!

Sally Fouhse

Synergetic Souls

The harsh clamor of my alarm roused me from placid slumber. Exhausted from working late the night before, a million tasks awaited me at home. All of this, combined with the fact that it was Labor Day, made it especially difficult to drag myself out of bed, but thankfully I did.

This was Monday, my regular volunteer day at the Bailey-Boushay House, an adult day-health and residential care facility for people living with AIDS and other life-threatening illnesses. When I first arrived, it was unusually quiet. After checking in with two different floors, I thought about heading home.

Just then one of the nurses came up to me and spoke of a patient who was having an especially hard time. "I can't stay with Igor right now, but could you go and sit by his side and calm him as best you can?"

"Sure. It doesn't look like much is going on this morning anyway." As I turned to walk down the hall, the nurse added, "By the way, I think you should know that Igor is a Russian concert pianist, and he is dying." I nodded silently and proceeded on my way.

As a volunteer, my first priority was to provide companionship, as well as to run errands for the residents and take them to their doctors' appointments. Each Monday brought a unique set of experiences.

When I walked into his room, I noticed that Igor was semicomatose. As I sat beside him, holding his hand and talking to him, I didn't feel as if I were making a connection. When I decided to move my chair to the other side of his bed, I found a letter sitting on the night table, so I decided to read it to him.

The letter was spiritual and heartfelt. It mentioned how much joy Igor and his music had brought to this world. His friend also reminded Igor how much he adored Beethoven, Bach and Schubert, and how Igor would soon be playing the piano for the angels in heaven.

All of a sudden Igor's eyes began to open, so I read the letter again. Then, without even thinking twice, I stood up, placed a CD in the stereo and pushed play. Beautiful piano music played as I placed my hand on his chest. It seemed like a soothing, peaceful and centering gesture.

Igor's chest muscles were tight and his breathing labored. "Igor, it's okay to go. It's time," I whispered. Softly I said, "Relax, take deep breaths and feel the music." Much to my surprise, he did. Igor's muscles calmed, and his breathing slowed. Then, like a proud coach, I said, "Wonderful. Do it again . . . Perfect!" Igor had a shining sparkle in his eyes.

I guess you have to be somewhat of a perfectionist to be a concert pianist, I deduced. Igor liked being perfect. It almost seemed as though he were performing his final concert. I continued speaking positive words of encouragement. At one point, I thought he might like me to place my hand on his forehead, but as I moved my hand, he reached up and brought it back to his chest.

At last, Igor took his last breath. I waited and asked, "Are you there yet?" When he started to come back, I said, "No . . . no," as I patted his chest. "You made it. I am proud of you." Then Igor let go.

I stayed with him about ten minutes and collected myself. I couldn't believe I had it in me to do something like that. Our souls had connected. I felt overwhelmed by the power of the human spirit.

As a nurse in a childbirth center, I'm accustomed to guiding women through labor almost every day. I surprised myself by saying the exact same things to Igor that I usually say to women in labor.

As I sat by Igor's side, I contemplated how these intense and magical experiences of birth and death are similar. From the moment of birth to the moment of death, we all need encouragement, love and the human touch.

Malinda Carlile

Top Ten List of Things a Volunteer Should Know

10. List your dreams and talents. Where do you excel? What have you always dreamed of doing? What do you really enjoy or would like to try? Is there a way to prepare, learn or try it as a volunteer?

9. Pick your duration. One size doesn't fit all, just like volunteer opportunities. I've found that volunteer projects come in three sizes: one-time, short-term, and "whad'ya doing for the rest of your life?"

8. Make a commitment. Sometimes a volunteer project is an acquired taste. Give yourself a chance to have good days, bad days and in-between days. If after three months you see no redeeming value, then at least you can feel you gave it a fair chance.

7. Watch and learn. Seasoned volunteers can teach you the "ropes" so to speak. Observe them and follow their lead. Have confidence in the knowledge that you are capable and trainable. Balance that confidence with a dose of humility, also.

6. Ability, need and desire. You must have the ability to do the service, there must be a need for the service,

and you must have the desire to be of service.

5. Unpaid doesn't mean unprofessional. "Anything worth doing is worth doing well." All that we do, we need to do with our most sincere effort. Anything less is a disservice to those we are helping and ultimately to ourselves.

4. Balance is key. Priorities add balance. Charity begins at home—keep the priorities straight. Balance out family, work and volunteering. If you become overwhelmed, stress will set in and you won't enjoy doing anything.

3. Stand back and admire. Sometimes people forget to say "thank you," so you will need to reward yourself. Be proud of your accomplishments—take the time to smell the roses, hear the raindrops on the pane, feel the snow on your nose, taste the cool clear water.

2. Find a home or make a change. Are you stale or still fresh? Are you learning, enthusiastic or approaching burnout? Check yourself periodically and act upon your honest answers.

1. Have fun! Life has enough drudgery; volunteering shouldn't be one of them. Giving of yourself should be uplifting and joyful. We are at our best when we learn, grow, play and serve each other with love and respect.

Donald Patrick Dunn

"Hello, I'm Matilda, a volunteer librarian. Our featured book of the millenium is 'From Here to Eternity.'"

Reprinted by permission of Charles Markman.

Who Is Jack Canfield?

Jack Canfield is one of America's leading experts in the development of human potential and personal effectiveness. He is both a dynamic, entertaining keynote speaker and a highly sought-after trainer. Jack has a wonderful ability to inform and inspire audiences toward increased levels of self-esteem and peak performance.

He is the author and narrator of several bestselling audio- and videocassette programs, including *Self-Esteem and Peak Performance, How to Build High Self-Esteem, Self-Esteem in the Classroom* and *Chicken Soup for the Soul—Live.* He is regularly seen on television shows such as *Good Morning America, 20/20* and *NBC Nightly News.* Jack has co-authored over fifty books, including the *Chicken Soup for the Soul* series, *Dare to Win, The Aladdin Factor, 100 Ways to Build Self-Concept in the Classroom, Heart at Work* and *The Power of Focus: How to Hit Your Business, Personal and Financial Targets with Absolute Certainty.*

Jack is a regularly featured inspirational and motivational speaker for professional associations, school districts, government agencies, churches, hospitals, nonprofit organizations, sales organizations and corporations. His clients have included the American Heart Association, the Children's Miracle Network, the Boys Club of America, Reading Fun, the American Dental Association, the American Management Association, AT&T, Campbell's Soup, Clairol, Domino's Pizza, GE, ITT, Hartford Insurance, Johnson & Johnson, the Million Dollar Round Table, NCR, New England Telephone, Re/Max, Scott Paper, TRW and Virgin Records.

Jack conducts an annual eight-day life-changing workshop to build self-esteem and enhance peak performance. It attracts educators, counselors, parents, corporate trainers, professional speakers, ministers and anyone else interested in transforming their lives and teaching those skills to others.

For further information about Jack's books, tapes and training programs, or to schedule him for a presentation, please contact:

Self-Esteem Seminars
P.O. Box 30880
Santa Barbara, CA 93130
phone: 805-563-2935 • fax: 805-563-2945
Web site: *www.jackcanfield.com*

Who Is Mark Victor Hansen?

Mark Victor Hansen is a professional speaker who, in the last twenty years, has made over four thousand presentations to more than two million people in thirty-two countries. His presentations cover sales excellence and strategies; personal empowerment and development; and how to triple your income and double your time off.

Mark has spent a lifetime dedicated to his mission of making a profound and positive difference in people's lives. Throughout his career, he has inspired hundreds of thousands of people to create a more powerful and purposeful future for themselves while stimulating the sale of billions of dollars worth of goods and services.

Mark is a prolific writer and has authored *Future Diary, How to Achieve Total Prosperity* and *The Miracle of Tithing*. He is coauthor of the *Chicken Soup for the Soul* series, *Dare to Win, The Aladdin Factor* and *The Power of Focus* (all with Jack Canfield) and *The Master Motivator* (with Joe Batten).

Mark has also produced a complete library of personal empowerment audio- and videocassette programs that have enabled his listeners to recognize and use their innate abilities in their business and personal lives. His message has made him a popular television and radio personality, with appearances on ABC, NBC, CBS, HBO, PBS and CNN. He has also appeared on the cover of numerous magazines, including *Success, Entrepreneur* and *Changes*.

Mark is a big man with a heart and spirit to match—an inspiration to all who seek to better themselves.

For further information about Mark write:

MVH & Associates
P.O. Box 7665
Newport Beach, CA 92658
phone: 714-759-9304 or 800-433-2314
fax: 714-722-6912
Web site: *www.chickensoup.com*

Who Is Arline McGraw Oberst?

Arline McGraw Oberst is a professional speaker, trainer and author. She has been a spokesperson for Prevent Child Abuse—New Jersey for more than five years. Educating the population of New Jersey on how to prevent child abuse in all its forms has become a passion for her.

While working with volunteers at Prevent Child Abuse—New Jersey, she noticed that stories about volunteers read more like a report to the media than a true experience. Arline is an avid reader of inspirational stories and quotes, and she wanted to create a book that was filled with the heart and soul of volunteering.

Volunteering as a staff member in 1997 for Jack Canfield's Facilitator Skills Seminar, Arline received permission to coauthor *Chicken Soup for the Volunteer's Soul*. She describes the next four years working on the book as a "labor of love."

In 1997, Arline began her own training and consulting company, Lifetime Resources for Women, Inc. She developed programs modeled after Jack Canfield's work on self-esteem. She is a member of the National Speakers Association and GreatWomenSpeakers.com.

Arline has always been a volunteer in her community of Essex County, volunteering for her church, homeschool association, political campaigns and service clubs. She continues in whatever way possible to serve others. Recently, Arline volunteered her speaking expertise as the keynote speaker at the New Jersey Governor's Conference on Volunteerism.

Arline has been married for more than forty years to her high-school sweetheart, Russell. They have two wonderful adult children, Russ Jr., who resides in Toms River, New Jersey, and Donna Jean Hanning of Virginia Beach, Virginia. Both Donna and Russ Jr. are very active in volunteering.

For further information about Arline's keynote speaking and trainings, you may contact her by e-mail at *ArlineO@aol.com* or visit her Web site at *www.ArlineOberst.com*.

Who Is John T. Boal?

John T. Boal is the Western Regional Manager for The Advertising Council, a private, nonprofit organization based in New York. Now celebrating its sixtieth anniversary, the Ad Council is the nation's leading producer of public-service announcements. Familiar campaigns include "Friends Don't Let Friends Drive Drunk," "Take a Bite Out of Crime" and "I Am an American," among many others. In 2001, Ad Council campaigns graciously received over $1.7 billion in donated media.

While an advertising executive in Pittsburgh, John moonlighted as a beer vendor at Three Rivers Stadium. There, a chance meeting with his hero, Pirates rightfielder Roberto Clemente, helped shape his first book.

After returning home to California in 1976, he became a sitcom writer at Paramount Studios; a Mr. Mom; an independent journalist with over five hundred credits in such publications as *Los Angeles Times* and *Modern Maturity;* and operated a successful public-relations consultancy for fifteen years.

In 1998, John published *Be a Global Force of One!* A national menu for visionary volunteers, the book is dedicated to Roberto Clemente who died as a volunteer trying to deliver earthquake supplies to Nicaragua on December 31, 1972.

A low-key activist, John has sponsored elementary-, middle- and high-school volunteer essay contests and donated over thirty pints of blood to the American Red Cross. He also conducts pro bono public relations for Knightsbridge International and Mentoring A Touch From Above, and is the volunteer outreach coordinator for a local chapter of the National Federation of the Blind.

John passionately feels if more people would drift away from our entertainment- and sports-driven culture toward "making those considered least, those considered most" in our society, then the everyday stewards of this new century could leave the most significant legacy in the history of mankind. Contact John at:

The Ad Council, Inc.
150 S. Glenoaks Blvd., #8054
Burbank, CA 91502
e-mail: *JBoal@AdCouncil.org*
or *JBoal202@cs.com*

Who Is Tom Lagana?

Tom Lagana is a professional speaker, author, professional engineer and was recognized in the 1994 Jefferson Awards in Delaware. He is a professional member of the National Speakers Association. With more than thirty-five years of experience in the corporate world, Tom has worked with successful teams throughout North America, Europe and the Far East.

Influenced by his mother who volunteered as a registered nurse for the American Red Cross, Tom's volunteering activities as a teenager started with fundraising projects for his school. In his adult years, he helped solicit funding from corporations and employees for the United Way of Delaware. Tom has volunteered extensively in the prison system throughout the United States, working with inmates. He is also a narrator for the Delaware Division for the Visually Impaired and a volunteer in the emergency room at Wilmington Hospital.

Tom is a graduate of Villanova University. He attended Jack Canfield's 1997 Facilitation Skills Seminar in Santa Barbara, California, and returned in 1998 to serve as an assistant. He has facilitated more than one thousand personal-development and management presentations nationally and internationally.

He is coauthor of the 1993 textbook, *Guidelines for Safe Automation of Chemical Processes* and coauthor of *Chicken Soup for the Prisoner's Soul*.

Tom presents keynotes and seminars to corporations and organizations. He and his wife, Laura, have been happily married for more than thirty years. They have two grown sons and a grandson. Laura and Tom work with the coauthors of other upcoming *Chicken Soup for the Soul* books.

For more information about Tom's training programs, and to schedule him for a keynote presentation, please contact:

Success Solutions
P.O. Box 7816
Wilmington, DE 19803
phone: 302-475-4825
e-mail: *TomLagana@yahoo.com*
Web site: *www.TomLagana.com*

Who Is Laura Lagana?

Laura Lagana is an author, speaker and registered nurse who delights in sharing real-life, personal experiences and healthy inspiration.

Since the age of fifteen, she has been a volunteer. During her junior year in high school, a friend persuaded Laura to volunteer as a hospital candy striper. Torn between pursuing a career in nursing or journalism, she thought the hospital volunteer experience would help her decide.

Four years later, she graduated from the Bryn Mawr Hospital School of Nursing and began working in the intensive-care unit of a Wilmington, Delaware area hospital. Within months, Laura met and married her soul mate, Tom.

In early 1997, after years of frequent corporate travel, Laura and Tom became business partners. Together they attended Jack Canfield's facilitation skills seminar in California in July—the catalyst that transformed both their lives.

Following her lifelong passion for writing, she began assisting Tom in his work as coauthor of *Chicken Soup for the Prisoner's Soul* in August 1997. After raising two sons and welcoming a grandson, Laura savors the privilege of working with her best friend, Tom.

Laura's stories have been published in *Chicken Soup for the Couple's Soul, Chicken Soup for the Prisoner's Soul, Chicken Soup for the Nurse's Soul* and *Chicken Soup for the Soul Christmas Treasury*. In addition, she is author and editor of *Touched by Angels of Mercy*, an inspirational anthology about nurses, patients and caregivers.

She is grateful for her volunteer experiences as surgical liaison for Christiana Care Health System, medical narrator for the Division for the Visually Impaired, facilitator for the American Cancer Society (Skin Cancer Prevention Program), speaker for the Arthritis Foundation, cantor and choir member, lunchtime parochial school nurse, classroom reading aide and library assistant.

For further information about Laura, please contact:

Success Solutions
P.O. Box 7816
Wilmington, DE 19803
e-mail: *LauraALagana@yahoo.com*
Web site: *www.LauraLagana.com*

Contributors

Candace F. Abbott is the founder of Delmarva Christian Writers' Fellowship. She is author of the book, *Fruit-Bearer*. Candy and her husband Drew are owners of Fruit-Bearer Publishing. She may be reached at P.O. Box 777, Georgetown, DE 19947; fax 302-856-7742; e-mail: *dabbott@dmv.com*; Web site: *www.fruitbearer.com*.

Mary Drew Adams is a wife, mother and grandmother. She lives near Gettysburg, Pennsylvania. She enjoys golfing, volunteering and writing. She has had short fiction and nonfiction published in several publications, including *Reader's Digest* and *Ideals*.

Sarah Ainslie, a former businesswoman and fiber artist, lives in St. Albert, Alberta, Canada, with her husband Gordon and her service dog, Tagalong Tickles. She has multiple sclerosis and uses a power wheelchair. She is a graduate of Newman Theological College and volunteers in pastoral care and a dog-assisted therapy program. Sarah and Tickles are also enjoying the challenge and the fun of the dog sport of agility.

George S. J. Anderson is a registered nurse of twenty-five years who has many experiences with oncology patients. He is the husband of a breast-cancer survivor and facilitates a support group for other husbands and significant others. He is a writer, poet and artist. He illustrated and published a book about the realities of breast cancer. He may be reached by e-mail at *CryTearEon@aol.com*.

Joan Wester Anderson is a magazine writer and book author for about thirty years. Her book, *Where Angels Walk*, was on the *New York Times* bestseller list for more than a year. Her latest offering is *Forever Young*, the biography of Loretta Young. She may be reached by e-mail at *angelwak@earthlink.net*; Web site: *www.mcs.net/~angelwak/home.html*.

Charlene Baldridge is a grieving mother, freelance writer, critic and essayist who specializes in the arts. She lives in San Diego. Now sixty-something, she's working at her seventh career. She may be contacted by e-mail at *charb81@cox.net*.

Beth Barrett was a successful trial attorney for eighteen years until an accident disabled her, allowing her to find her life purpose: to inspire and motivate others to reach their full potential. She is authoring a book entitled, *You Are Not Your Body: Lessons on Living a Joyous and Fulfilling Life for the Physically Challenged*. She may be reached by e-mail at *babarracuda@worldnet.att.net*.

Victoria Harnish Benson has published numerous articles, columns and stories on the Internet and has written a column for an alumni magazine for twenty-five years. Her first book, *To No Man's Glory*, her husband's memoirs of the Holocaust and spiritual healing, was released in February 2000. She may be reached at e-mail: *WrytRyt@aol.com*; P.O. Box 4211, Medford, OR 97501.

Chris Bibbo is the Campus Chapters and Youth Programs Manager for Habitat for Humanity International's West and Mountain States regions. He trains and supports Habitat's high school and college chapters, preparing students to be leaders in the effort to eliminate substandard housing. A native of Somers, New York, Chris currently resides in Denver, Colorado, and can be reached at *cbibbo@aol.com*.

Nancy Blain was born in a small town in southern Alberta, Canada, called Didsbury. Affected by the drug thalidomide, life has been character-building. With the love of friends and family, she graduated from college and university. Her chosen profession is Volunteer Management. She is passionate about travel, music, writing, shopping and friends. She can be reached by e-mail at *nancy_blain@hotmail.com*.

Doc Blakely, CSP, CPAE, is a professional speaker, humorist, fiddler, holder of every major award given by the National Speakers Association, and is in the speaker's Hall of Fame. Doc and Mike Blakely are professional performers at conventions throughout America. For more about them, see *www.platform professionals.com* and *www.mikeblakely.com*.

Sheila A. Bolin is the head tennis professional at Orange Lake Resort & Country Club in Orlando, Florida, and founder of Tennis with a Different Swing. A coauthor of two books for law enforcement, she is working on a project dealing with the use of a vaccine to mitigate swan deaths caused by botulism. Sheila can be reached at *Bolin.S@att.net*.

Wynell Glanton Britton is a volunteer for hospice in Athens, Alabama. Gardening has always been the love of her life, and she continues to give to the community through the bounty of her garden.

Margaret Buckingham is an event planner who initiates and organizes programs and then manages entire fund-raising campaigns, social events and volunteer functions. Her clients' areas of expertise include arts and culture, civic affairs, education, environment, health and social services. While her dad, Ed, saved the Opening Ceremonies, Margaret was Manager of Volunteer Services for the 1984 Los Angeles Olympic Organizing Committee.

Sandra J. Bunch lives in Kansas City, Missouri with her husband, Rick, and two daughters. She is a homemaker and freelance writer previously published by DaySpring Greeting Cards. They are currently attending Midwestern Baptist Theological Seminary in preparation for ministry. Sandra can be reached by e-mail at *APensPal@aol.com*.

Bill Canty's cartoons have appeared in many national magazines, including the *Saturday Evening Post, Good Housekeeping, Better Homes and Gardens, Woman's World, National Review* and *Medical Economics*. His syndicated feature *All About Town* runs in thirty-five newspapers. Bill can be reached at P.O. Box 1053, S. Wellfleet, MA 02663; phone and fax 508-349-7549; e-mail: *wcanty@attbi.com*; Web site: *www.reuben.org/Canty*.

Malinda Carlile is a labor and delivery nurse who lives in Seattle, Washington. Her volunteer work includes supporting individuals diagnosed with HIV at the Bailey Boucher House in Seattle. In addition, she participates in Operation Smile, an organization providing reconstructive sugery and related health services to children in developing countries. E-mail Malinda at *mcarlile38@ hotmail.com.*

Jenna Cassell is a media producer, author, consultant, educator, interpreter and founder of Pathwalk Productions, a company specializing in inspirational media. She has received more than twenty media production awards and is included in multiple *Who's Who* directories. Jenna can be reached by e-mail at *jencass@san.rr.com.*

Nansie Chapman has a master of arts degree in clinical psychology and is the managing editor and copublisher of *Santa Barbara Family Life* magazine at Web site: *www.sbfamilylife.com.* She can be reached at SBFL, P.O. Box 4867, Santa Barbara, CA 93104; 805-965-4545; e-mail: *nansie@sbfamilylife.com.*

Tara Church cofounded Tree Musketeers at age eight and grew it from grassroots to the nation's leading youth environmental organization with campaigns that empower millions to become leaders of community change. Tara currently attends Harvard Law School where she continues her commitment to public service and the promise of youth leadership. She can be reached through her Web site at *Tara@TreeMusketeers.org.*

Charles W. Colson was a well-known public figure, convicted and imprisoned for seven months because of his involvement in the Watergate scandal as Nixon's Special Counsel. A year after his release he started a prison ministry. In 1993, he was awarded the Templeton Prize for Progress in Religion. He is now a nationally recognized speaker and founder of Prison Fellowship® Web site: *www.prisonfellowship.org.*

Casey Crandall is a student at Randolph High School in New Jersey. She is an active member of her church and a two-year volunteer for the Appalachia Service project. Her outside interests include color guard, skiing, being a hospital volunteer and dance. She can be reached by e-mail at *ASP98PTP@aol.com.*

Rod Delisle is a numeric control programmer in Petersfield, Manitoba, Canada. He was a member of the Rotaract Club of Winnipeg-Charleswood before joining the sponsoring Rotary Club. An award-winning newsletter editor, Rod continues to serve his community through Rotary. He can be reached at *rod_delisle@hotmail.com.*

Donald Patrick Dunn holds a bachelor of science degree from Roberts Wesleyan College in Organizational Management. He enjoys volunteering, motorcycling, scuba diving, kite flying, reading and is a licensed amateur radio operator. He is employed in the nuclear industry and resides in Webster, New York.

Mack Emmert volunteers with HIV-AIDS patients at Christian Care in Wilmington, Delaware. He has also volunteered with Puppeteers of America, the American Cancer Society, and AIDS—Delaware. In 1997, he received the prestigious Legacy Award from AARP and Centrum Silver vitamins, which is given to only four individuals every two years. He may be reached at 302-652-1800.

Tammie L. Failmezger is a writer who penned numerous poems and articles to help manage her grief following Leigh Ann's death. She's also written articles to help other bereaved families who have lost a child. She can be reached by e-mail at *sargefail@hotmail.com*.

Kayte Fairfax is a social researcher, creative writer and social justice activist. Over ten years, she's been involved in various efforts to campaign for human rights and the environment, including work in Thailand and India. She can be reached by e-mail at *kfx6@yahoo.com* or 41 Brendan Beach, Pukerua Bay, Wellington, New Zealand-Aotearoa.

Gary K. Farlow is a native tarheel with a juris doctorate from Heed University. His works have appeared in two poetic anthologies, *Essence of a Dream* and *Best Poems of 1998*. His works, *Conferring with the Moon* and *After Midnight*, two volumes of poetry, may be ordered from Carolyn Jackson, 915 Benjamin Benson St., Greensboro, NC 27406.

Rusty Fischer is a former teacher living in Orlando, Florida. Through his work with local schools and church groups, he enjoys sharing his love of the written word with others. He also enjoys spending time with his beautiful wife of seven years, Martha. He may be reached by e-mail at *writestuff86@yahoo.com*.

Meganne Forbes is the artist who created the beautiful watercolor painting for our book cover. Her artwork can be seen in galleries in Hawaii, collections around the world, and in the Santa Barbara area where she lives. Since graduating from the University of California Santa Barbara in the seventies, she has painted the awesome beauty of nature. Please contact her at 805-684-8357 or e-mail *meggidev@yahoo.com*. Her Web site is *www.meganneforbes.com*.

Sally Fouhse is a business manager for the Santa Barbara Trust for Historic Preservation in Santa Barbara, California. A California native, she has a B. A. from University of California Davis in German and History and is pursuing her C. P. A. license. She happily contributes her Type A personality to the mix of mostly Type B folks in the not-for-profit field. Sally can be reached by e-mail at *sally@sbthp.org*.

Holly Frederickson resides in Victoria, British Columbia, where she facilitates workshops on customer service, public speaking and effective communication skills. She is currently pursuing her love of writing. While her volunteer experience is extensive and varied, she is drawn to projects supporting children. Camp Goodtimes ranks first in her favorites!

Natasha Friend is the director of the Brimmer and May Summer Camp in Chestnut Hill, Massachusetts. She spends her noncamp time writing everything from poetic parodies to song lyrics to children's fiction. Her latest venture, a middle-grade novel titled *Halo Effect*, is currently being revised for publication.

Elaine L. Galit is an award-winning freelance writer. Her published articles and photograph credits include *Writer's Digest, Cowboy Sports and Entertainment, Memorial West Magazine, Houston Maturity Magazine* and *Woman's World.* She is coauthor of *Exploring Houston with Children.* She may be reached at 14354 Memorial Dr., PMB 1087, Houston, TX 77079; e-mail: *EHWC123@aol.com.*

Cynthia Polansky Gallagher is a freelance writer in Annapolis, Maryland, whose work has appeared in various print, video and on-line publications. Her first novel, *Far Above Rubies,* is based on a Holocaust survivor's story that she heard while volunteering with Facing History and Ourselves. She may be reached by e-mail at *Author40@aol.com;* Web site: *http://author40.tripod.com.*

David Garnes is a former high-school English teacher and a longtime academic reference librarian, specializing in the health sciences. His writings have appeared in numerous anthologies, including *Stories from the Other Side: Thematic Memoirs, The Isherwood Century* and *Connecticut Poets on AIDS.* He may be reached by e-mail at *davidgarnes@msn.com.*

Karen Garrison is an award-winning writer specializing in stories that encourage faith and uplift the spirit. A wife and mother of two, she is working on her second inspirational novel when she's not chasing her two small clowns-in-training, Abigail and Simeon. You may reach her at *INNHEAVEN@aol.com* or 740-283-3895.

Johnnie Ann Gaskill writes a weekly inspirational column for two newspapers. A former teacher and education director, Johnnie enjoys having extended time to write. She and her husband live in Thomaston, Georgia, where their two daughters often bring grandchildren for them to spoil. She may be reached by e-mail at *jjgask@charter.net.*

Debby Giusti is a medical technologist and freelance writer who lives in the Atlanta area. She writes for Advance Magazine for Administrators of the Laboratory and serves on their Editorial Advisory Board. Her work has appeared in numerous publications, including *Woman's World, Army Magazine, Family* and *Our Sunday Visitor.* She may be reached by e-mail at *willoworks@ mindspring.com.*

David "Goose" Guzzetta is a vagabond, writer, artist and volunteer. He enjoys climbing, backpacking and bike touring with his big dog, Kyma. David hopes to write the Great American Novel or at least the Mediocre Short Story. To contact, harass, employ or pass on great recipes, he may be reached by e-mail at *guzzu22@hotmail.com.*

Carl Hammerschlag, M.D., is a speaker, author and psychiatrist. He spent nearly twenty years as a physician among Native Americans in the Southwest. He is a member of the faculty of the University of Arizona School of Medicine. He may be reached at 3104 E. Camelback Rd., Suite 614, Phoenix, AZ 85016; fax: 602-954-8560; e-mail: *info@healingdoc.com;* Web site: *www.healingdoc.com.*

Ruth Hancock has been published in magazines, hospice journals and newspapers writing short stories based on her life and interests as a hospice volunteer, wife of an Episcopal priest, mother, a twenty-five-year career in the fashion industry as model, fashion director and commentator and as a dedicated Christian. She can be reached by e-mail at *rahancock@worldnet.att.net*.

Eve M. Haverfield is the founder and director of Turtle Time, Inc., a nonprofit organization dedicated to the recovery of marine turtles. A winning member of Eckerd's Salute 100 Women Volunteers in 1998, Eve supervises one hundred volunteers and coordinates an extensive environmental education program. With the beach as her "office," Eve can be contacted via e-mail at *whaverfi@peganet.com*.

Jonny Hawkins is a nationally published cartoonist whose work has appeared in over 250 publications, such as *Reader's Digest, Guideposts, Barron's, Harvard Business Review, Woman's World* and hundreds of other places. He can be reached at 616-432-8071 and P.O. Box 188, Sherwood, MI 49089 or *cartoonist@anthill.com*.

Sarah Hawkins majored in Spanish and Public Policy at Duke University. Her volunteer interests include returning to work in a school in Kenya that she visited in the spring of 2000. Sarah aspires to one day create and run a nonprofit organization. She may be reached by e-mail at *Sashawk@aol.com*.

Susana Herrera teaches English at Los Altos High School in Los Altos, California. Her Peace Corps experience became her first novel, *Mango Elephants in the Sun: How Life in an African Village Let Me Be in My Skin* (Shambhala Publications, 2000). She is hopeful of selling her screenplay on *Mango Elephants* and can be reached at *mangosun@yahoo.com*.

Elaine Ingalls Hogg is a Palliative Care volunteer. "Discovering each pupil's abilities," has been her teaching motto for more than twenty-five years. She is the author of the fully illustrated children's book, *Remembering Honey*, an award-winning story to help young children express their emotions after the loss of a pet. She may be reached at *www.elainehogg.tripod.com/webpages/*.

Françoise Inman is the stay-at-home mom of four boys. She anticipates that she will be a den leader for many years to come. She has written a community column for a local newspaper and has been published in *Chicken Soup for the Expectant Mother's Soul*. She can be reached by e-mail at *inmancorp@n2mail.com*.

Ellen Javernick lives in Loveland, Colorado. A first-grade teacher and freelance writer, she's the author of ten books for children. She has five grown children and two darling granddaughters. E-mail Ellen at *javernicke@aol.com*.

Carolyn E. Jones is an Alaskan and lawyer of thirty-three years who is "reinventing herself." An only child born to parents who were told they could never have children, Carolyn reasons her birth is being fulfilled by trying to help the hundreds of thousands of suffering Russian children. By helping them defy the odds, she's completing the circle of life.

Bil Keane created The Family Circus based on his own family in 1960. It now appears in well over 1,500 newspapers and is read daily by 188 million people. The award-winning feature is the most widely syndicated panel cartoon in America. Check out *The Family Circus* Web site at *www.familycircus.com.*

Patsy Keech is a mother, teacher, author and motivational speaker. She and her husband, Robb, founded the Spare Key Foundation as a tribute to their son, Derian. This nonprofit organization assists families with critically ill children with a one-time mortgage payment during extended hospitalizations. Her book, *Mothering an Angel,* is based on a critically ill child. Patsy can be reached at *pkeech@sparekey.org.*

Diane Kelber is a professional actress, singer and dancer who has performed in areas as diverse as cruise ships in the Caribbean to opera in Cincinnati; TV movies to commercials. She has cowritten two one-act plays and performed her first solo show titled *Two Peas in a Pod.* She can be reached at *Dkelber@rfbd.org.*

Nate Klarfeld is a retired dentist whose volunteer commitments have included cofounding a free dental clinic for inner-city transients, serving on the boards of several civic and religious organizations and being a Child Life Volunteer at Children's Mercy Hospital in Kansas City, Missouri. He can be reached by e-mail at *monkeyteach@aol.com.*

Dave Krause has more than twelve years of nonprofit experience with organizations such as Boys and Girls Clubs of America, YMCA and Big Brothers Big Sisters. He is a motivational speaker and has been successful in recruiting volunteers and donors who have contributed more than seven million dollars to these various charities. He may be reached through his business Web site: *www.volunteer-appreciation.com.*

Tom Krause is a frequent contributor to *Chicken Soup for the Soul* series and coauthor of the upcoming *Chicken Soup for the Coach's Soul.* He is a motivational speaker, teacher and coach. He is the author of *Touching Hearts—Teaching Greatness,* a motivational/inspirational book for teenagers and adults. Tom resides in Nixa, Missouri, with his wife Amy and stepson Tyler. His Web site is *www.coachkrause.com.*

Pooja Krishna is a banker, who writes in her spare time. She has been involved in a variety of community support initiatives including those for the visually impaired and Adult Literacy. She currently makes her home in Toronto, Canada with her husband. She can be reached at 39 Pemberton Avenue #315, Toronto, Ontario, M2M 4L6, Canada; 416-590-0002; e-mail: *poojak@mail.com.*

Santina Lonergan is a lifelong resident of northeastern Pennsylvania. She has earned Bachelor's and Master's Degrees in European History from Marywood University, Dunmore, Pennsylvania. Married for thirty-two years to Brian Lonergan, they have three adult children. She is a teacher in the Pittston Area Senior High, teaching European and American History. She may be reached by e-mail at *sanfran.31@adelphi.net.*

Charles Markman has been in the art business since high school. He operated a graphic-design school in Oak Park, Illinois, and sneaked cartoons into advertisements as often as possible. He still draws and works as a volunteer docent at the International Museum of Cartoon Art in Boca Raton, Florida. He may be reached at 18549 Sunburst Lane, Boca Raton, FL 33496; 561-451-0610; fax: 561-451-2927; e-mail: *cngmarkman@aol.com*.

Matt Matteo is an award-winning artist, author of two cartoon series, book illustrator and adult tutor. He contributes much of his work to benefit charities. He is originally from Derry, Pennsylvania and may be contacted at 801 Butler Pike BS-7345, Mercer, PA 16137.

Donna McDonnall is a registered nurse and freelance writer. She was a 1991 recipient of the Nightingale Award and 1998 Colorado School Nurse of the Year. She's had numerous articles, devotions, and vignettes published in magazines, newspapers, and books. She may be reached at 614 Willow Valley, Lamar, CO 81052; e-mail: *mcdonnall1@mindspring.com*.

Pat Mendoza is an internationally acclaimed storyteller, singer, composer, humorist and musician. He has appeared throughout the United States, Canada and the British Isles since 1976. He is author of: *Song of Sorrow, Four Great Rivers to Cross, Extraordinary People in Extraordinary Times* and *Between Midnight and Morning*. He may be contacted by e-mail at *PatMendoza@aol.com* or write him at 1566 Adams St., Denver, CO 80206.

Barb Mestler has volunteered with the Compeer Program since 1974. A graduate of Rochester Institute of Technology, she is a member of its adjunct faculty. Formerly an employment director, she currently works as a human-resource specialist. She received the New York State Governor's Service Award and was named a Point of Light. Her main interests include family, friends, traveling and, of course, volunteering!

Liz Murad is involved with the General Federation of Women's Clubs and the Local PTA. She and her husband, Ron, a mason and Sunday school teacher, are raising two beautiful daughters in New Jersey and teaching them the importance of volunteering. Liz might return to teaching music some day, but is currently offering inspirational and whimsical calligraphy. She may be reached at her Web site: *www.inkybiz.com*.

Maureen Murray is a speaker, writer and success coach from Pittsburgh, Pennsylvania whose life work is helping people to develop a positive perspective and best use their talents to create satisfying lives. She is the author of *How to Sing in the Rain with a Frog in Your Throat*. She may be e-mailed at *MMurray HA@aol.com*.

Vera Nicholas-Gervais is a former diplomat who is building a new career as a Personal Coach for women, at-home mother and writer. She has written a book about the emotional lives of stay-at-home moms and is a monthly columnist for a parenting news magazine. She lives near Ontario, Canada, and can be reached at 613-489-2224; Web site: *www.soulgoals.com*; e-mail: *vera@soulgoals.com*.

Jinny Pattison is a college student studying psychology and Spanish. While in high school, she spent two summers on Teen Missions trips, one to Mozambique and the other to Honduras. She may be e-mailed at *jinnybo@aol.com.*

Terry Paulson, Ph.D., CSP, CPAE, of Agoura Hills, California, is the author of *50 Tips for Speaking Like a Pro* and *They Shoot Managers, Don't They?* As a psychologist and professional speaker, he helps leaders and teams make change work. He may be reached by e-mail at *terry@terrypaulson.com;* Web site: *www.terrypaulson.com;* or 818-991-5110.

Denise Peebles is a homemaker and mother of two children, Ashley and Jonathan. She loves to write stories about her family. She is published in a book about Lauderdale County History, which is on display in libraries across Alabama. She may be reached at *SPeeb47489@aol.com.*

Bob Perks is president of Creative Motivation and author of the book *The Flight of a Lifetime.* He is a Member of the National Writers Association and a training consultant with the state of Pennsylvania. He may be reached at P.O. Box 1702, Shavertown, PA 18708-1024; fax: 570-696-1310, e-mail: *Bob@BobPerks.com;* Web site: *www.bobperks.com.*

Tom Prisk has been a published cartoonist since 1977. His work has appeared in *The Saturday Evening Post, The Best Cartoons from The Saturday Evening Post, Woman's World, Reader's Digest, Yankee Magazine, Writer's Digest, Leadership,* and *The Best Cartoons from Leadership,* among others. He may be e-mailed at *tprisk@up.net.*

Norma Reedy, the mother of Phil Reedy, is a freelance writer residing in Virginia. She is a legal secretary in Washington, DC. She has been writing for fifteen years as a columnist and contributing editor for church publications. She has two surviving children, Danny and Leigh Anne, and granddaughter Brittney. She may be reached by e-mail at *NRReedy@venable.com.*

Rosemarie Riley was born in Australia and moved to the U.S. in 1990. She is a teacher and author, a member of Australian Society of Authors, Society of Children's Writers and Illustrators and American Association of University of Women. She can be contacted at 847 Embree Crescent, Westfield, NJ 07090; e-mail: *rosemariejriley@yahoo.com.*

Diane Rodecker is a freelance writer. Her award-winning weekly column, "Challenger," has appeared in the *Orange County Register* since 1993. Her column and advocacy for disabled people help empower those with disabilities and promote volunteerism in Southern California. A University of Southern California graduate, she raised four children with disabilities; one son died in 1992. Diane can be reached at *Chalwriter@aol.com.*

Father Domenic Jose Roscioli spends his summers as a volunteer at Paul Newman's Hole In The Wall Gang Camp for children with life-threatening illnesses. At home in Kenosha, Wisconsin, he continues to battle to improve the quality of life in his inner-city Columbus Park neighborhood. He can be reached at The New Earth Store, 5439 22nd Ave., Kenosha, WI 53140 or by calling 262-657-4463.

Dorothy Rose is a registered nurse. She is a wife, the proud mother of three sons and grandmother of seven grandchildren. Her passions are reading and traveling. She finds great fulfillment in volunteering her time, especially where children are concerned. She may be reached by e-mail at *Dotjoer@aol.com*.

George M. Roth is an inspirational writer and speaker. His dynamic keynote speeches emphasize his unique program "Volunteer for Success." He is author of *Sometimes Life Just Isn't Fair* and contributing author to *Chicken Soup for the Prisoner's Soul*. He belongs to National Speakers Association, Screen Actors Guild and AFTRA. He may be reached by e-mail at *GMR@georgeroth.com*; Web site: *www.georgeroth.com*.

Jack Schmidt is a graduate of Albright College in Reading, Pennsylvania, and a former navy flight instructor. He is a volunteer at a local library and an association for the blind. He has drawn cartoons since 1961 and is published in many trade journals, as well as *The Saturday Evening Post, Saturday Review, National Enquirer, Reader's Digest, Good Housekeeping, American Legion, Woman's World* and *Nursing Spectrum*.

Stephanie Sheen is a senior at Murray High School in Salt Lake City, Utah. She is editor of her school newspaper and is the recipient of several prestigious awards for her writing. She will be attending Boston University in the fall, where she will major in journalism. E-mail *Secndhidu@aol.com*.

Pamela B. Silberman is a recreational and group therapist in Baltimore, Maryland. Her greatest honor has been enjoying the experiences of many personal transformations when people truly care within health care settings. Pamela also presents workshops on Stress Management and Self-Esteem for adults and teens. She can be reached at *WthSpirit@aol.com*.

Steve Smeltzer is a native of Indiana. In addition to cartooning, he makes his living by teaching and playing drums. He and his wife, Cynthia, enjoy traveling to small-town diners. Steve's cartoons have appeared in *Better Homes & Gardens, Good Housekeeping, Reader's Digest, Saturday Evening Post, USA Weekend* and *Woman's World*. His Web address is *www.smeltzercartoons.com*.

P. Christine Smith is a writer and reporter who is published in newspapers, magazines and website magazines. She studied Communication Arts and English at Marist College in Poughkeepsie, New York. She is the wife of a career Navy man and writes for web and print publications dedicated to military families, in addition to civilian publications. She may be reached by e-mail at *trentandchristine@hotmail.com*.

Christian Snyder is a freelance cartoonist and illustrator. He specializes in magazine gag cartooning and creating cartoons for specialized trade journals. Christian is also experienced in political/editorial cartooning and book cover illustrations, and is currently seeking professional assignment. He may be reached at WCF #93A3574, P.O. Box 501, Attica, NY 14011.

Cathryn Pearse Snyders is a speech pathologist for the Children's Hospital of the King's Daughters in Norfolk, Virginia. A native of Tennessee, she attended and graduated from the University of Virginia. She is married to a pediatrician, and they have two incredible children. All family members are actively engaged in various children's causes.

Pamela Strome-Merewether and her husband Timothy have one very special son named Taylor. She has worked at a community college in Albuquerque, New Mexico, for several years. She may be reached by e-mail at *pstrome@ tvi.cc.nm.us.*

Lois Clark Suddath was born and reared in Illinois and spent most of her adult life in New Mexico. Following a thirty-year career in banking, she moved to Arizona with her husband Bob. She volunteers for Sun Health at Boswell Memorial Hospital. She is president of the Sun City Calligraphy Society and can be reached by e-mail at *callicolor@juno.com.*

LeAnn Thieman is a nationally acclaimed speaker and author. A member of the National Speakers Association, she inspires audiences to balance their lives, truly live their priorities, and make a difference in the world. She has written stories for seven *Chicken Soup for the Soul* books and is coauthor of *Chicken Soup for the Nurse's Soul.* She may be reached at 6600 Thompson Drive, Fort Collins, CO 80526; Web site: *www.LeAnnThieman.com;* phone: 877-THIEMAN.

Elizabeth T. Verbaas is a volunteer in the Foster Grandparent Program at the Area Agency on Aging of Palm Beach/Treasure Coast in Florida. An avid reader and writer, she is penning a book titled *From Here.* She may be reached by e-mail at *greenfeet@juno.com.*

Melanie Washington is a supplier management analyst with the Boeing Co. in Long Beach, California. A winner of the William Allen Award as Boeing's Volunteer of the Year in the Southwest region in 2000, Melanie is currently mentoring the young man who killed her son. Web site: *www.matfa.org.*

Tony Webb studied anthropology at the University of Utah. His writings have been featured in international newsletters, magazines, on-line publications and anthologies, including *Chicken Soup for the Prisoner's Soul.* He may be reached at P.O. Box 442, Liverpool, TX 77577.

Jamie Winship was an English Literature teacher at the Bandung Alliance International School in West Java, Indonesia. He and his wife have lived in Indonesia for eight years and have been involved in various educational and literacy projects throughout the archipelago. He may be reached by e-mail at *jwnics@bbnp.com.*

Bob Zahn has had thousands of his cartoons in all the leading publications, including *Woman's World, Better Homes & Gardens, Reader's Digest, First* and many others. Hundreds of his greeting cards have been published by major greeting-card companies. Six of his humor books have been published. Bob's e-mail address is *zahntoons@aol.com.*

Karen Zangerle is Associate Director at PATH Crisis Center. Karen interviews, trains and supervises approximately 120 crisis line volunteers. She has won a number of awards over the years for her work in social services. She believes she has the best job in the world working with more than 1,200 wonderful volunteers. She may be reached by e-mail at *karen.zangerle@verizon.net*.

Linda Jin Zou, Ed.D., received her doctorate from Oklahoma State University. She is working on a book, *Her Choices*, portraying a Chinese woman as she confronts changes and moral dilemmas affected by the new economic and political landscape in China. She can be reached by e-mail at *imark4@attbi.com*.

Permissions

We would like to acknowledge the many publishers and individuals who granted us permission to reprint the cited material. (Note: The stories that were penned anonymously, that are in the public domain, or that were written by Jack Canfield, Mark Victor Hansen, Arline McGraw Oberst, John T. Boal, Tom Lagana or Laura Lagana are not included in this listing.)

Volunteer's Creed. Reprinted by permission of Tom Krause. ©1999 Tom Krause.

When Two or More Gather. Reprinted by permission of Maureen C. Murray. ©2001 Maureen C. Murray.

Something Worthwhile. Reprinted by permission of Tony Webb. ©2001 Tony Webb.

The Sounds of Hope. Reprinted by permission of Cathryn Pearse Snyders. ©2000 Cathryn Pearse Snyders.

The Yellow Birds. Reprinted by permission Karen Garrison. ©2001 Karen Garrison.

Keep Your Head Up. Reprinted by permission of Susana Herrera. ©2000 Susana Herrera.

How Many Grapes Does It Take? Reprinted by permission of Natasha Friend. ©2000 Natasha Friend.

The Hug of a Child. Reprinted by permission of Victoria Harnish Benson. ©1999 Victoria Harnish Benson.

We've Got Mail. Reprinted by permission of Gary K. Farlow. ©2000 Gary K. Farlow.

With a Little Help from Her Friends. Reprinted by permission of Eve M. Haverfield. ©2000 Eve M. Haverfield.

A Second Chance. Reprinted by permission of Jenna Cassell. ©2000 Jenna Cassell.

Pegasus's Wings. Reprinted by permission of Vera Nicholas-Gervais. ©2000 Vera Nicholas-Gervais.

The Quilting Bee. Reprinted by permission of Joan Wester Anderson. ©1987 Joan Wester Anderson. Originally published in *Catholic Digest,* 1987.

Don't You Just Feel Like Singing? Reprinted by permission of Terry Paulson, Ph.D. ©2001 Terry Paulson, Ph.D.

Beyond the Huddle. Reprinted by permission of Charlene Baldridge. ©2000 Charlene Baldridge.

A Cure for Restlessness. Reprinted by permission of Linda Jin Zou. ©2001

Linda Jin Zou.

Giving Something Back. Reprinted by permission of Wynell Glanton Britton. ©1999 Wynell Glanton Britton.

Daddy Bruce Randolph. Reprinted by permission of Pat Mendoza. ©2000 Pat Mendoza.

Coats for Kosovo. Reprinted by permission of Debby Giusti. ©2000 Debby Giusti.

I'll Never Forget. Reprinted by permission of P. Christine Smith. ©2000 P. Christine Smith.

Dave. Reprinted by permission of Jamie Winship. ©2000 Jamie Winship.

A Touch of Love. Reprinted by permission of Kayte Fairfax. ©2000 Kayte Fairfax.

A Volunteer's Prayer. Reprinted by permission of Lois Clark Suddath. ©1999 Lois Clark Suddath.

A Touch from Above. Reprinted by permission of Melanie Washington. ©2000 Melanie Washington.

Treasured Visits. Reprinted by permission of Rosemarie Riley. ©1998 Rosemarie Riley.

A Brief and Shining Moment. Reprinted by permission of George S. J. Anderson. ©2000 George S. J. Anderson.

The Lady with the Smiley Voice. Reprinted by permission of Diane Kelber. ©2000 Diane Kelber.

Big Sisterhood. Reprinted by permission of Beth Barrett. ©1998 Beth Barrett.

What's a Big Brother? Reprinted by permission of Norma Reedy. ©1999 Norma Reedy.

Drawing Out the Truth. Reprinted by permission of Nate Klarfeld. ©2000 Nate Klarfeld.

A Reason for Living and *The Bread of Life.* Reprinted by permission of Ellen Javernick. ©2000 Ellen Javernick.

The Pillow. Reprinted by permission of Casey Crandall. ©2000 Casey Crandall.

A Twist of Fate. Reprinted by permission of Patsy Keech. ©2000 Patsy Keech.

A Tiny Denim Dress. Reprinted by permission of Jinny Pattison. ©2000 Jinny Pattison.

Reunion. Reprinted by permission of LeAnn Thieman. ©2000 LeAnn Thieman.

Chicken Soup for the Soul®

Improving Your Life Every Day

Real people sharing real stories—for nineteen years. Now, Chicken Soup for the Soul has gone beyond the bookstore to become a world leader in life improvement. Through books, movies, DVDs, online resources and other partnerships, we bring hope, courage, inspiration and love to hundreds of millions of people around the world. Chicken Soup for the Soul's writers and readers belong to a one-of-a-kind global community, sharing advice, support, guidance, comfort, and knowledge.

Chicken Soup for the Soul stories have been translated into more than 40 languages and can be found in more than one hundred countries. Every day, millions of people experience a Chicken Soup for the Soul story in a book, magazine, newspaper or online. As we share our life experiences through these stories, we offer hope, comfort and inspiration to one another. The stories travel from person to person, and from country to country, helping to improve lives everywhere.

Chicken Soup
for the Soul®

Share with Us

We all have had Chicken Soup for the Soul moments in our lives. If you would like to share your story or poem with millions of people around the world, go to chickensoup.com and click on "Submit Your Story." You may be able to help another reader, and become a published author at the same time. Some of our past contributors have launched writing and speaking careers from the publication of their stories in our books!

Our submission volume has been increasing steadily — the quality and quantity of your submissions has been fabulous. We only accept story submissions via our website. They are no longer accepted via mail or fax.

To contact us regarding other matters, please send us an e-mail through webmaster@chickensoupforthesoul.com, or fax or write us at:

Chicken Soup for the Soul
P.O. Box 700
Cos Cob, CT 06807-0700
Fax: 203-861-7194

One more note from your friends at Chicken Soup for the Soul: Occasionally, we receive an unsolicited book manuscript from one of our readers, and we would like to respectfully inform you that we do not accept unsolicited manuscripts and we must discard the ones that appear.

Chicken Soup for the Soul®

The Power of Positive

101 Inspirational Stories about **Changing Your Life** through **Positive Thinking**

Jack Canfield,
Mark Victor Hansen,
and Amy Newmark

Attitude is everything. And this book will uplift and inspire readers with its 101 success stories about the power of positive thinking and how contributors changed their lives, solved problems, or overcame challenges through a positive attitude, counting their blessings, or other epiphanies.

978-1-61159-903-9

Every cloud has a silver lining. Readers will be inspired by these 101 real-life stories from people just like them, taking a positive attitude to the ups and downs of life, and remembering to be grateful and count their blessings. This book continues Chicken Soup for the Soul's focus on inspiration and hope, and its stories of optimism and faith will encourage readers to stay positive during challenging times and in their everyday lives.

978-1-935096-56-6

Chicken Soup for the Soul
Find Your Happiness

101 Inspirational Stories
about Finding Your
**Purpose,
Passion,** and **Joy**

Jack Canfield,
Mark Victor Hansen & Amy Newmark
Foreword by Deborah Norville

Others share how they found their passion, purpose, and
joy in life in these 101 personal and exciting stories that
are sure to encourage readers to find their own happiness.
Stories in this collection will inspire readers to pursue
their dreams, find their passion and seek joy in their life.
This book continues Chicken Soup for the Soul's focus on
inspiration and hope, reminding readers that they can
find their own happiness.

978-1-935096-77-1

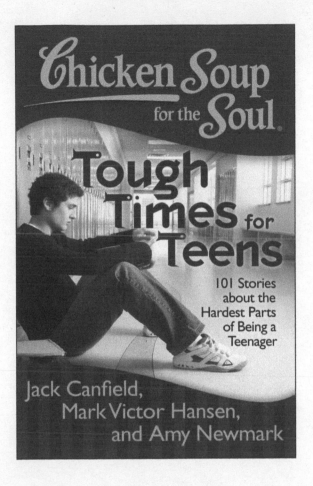

The teenage years are tough, and when bad things happen, the challenges can be overwhelming. Faced with illness, car accidents, loss of loved ones, divorces, or other upheavals, the obstacles to happiness can seem insurmountable. The 101 stories in this book describe the toughest teenage challenges and how other teens, with the same struggles, overcame them. This collection will be a support and companion for teenagers and will encourage, comfort, and inspire them, showing them that, as tough as things can get, they are not alone.

978-1-935096-80-1